The Blasket Islandman

The Life and Legacy of Tomás Ó Criomhthain

GERALD HAYES lives in Massachusetts and holds dual citizenship in the United States and Ireland. He has degrees from the College of the Holy Cross and the Harvard Graduate School of Education. His late father-in-law, Mike Carney, gave him a gift that was to substantially influence him: the story of the human drama that unfolded at the dawn of the twentieth century on the Great Blasket, Carney's beloved homeland. Hayes is co-author with Carney of *From The Great Blasket to America: The Last Memoir by an Islander* (2013) and with Eliza Kane of *The Last Blasket King* (2015). His hope is to share the island's story with the world.

The Blasket Islandman

The Life and Legacy of Tomás Ó Criomhthain

GERALD HAYES

2018

Maureen :.

I hope you enjoy my latest literary effort!

Love,

Jerry

The Collins Press

FIRST PUBLISHED in 2018 by
The Collins Press
West Link Park
Doughcloyne
Wilton
Cork
T12 N5EF
Ireland

Paperback ISBN: 978-1-84889-340-5

Maps by Dómhnal Ó Bric, Dún Chaoin, County Kerry

Typesetting by Carrigboy Typesetting Services
Typeset in Garamond Premier Pro
Cover design by Artmark
Printed by Melita Press in Malta

Dedication

This book is dedicated to my late paternal grandfather, Daniel J. Hayes. Dan was born in 1883 in Ballyshonakin, Effin, Kilmallock, County Limerick, Ireland. He emigrated to the United States at the age of twenty-seven, settling in Springfield, Massachusetts, where he married Katherine Healy, another Irish 'come-over'. The couple raised two sons, my father, Edward, and his younger brother, William.

Dan's mettle was severely tested as he approached his sixties. His beloved Katherine passed away in 1940 at just fifty-two years of age. Two years later, his son William was killed at the age of twenty when his ship, the USS *Juneau*, was sunk by a Japanese torpedo during the Battle of Guadalcanal in the Second World War.[1] Dan proudly wore a Gold Star lapel pin in his deceased son's honour for the rest of his life.

Overcoming this double loss, Dan was steadfast in his commitment to his remaining family, focusing his energies on the well-being of his many grandchildren, grandnephews and grandnieces. And he never forgot his family back in County Limerick. Several times a year, Dan sent money and clothing to his brother Mick, who continued to work his Limerick dairy farm.

Known for his physical strength and varied skill set, Dan had a series of jobs in public works, manufacturing and security. In his golden years, he enjoyed an occasional Sunday afternoon visit to Springfield's John Boyle O'Reilly Club, where he met my future father-in-law, native Blasket islander Michael J. Carney. They quickly became great friends.

In 1973, at the age of ninety, some sixty-three years after emigrating, Dan took his first trip back to Ireland to visit Mick. He returned to Limerick twice more over the ensuing years.

Dan died in 1979 at the age of ninety-six after a long life of adventure, hard work and an abiding love of family that sustained him in difficult times. He was the patriarch of the Hayes, Crowley and Buckley clan in the Springfield area. He is still sorely missed.

I am for ever indebted to Dan for shepherding me through challenges in my own life, including my mother's death when I was thirteen. Dan did his very best to help me and my five younger siblings navigate very trying circumstances. I will be forever grateful to Dan for the stabilising role he played in our lives.

The dedication of this book to Dan is entirely appropriate, given the striking similarity in the stoic manner in which he and Tomás Ó Criomhthain dealt with the tragedies that came their way. Both these great Irishmen exhibited enormous grace and fortitude in the face of heartbreak that would surely break a lesser man.

GERALD HAYES

Contents

Ó Criomhthain Family Tree

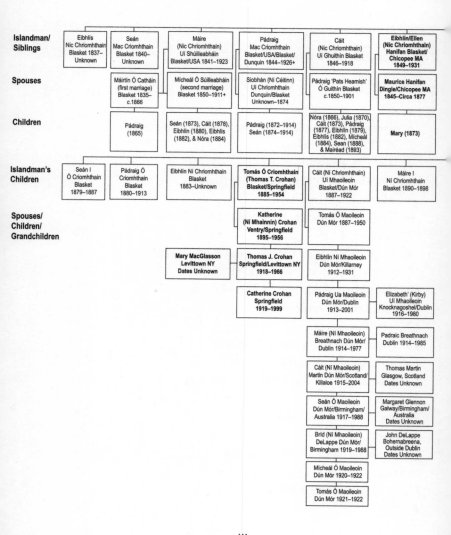

Grandparents

Parents

Islandman/Siblings

| Eibhlís Nic Chríomhthain Blasket 1837–Unknown | Seán Mac Críomhthain Blasket 1840–Unknown | Máire (Nic Chríomhthain) Uí Shúilleabháin Blasket/USA 1841–1923 | Pádraig Mac Críomhthain Blasket/USA/Blasket/ Dunquin 1844–1926+ | Cáit (Nic Chríomhthain) Uí Ghuithín Blasket 1846–1918 | **Eibhlín/Ellen (Nic Chríomhthain) Hanifan Blasket/ Chicopee MA 1849–1931** |

Spouses

| | Máirtín Ó Catháin (first marriage) Blasket 1835–c.1866 | Mícheál Ó Súilleabháin (second marriage) Blasket 1850–1911+ | Siobhán (Ní Céitinn) Uí Chríomhthain Dunquin/Blasket Unknown–1874 | Pádraig 'Pats Heamish' Ó Guithín Blasket c.1850–1901 | **Maurice Hanifan Dingle/Chicopee MA 1845–Circa 1877** |

Children

| | Pádraig (1865) | Seán (1873), Cáit (1878), Eibhlín (1880), Eibhlís (1882), & Nóra (1884) | Pádraig (1872–1914) Seán (1874–1914) | Nóra (1866), Julia (1870), Cáit (1873), Pádraig (1877), Eibhlín (1879), Éibhlís (1882), Mícheál (1884), Sean (1888), & Mairéad (1893) | **Mary (1873)** |

Islandman's Children

| Seán I Ó Críomhthain Blasket 1879–1887 | Pádraig Ó Críomhthain Blasket 1880–1913 | Eibhlín Ní Chríomhthain Blasket 1883–Unknown | **Tomás Ó Críomhthain (Thomas T. Crohan) Blasket/Springfield 1885–1954** | Cáit (Ní Chríomhthain) Uí Mhaoileoin Blasket/Dún Mór 1887–1922 | Máire I Ní Chríomhthain Blasket 1890–1898 |

Spouses/ Children/ Grandchildren

| **Katherine (Ní Mhainnín) Crohan Ventry/Springfield 1895–1956** | Tomás Ó Maoileoin Dún Mór 1887–1950 |

| **Mary MacGlasson Levittown NY Dates Unknown** | **Thomas J. Crohan Springfield/Levittown NY 1918–1966** | Eibhlín Ní Mhaoileoin Dún Mór/Killarney 1912–1931 |

| **Catherine Crohan Springfield 1919–1999** | Pádraig Ua Maoileoin Dún Mór/Dublin 1913–2001 | Elizabeth' (Kirby) Uí Mhaoileoin Knocknagoshel/Dublin 1916–1980 |

| Máire (Ní Mhaoileoin) Breathnach Dún Mór/ Dublin 1914–1977 | Padraic Breathnach Dublin 1914–1985 |

| Cáit (Ní Mhaoileoin) Martin Dún Mór/Scotland/ Killaloe 1915–2004 | Thomas Martin Glasgow, Scotland Dates Unknown |

| Seán Ó Maoileoin Dún Mór/Birmingham/ Australia 1917–1988 | Margaret Glennon Galway/Birmingham/ Australia Dates Unknown |

| Bríd (Ní Mhaoileoin) DeLappe Dún Mór/ Birmingham 1919–1988 | John DeLappe Bohernabreena, Outside Dublin Dates Unknown |

| Mícheál Ó Maoileoin Dún Mór 1920–1922 | |

| Tomás Ó Maoileoin Dún Mór 1921–1922 | |

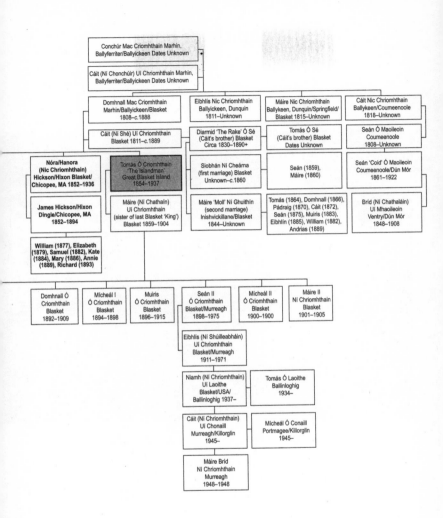

Conchúr Mac Críomhthain Marhin, Ballyferriter/Ballyickeen Dates Unknown

Cáit (Ní Chonchúir) Uí Chríomhthain Marhin, Ballyferriter/Ballyickeen Dates Unknown

Domhnall Mac Críomhthain Marhin/Ballyickeen/Blasket 1808–c.1888

Eibhlís Nic Chríomhthain Ballyickeen, Dunquin 1811–Unknown

Máire Nic Chríomhthain Ballykeen, Dunquin/Springfield/ Blasket 1815–Unknown

Cáit Nic Chríomhthain Ballykeen/Coumeenoole 1818–Unknown

Cáit (Ní Shé) Uí Chríomhthain Blasket 1811–c.1889

Diarmid 'The Rake' Ó Sé (Cáit's brother) Blasket Circa 1830–1890+

Tomás Ó Sé (Cáit's brother) Blasket Dates Unknown

Seán Ó Maoileoin Coumeenoole 1808–Unknown

Nóra/Hanora (Nic Chríomhthain) Hickson/Hixon Blasket/ Chicopee, MA 1852–1936

Tomás Ó Criomhthain 'The Islandman' Great Blasket Island 1854–1937

Siobhán Ní Cheárna (first marriage) Blasket Unknown–c.1860

Seán (1859), Máire (1860)

Seán 'Coid' Ó Maoileoin Coumeenoole/Dún Mór 1861–1922

James Hickson/Hixon Dingle/Chicopee, MA 1852–1894

Máire (Ní Chathaín) Uí Chríomhthain (sister of last Blasket 'King') Blasket 1859–1904

Máire 'Moll' Ní Ghuithín (second marriage) Inishvickillane/Blasket 1844–Unknown

Tomás (1864), Domhnall (1866), Pádraig (1870), Cáit (1872), Seán (1875), Muiris (1883), Eibhlín (1885), William (1882), Andrias (1889)

Bríd (Ní Chathaláin) Uí Mhaoileoin Ventry/Dún Mór 1848–1908

William (1877), Elizabeth (1879), Samuel (1882), Kate (1884), Mary (1886), Annie (1889), Richard (1893)

Domhnall Ó Criomhthain Blasket 1892–1909

Mícheál I Ó Criomhthain Blasket 1894–1898

Muiris Ó Criomhthain Blasket 1896–1915

Seán II Ó Criomhthain Blasket/Murreagh 1898–1975

Mícheál II Ó Criomhthain Blasket 1900–1900

Máire II Ní Chríomhthain Blasket 1901–1905

Eibhlís (Ní Shúilleabháin) Uí Chríomhthain Blasket/Murreagh 1911–1971

Niamh (Ní Chríomhthain) Uí Laoithe Blasket/USA/ Ballinloghig 1937–

Tomás Ó Laoithe Ballinloghig 1934–

Cáit (Ní Chríomhthain) Uí Chonaill Murreagh/Killorglin 1945–

Mícheál Ó Conaill Portmagee/Killorglin 1945–

Máire Bríd Ní Chríomhthain Murreagh 1948–1948

Principal residence in the United States = BOLD
Information condensed for presentation purposes
Blasket = Great Blasket Island

ix

'... the like of us will never be again'

Introduction

I can see him in my mind's eye. It is well past sunset on the Great Blasket. While other islanders gather for another session of song, dance and storytelling, Tomás Ó Criomhthain is hunched over a table in the house he built with his own hands with stones he found on the island. He is deep in concentration. His face is creased by nearly seven decades in the sun, wind and rain. The wind is howling outside, but there is a warm glow from his fireplace. His work is illuminated by a single seal-oil lamp. He is writing on oversized foolscap paper with a Waterman pen given to him by his young mentor, Brian Ó Ceallaigh. His handwriting is meticulous, a work of art. He takes an occasional puff on his glowing pipe and the house gradually fills with smoke and the aroma of burning tobacco. This work continues almost nightly for more than six long years.

The result of his dedicated labour is monumental and includes the original manuscripts of his classic works, *Allagar na hInise (Island Cross-Talk)* and *An tOileánach (The Islandman)*. His writing is the thoughtful product of a true craftsman of words. He is tired, but he persists with his task. After all, he is creating a permanent record of people who, in his immortal words, will 'never be again'. He is highly motivated. He is determined that the story of his community will be remembered, unlike so many ancient folktales that have vanished from memory without the benefit of being transcribed for posterity. He is the authentic Blasket islandman.

Inspired by my late father-in-law, Michael J. Carney, I have spent much of the last seven years immersed in writing about the Great Blasket. Until he passed away in August 2015, Mike was the oldest of just eight surviving native islanders. He was one of the island's most outspoken advocates over the last half century of his life. His enormous passion for the island kindled my interest in the Great Blasket. I am deeply grateful to Mike for encouraging me to write about his now-abandoned but much-beloved isle in the Atlantic.

This is my third book about important figures in the island's history, a Blasket trilogy. My first, *From the Great Blasket to America – The Last Memoir by an Islander*, was written in collaboration with Mike. It tells the story of his life, his youth on the island, his ten years in Dublin and then his emigration to Springfield, Massachusetts. My second, *The Last Blasket King – Pádraig Ó Catháin, An Rí*, was written in collaboration with Eliza Kane, the great-great-granddaughter of the island's last king. A contemporary of Tomás, Ó Catháin played the key leadership role on the island in the first quarter of the twentieth century.

This third book, a biography of Tomás, the widely renowned 'islandman', has proved to be my greatest challenge. It is daunting to write about such a well-known personality and to present a value-added perspective. Tomás' prominence and historical significance place a heavy burden on his biographer.

Tomás' own autobiographical works, *Allagar na hInise* and *An tOileánach,* have been in circulation for over ninety years. They have been read throughout Ireland and around the world – tens of thousands of copies are in print. Tomás is also prominently referenced in virtually all of the many books that have been written about the island. He enjoys the greatest fame of any Blasket islander, although his contemporary Peig Sayers is a close second. He is one of those people of great

Tomás in a 1932 photo by Thomas Waddicor with his characteristic intensity on full display.

stature known only by a single name – 'Tomás' – as if further elaboration is unnecessary to identify him. I will generally refer to him by this famous given name.

It is somewhat surprising that there is no single work, other than *An tOileánach*, that is devoted exclusively to telling

Tomás' life story. And *An tOileánach* tells only a portion of the tale. This book is intended to fill this gap in the Blasket literature, to describe the circumstances and forces that influenced his writing and to delineate his literary and cultural impact. This book centres on Tomás' own accounts of his life, with additional material drawn from many other sources.

Tomás' writing was edited, sometimes heavily. *An tOileánach*, for example, has been edited and published three times, with each edition based on Tomás' original Irish manuscripts. Two editions have been translated from Irish into English. All this involved interpretation of his original meaning, as dedicated scholars sought to understand and express the precise meaning of his words.

Further, Tomás' works have been analysed by scholars from all over the globe. Indeed, Tomás could never have imagined the amount of dissection and analysis to which his writing has been subjected. The reason for such extensive scrutiny is clear. Tomás provides a first-hand insight into the social dynamics of this celebrated island. His words are critically important to gaining an understanding, not only of life on the Great Blasket, but of the language and culture of Ireland as a whole. He provides a unique and irreplaceable window on a bygone place and time.

This is a work of biography, not literary criticism. My intent is to tell the tale of this extraordinary man, but to leave the literary criticism to others more qualified in that arena. The literature includes numerous essays and articles in academic journals and elsewhere critiquing Tomás' work. I have included a summary of this criticism (see Chapter 14), but I highly recommend the many original sources to the reader seeking a more in-depth exploration of Tomás as an author.

A couple of editorial comments are in order …

When referencing Tomás' major works, I will quote primarily from Tim Enright's English translation of *Allagar na hInise*, entitled *Island Cross-Talk*, and Robin Flower's English translation of *An tOileánach*, titled *The Islandman*. While these books are at least once removed from the author's own words, they are the versions in the widest circulation. I will also quote from *The Islander*, an unabridged English version of *An tOileánach* by Gary Bannister and David Sowby, for passages from the original manuscript that were not included in *The Islandman*. This approach raises the valid issue of separating Tomás' writing from his original Irish, but since this author is not fluent in Irish, it was the only practical methodology. With respect to other source material in Irish, my translators have made every effort to convey the meaning intended by the original author. I sincerely regret any errors.

I have generally used the English spelling for words, including names, places, artefacts and selected expressions. The Irish that seems closest to the local Irish convention in West Kerry is presented in parentheses immediately after the first use of such a word. With respect to names, I have used the form that was typically used during the subject's lifetime, in either Irish or English. For persons known by multiple names, both forms are indicated at their first mention (e.g. Tomás Ó Criomhthain and Thomas O'Crohan). Nicknames are presented in quotation marks (e.g. Pádraig 'An Rí' Ó Catháin). Patronymics and matronymics are presented without quotation marks (e.g. Pádraig Peats Mhicí Ó Catháin). Maiden names are given in parentheses.

Tomás provides quite a few dates for significant events, but I have found that many of these dates lack historical accuracy. This is entirely understandable. Tomás wrote *An tOileánach* when he was in his late sixties and early seventies. He recounts many events that took place much earlier in his life, and he did

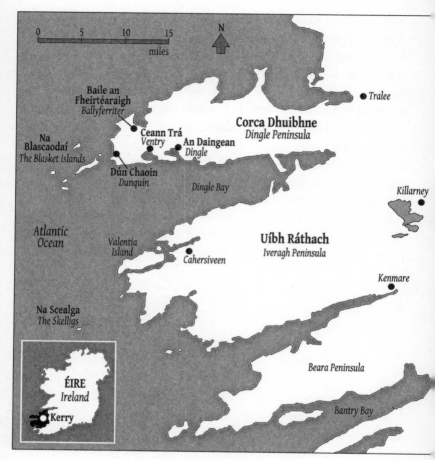

Ireland/West Kerry

not have access to reference material that would have enabled him to verify exact dates. Further, as an experienced raconteur, he probably didn't focus a great deal on precision in the dates he cited. He approached his writing as a storyteller, not as a historian. Thus, many of the dates Tomás gives in his writing reflect only his best approximation of the timing of events.

Introduction

In this work, I have made every effort to corroborate Tomás' timeline using whatever reliable documentation was available. Where appropriate, I have incorporated the evidentiary date rather than Tomás' best estimate, with any difference noted in the narrative or endnotes. In other instances, dates or events are presented as 'likely' if there is a high degree of probability, but less than conclusive verification.

Over eighty years have now elapsed since Tomás' passing. His literary stature has grown significantly, and deservedly so. I hope this book is a fitting tribute to this genuine Blasket giant, Tomás Ó Criomhthain, the eminent islandman, as well as a valuable resource to those who seek to understand his life, times, and legacy.

Tomás Ó Criomthain outside his house, courtesy of the Blasket Centre.

1. Tomás Ó Criomhthain: The Blasket Islandman

Tomás Ó Criomhthain (pronounced 'O-krih-hin' and anglicised as Thomas O'Crohan) was one of Ireland's foremost Irish language authors. He was born in 1854 on the Great Blasket (*An Blascaod Mór*), located off Ireland's rocky southwest coast. He lived virtually his entire life on this stunningly beautiful but isolated island, making only occasional trips to the mainland. He was probably the first native Blasket islander to achieve full literacy in the Irish language, largely through his own determined effort as he approached middle age. Against all odds, Tomás emerged from a humble background and a limited formal education to chronicle the story of this tiny island community as it began slipping inexorably into history during the first half of the twentieth century.

As an author, Tomás was a key participant in Ireland's transition from its thousand-year-old oral folklore tradition to an emerging written form of storytelling. Among his literary achievements are two Irish-language classics, *Allagar na hInise* (*Island Cross-Talk*) and *An tOileánach* (*The Islandman*). Tomás began writing them when was in his mid-sixties and they were published when he was in his mid-seventies, an enormous accomplishment. He later wrote a third book, *Dinnseanchas na Blascaodaí*, in which he described the physical features of

Tomás outside his house.

the Blasket Islands (*Na Blascaodaí*). A collection of fifty-two of his folktales and poems was published years later as *Seanchas ón Oileán Tiar*. Another volume comprising more diary entries, was eventually published as *Allagar II*. Tomás was also a frequent contributor to several Irish-language periodicals, with about 150 published pieces to his credit. His stories, poems and articles have been collected in three anthologies, *Bloghanna ón mBlascaod*, *Scéilíní ón mBlascaod* and *Cleití Gé ón mBlascaod Mór*. For a writer who got a late start, Tomás was a prolific author indeed.

Tomás was dubbed 'The Islandman' by his principal editor, Pádraig 'An Seabhac' (pronounced 'On showuk' meaning 'The Hawk') Ó Siochfhradha. An Seabhac was an organiser for the Gaelic League, a leader of the Celtic Revival, a businessman and later a member of Seanad Éireann. 'The Islandman' is an entirely appropriate nickname. It is recognised far and wide and it has easily withstood the test of time.

Tomás was one of the most important Irishmen of the early twentieth century. His growth and development as a writer coincided with some of the most turbulent times in Irish history, including the Easter Rising (1916), the Irish War of Independence (1919–1922), the establishment of the Irish Free State (1922) and the Irish Civil War (1922–1923). He played a crucial supporting role in the ongoing Celtic Revival by providing inspiring first-person descriptions in Irish of an authentic folk culture that was largely uncorrupted by the influence of Great Britain.

Given his simple background as a fisherman and a farmer, Tomás was a highly unlikely candidate for literary fame. It is a tribute to his intelligence and initiative that he acquired the basic skills needed to memorialise Blasket life. He was then persuaded by island visitors to share the island's unique story with a wide audience through the medium of his writing. Then, with indefatigable persistence, he used his acute powers of observation together with his budding writing ability to produce fascinating literature that documented his life and times for posterity.

Tomás was not a physically imposing man. He was no more than five feet four inches tall and built like a barrel, weighing about 83 kg (13 stone). But he had an intensity that was reflected in his deep-set eyes and in his writing. Robin Flower, a British scholar and frequent visitor to the Great Blasket, as well as a close friend of Tomás for over a quarter of a century (see Chapter 9), wrote that he was 'a slight but confident figure'.[1] Flower further described him in striking terms:

> He was in those days [around 1910] a small, lively man, with a sharp, intelligent face, weathered and wrinkled

by the sun and rain and the flying salt of the sea, out of which two bright, observant eyes looked critically upon the world.[2]

The early twentieth-century Irish scholar Daniel Binchy wrote: 'I can still see him as he stood by the hearth in his own kitchen, a trim lithe figure with finely chiseled features and keen bright eyes that seemed to survey the world with friendly and somewhat ironic detachment. His voice still lingers in my ear, clear and musical like a silver bell.'[3] Tomás almost always wore a distinctive black broad-brimmed hat. In his old age, he was a bit stooped. He was very bright and had an even temperament. His son, Seán Ó Criomhthain, said that he 'didn't like any fighting or quarrelling or bickering, and he was anxious that everything would be nice and civil.'[4]

Mícheál de Mórdha, the now-retired long-time director of the Blasket Centre (*Ionad an Bhlascaoid Mhóir*) in Dunquin (*Dún Chaoin*), West Kerry, wrote in his extensive history of the island, *An Island Community – The Ebb and Flow of the Great Blasket Island*:

> In many ways, Tomás Ó Criomhthain was a person apart, and his view of life was different to that of his fellow islanders. At the same time, Tomás was a Blasket islander the same as the rest, who lived on the island his entire lifetime. It is because of that, more than anything else, that Tomás's writing is so appealing.[5]

Tomás was primarily a fisherman and lobsterman by trade. He also cut turf for fuel, grew potatoes and worked on a series of important island building projects. He participated enthusiastically in the social and cultural life of the island. He experienced great joy and horrific sorrows. He may have become an author of great national significance, but he worked hard and struggled to get by just like everybody else on the island.

Tomás was one of the most prominent residents of the Great Blasket during his lifetime. His lifelong friend and eventual brother-in-law, Pádraig Peats Mhicí Ó Catháin, the last island king, played the key civic leadership role on the island during their adulthood. In contrast, Tomás' importance was more as the island's resident scholar and as an acknowledged master of the Irish language. The two men complemented each other.

As he aged, Tomás participated in decision-making about practical issues of common concern as a member of the island's informal 'council of elders'. He was highly opinionated, and he would not have hesitated to express his views on a wide range of subjects. He had a tendency to be somewhat of a contrarian. He was not, however, a dominating presence in a leadership sense.

Tomás was a skilled practitioner of several forms of Irish folk culture including poetry, singing, stepdancing and, of course, storytelling. He came to appreciate the critical importance of the Irish language and in his later years devoted himself to its preservation and advancement through his writing.

Over the course of his life, Tomás gained broad general knowledge that far exceeded the bounds of his limited national school education. He routinely brought higher-level thoughts to everyday life. Robin Flower wrote, for example:

> Lying under the lee of a turf-rick, or sitting in his own house or the King's kitchen, he would pour out tales and poetry and proverbs, quickening the whole with lively comments and precise explanations of difficult words and interspersing memories of his own life and of the island past.[6]

Flower once told a modest little story about a return trip to the Great Blasket that provides a glimpse into the lighter side of Tomás' personality:

> The day after my arrival on the Island, Tomás has been fishing all the morning over by Beiginis, and comes into the kitchen early in the afternoon carrying a large bream.
>
> 'That's a fine fish you have,' I say.
>
> 'It is for you, for I thought on the first day of your coming back to the Island you should have a good fish for supper.'
>
> I take the fish and lay it down on the table, and begin to thank him in my halting Irish.
>
> 'Don't thank me till you have heard all my story,' says he.
>
> 'Well,' I say, 'no story could make any difference to my thanks.'
>
> 'Listen then. When I came back from fishing this morning I had two bream, one larger and one smaller. That one there is not the larger of the two.'
>
> 'How comes that?' I say, smelling a jest in the wind.
>
> 'Well, it was this way. I came into my house, and I laid the two fish down on the table, and I said to myself: "Now which of these two fish shall I give the gentlemen from London?" And there came into my head the old saying, "When the Lord God made Heaven and earth at the first, He kept the better of the two for himself." And where could I find a higher example?'
>
> Laughing together over this artfully prepared comedy … we sit down at the table in front of the window, through which the eye ranges over the strait to the naked line of the coast of Ireland, and the business of the afternoon begins.[7]

Tomás was a husband, a father and a grandfather. His personal life was marked by great disappointments and terrible tragedy. His marriage was arranged by his family despite his love for another woman. Of his twelve children, only three lived into their twenties, and only two outlived him.

Tomás was very thoughtful and self-aware. As he aged, he became a man on a mission, seeking to preserve his story and to achieve a form of immortality in the process. In the deeply personal concluding words of *An tOileánach*, he wrote:

> I remember being a boy; I remember being a young man; I remember the bloom of my vigour and my strength. I have known famine and plenty, fortune and ill-fortune, in my life-days till to-day. They are great teachers for one that marks them well.
>
> One day there will be none left in the Blasket of all I have mentioned in this book – and none to remember them. I am thankful to God, who has given me the chance to preserve from forgetfulness those days that I have seen with my own eyes and have borne their burden, and that when I am gone men will know what life was like in my time and the neighbours that lived with me.
>
> Since the first fire was kindled in this island none has written of his life and his world. I am proud to set down my story and the story of my neighbours. This writing will tell how the Islanders lived in the old days.[8]

After the publication of *Allagar na hInise* and *An tOileánach* in the late 1920s, Tomás achieved a degree of fame throughout Ireland. His neighbours on the island must have been impressed by the acclaim his writing generated and the procession of visitors to the island seeking to meet him. But the islanders didn't hesitate to voice some criticism too (see Chapter 14).

Beyond the Great Blasket, Tomás' renown spread as his books were more widely read. Much of his fame came after his death in 1937.

Tomás' style as a writer is a reflection of his modest upbringing, his many heartbreaks, his arduous life and his stoic temperament. His writing was direct, spare and ironic, with a smattering of humour. He focused on recounting the major elements of island life and his own life story without much adornment or nuance. Since his own life was so similar to those of his island neighbours, his autobiography, *An tOileánach*, is effectively a detailed record of the life of the Blasket community as a whole.

Tomás was an intriguing man. He was a pivotal figure in the history of the Great Blasket and a giant in Irish language literature. His literary accomplishments in the Irish language, given their overall context, are nothing short of astounding. His contributions to Irish culture and literature are of epic proportions. He remains the quintessential 'islandman' and his legacy will endure forever.

2. A Blasket Homeland

Tomás was born, raised, lived and died on the Great Blasket during the late nineteenth and early twentieth centuries. He was steeped in island life. The profound impact of the island on Tomás as a person and as an author is evident in all his writing. Understanding the dynamics of life on the Great Blasket is essential to understanding this remarkable man.

During Tomás' lifetime, the Great Blasket was the breathtaking setting for a drama of overarching cultural, linguistic, political and historical significance. As Tomás aged, the island community was gradually fading into history. Its decline played out while Ireland itself was engrossed in yet another phase of its long and difficult struggle to achieve independence from Great Britain and then to establish its own standing as a nation. Essentially, the Blasket community was dying as a sovereign Ireland was being born.

Although Tomás occasionally made visits to the mainland, he never travelled outside westernmost County Kerry (*Contae Chiarraí*). He had some limited exposure to the world beyond the Great Blasket from newspapers, visitors to the island, a selection of books, and letters from America and elsewhere. But it was primarily the rigours of day-to-day life on the Great Blasket, as he personally experienced them, that informed his writing.

The abandoned village on the Great Blasket in 2012 from Blasket Sound.
Note the natural bowl that provided the village with some protection from
the fierce winds.

While Tomás' lens on the world was fairly narrow, he
suffered no lack of powerful material for his literary efforts.
This unique island, with its exceptional physical beauty, its
small population of fascinating residents and its ongoing
sequence of historic events, truly comes alive in Tomás' writing.

The Great Blasket is the largest of the six islands located
off southwest Ireland's Dingle Peninsula (*Corca Dhuibhne*)
that comprise the Blasket archipelago. These islands, the
Blaskets, lie at the very westernmost edge of Europe. The
other five Blaskets are Beginish (*Beiginis*), Inishnabro (*Inis na
Bró*), Inishvickillane (*Inis Mhic Uileáin*), Inishtooskert (*Inis
Tuaisceart*), and Tearaght (*An Tiaracht*).

The Great Blasket itself is about 2.4 km (1.5 miles) off the
mainland. It measures about 6 km (3.7 miles) long and 1 km

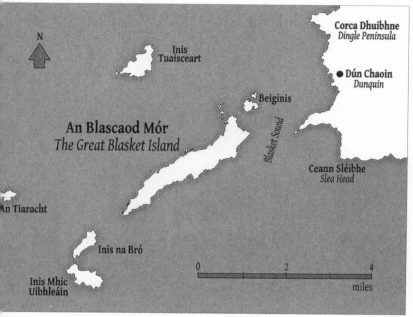

The Blasket Islands with Dunquin on the mainland to the east.

(two-thirds of a mile) wide. The terrain is mountainous with minimal flat land. The highest point is 'the Crow' (*An Cró*), standing 292 m (958 feet) above sea level. The island is shaped like an elongated triangle with towering cliffs along its north and south sides. The rocky landscape is totally devoid of trees. A sandy beach called the White Strand (*An Tráigh Bhán*) and an adjacent gravel beach (*An Tráigh Ghearraí*) look out across Blasket Sound (*An Bealach*) toward the mainland. The island comprises about 460 hectares (1,132 acres) of land, but only about 25 hectares (60 acres) was suitable for cultivation.

The island village (*An Baile*) of about thirty-five small homes was situated in a natural bowl that is tilted east toward the mainland. These houses were huddled together with a maze of footpaths running between them. Virtually all the homes

In one of the first photos of the island, taken in 1897, chimney smoke is blowing across the island village. Note the upside-down *naomhóg* (currach) in the foreground and the people to the far right.

faced south to avoid the onslaught of the wind, to afford some interior daylight and to capture warmth from the sun.

The views towards the mainland from the Great Blasket are spectacular. No less authoritative a source than *National Geographic Traveller* has declared this stretch of Ireland's southwest coast 'the most beautiful place on earth.'[1]

Of the six Blaskets, only the Great Blasket was occupied on a sustained basis over time. The first inhabitants probably arrived at the end of the Stone Age. They were followed by monks seeking to live an ascetic life. The Vikings came next, but they used the island only as a base for raids on the mainland. Their legacy includes the name of the islands, which may be an adaptation of the Norse word *brasker*, meaning 'sharp reef'.

In the early thirteenth century, the Normans arrived and British control of the Blaskets began. The Earl of Desmond leased the Great Blasket to the Ferriter family for a rent of two hawks per year. The Ferriters built a small 'castle' on the Great Blasket at Castle Point (*Rinn an Chaisleáin*) overlooking the island's small harbour. Its site was eventually used as an unconsecrated graveyard for unbaptised babies, the victims of shipwrecks and suicides.

By the sixteenth century, the Desmonds had become so assimilated into Irish culture that Queen Elizabeth I felt it necessary to dispatch her army to assert the authority of the Crown. The Irish resisted mightily, with help from troops sent by Pope Gregory XIII. In 1580, a key battle at Árd na Caithne (Smerwick), a coastal community not far from the Great Blasket, ended with the merciless slaughter by the British of 600 men who had surrendered. The hard-fought Desmond Rebellion was ultimately crushed by 1583.

In 1586, the Blaskets fell into the hands of two supporters of the Crown as spoils of war. They, in turn, sold them to Sir Richard Boyle, later the Earl of Cork. The Ferriters continued to rent the island until Piaras Ferriter (*Piaras Feiritéar*) was forced to sign over the family's interest to the Earl in 1629. As for poor Piaras, he was hanged on 16 October 1653 in Killarney (*Cill Airne*) after a group of Irish insurgents were defeated by the British (see Chapter 7).

The first long-term inhabitants of the Great Blasket were tenant farmers who migrated to the island, probably in the late seventeenth century. By the mid-eighteenth century, there were 'five or six'[2] families living on the Great Blasket. The population grew as more people fled to the island in search of a better life. Seán Ó Criomhthain, Tomás' son, said:

> The last line of people to live on the Island went there not more than two hundred years ago, if it is even that

much. They went there from the parish of Ventry [*Ceann Trá*], from Dunquin and from the parish of Ballyferriter [*Baile an Fheirtéaraigh*], not because of high spirits nor on holidays. It was the very opposite. Want, hunger and poverty caused them to go there.[3]

At first, fishing was conducted along the island's rocky coast with hand-lines. The catch was fairly limited and intended only for consumption on the island. The islanders began fishing as a commercial enterprise about 1820.

The so-called 'Souper School' (*Scoil an tSúip*) was established in 1840 and operated with limited enrolment until 1863. It was sponsored by the Church of Ireland, the official Church at the time. The school's nickname refers to the soup that the church missionaries distributed as part of their proselytisation efforts.

The island's national school opened in 1864 and operated for over three-quarters of a century (see Chapter 4). The average enrolment was about thirty students. English was the official medium of instruction, but it was not generally spoken by the islanders outside the school. Irish was the everyday language of the island. Children typically attended school for about seven or eight years. By the time they left, they had at least some ability to speak, read and write English and some competency in other subjects such as maths and geography.

The islanders felt considerable resentment about the rent and taxes they were required to pay, and attempts to collect these payments often resulted in confrontation, resistance and scorn (see Chapter 7). Rent was payable in cash, which the islanders raised by selling fish and livestock, mostly in Dingle (*An Daingean*). But the islanders had no long-term control over the rocky land they worked so hard.

The Blasket population reached 153 in 1841. It declined by about 29 per cent to 109 during the Great Famine in the

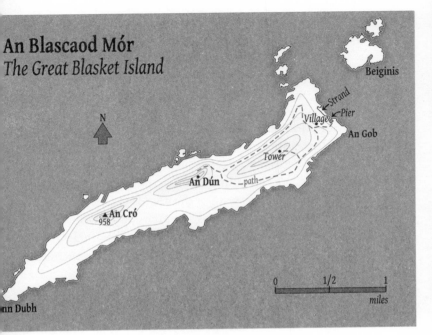

The Great Blasket.

mid-1800s. Percentage-wise, this drop was somewhat less than on the mainland. According to legend, no islander died of starvation, perhaps because of a varied diet that included both fish and shellfish, such as limpets and periwinkles, as well as home-grown vegetables. It may be that the rise in island deaths during this period was due to disease. Not surprisingly, the population began to grow again after the Famine.

The Great Blasket experienced particularly difficult times in the late 1870s and 1880s. The government was forced to send relief ships with food and supplies that helped the impoverished islanders survive. Despite their dire straits, the pressure to pay rent and taxes was unrelenting.

By 1891, conditions began to improve with the delivery of seed potatoes from the government. The fishing was better, too. Relative prosperity continued through the early part of the twentieth century. There was a viable balance between the number of men and of women. And the population continued to rise.

Civic leadership on the island during the nineteenth and early twentieth centuries was provided by a designated 'King' (*Rí*). The island King exerted great influence, but he exercised no real governmental authority. Important island-wide decisions were generally made by consensus of the island's elders.

An effort to resolve the persistent tension between the Earl of Cork and his island tenants was undertaken in 1907. The Congested Districts Board, an agency of the British government and a forerunner of the Irish Land Commission, purchased the Great Blasket from the Earl of Cork. The islanders' rent was reduced and an instalment purchase arrangement was instituted. The Board then reorganised parcel boundary lines on a more equitable basis. It also made a series of important physical improvements on the island (see Chapter 7).

On 15 April 1921, the islanders finally purchased their leasehold interests from the Board and became landowners with a vested interest in the island's future. But the steadily deteriorating economic conditions, in tandem with the constant temptation of emigration (see below), meant that the future of the Great Blasket grew increasingly bleak.

The islanders themselves consistently described their living conditions as 'tough'. There was no reliable communication with the mainland and transportation across Blasket Sound was infrequent and inconsistent. The weather was often horrible, with wind and rain pounding away at the island. The islanders focused their energy on eking out a meagre living. While the island was beautiful, it was an inhospitable place to live.

Robin Flower described the Great Blasket as a 'community imprisoned by the sea'.[4] Ironically, its residents were utterly dependent on the sea for their sustenance. In describing their susceptibility to the brutal forces of nature, Tomás wrote:

> This [the island] is a crag in the midst of the great sea, and again and again the blown surf drives right over it before the violence of the wind, so that you daren't put your head out any more than a rabbit that crouches in its burrow ... when the rain and the salt spume are flying.[5]

The Blasket economy was based on fishing (see Chapter 7), a business that was dangerous and produced erratic results. There was increasing competition from other fishermen as well as fluctuations in the price of fish. Finally, in 1921, a new American tariff on mackerel undercut the market, and fishing was no longer profitable. In subsequent years, lobstering generated much-needed income for the islanders. But a decision by the French government to ban Irish shellfish eventually curtailed this business too.

The islanders also raised livestock, including sheep and pigs, for sale on the mainland. They managed to grow a variety of crops, primarily for their own consumption, including potatoes, cabbage, turnips, carrots, parsnips, onions; and grains such as wheat, oats, rye and corn. But all this was secondary to the island's sea-based economy.

The islanders lived in small whitewashed stone houses. Most houses were built with their west wall facing into the rising hill. The earthen floors were damp and sand was frequently spread on them to keep them relatively dry. A turf fireplace was used for cooking and heat. Fresh water came from two spring-fed wells. Tomás wrote that some of the island houses 'had a handsomer appearance than the rest, and others were pretty wretched'.[6]

The difficult trip between Dunquin on the mainland and the Great Blasket only exacerbated the isolation of the island. The islanders' sea-going currachs, called *naomhóga*, were about 7.5 metres (24 feet) in length. They were either purchased on the mainland or built by the islanders themselves using animal skins or canvas stretched over a wooden frame and covered with tar as waterproofing. The trip from Dunquin to the island typically took about forty-five minutes. The only regularly scheduled crossings were to deliver and retrieve the post on Tuesdays and Fridays, weather permitting. In bad weather, crossings had to be postponed, no matter how urgent the mission. Tomás described being marooned in Dunquin, after attending a wedding on the mainland, for an incredible twenty-one days after the weather deteriorated.

The Norwegian Carl Marstrander, who visited the island in 1907 (see Chapter 9), once wrote, 'I have never met people who have demanded so little of life as these … I hope they're in their own way happy in all their misery.'[7] Blasket native Michael 'Mike' Carney (*Mícheál Ó Ceárna*) of Springfield, Massachusetts said: 'The island was a bare knuckle place. There was no police department, no courthouse, no post office, no general shop, no doctor, no running water, no electricity, no church and no pub. The islanders had to make do with what they had, which was not much.' Despite the trying conditions, the islanders were not given to complaining. Referring to their steady persistence in the face of adversity, Carney once said, 'They were saintly people, but they did not know it.'[8]

Describing the island, Robin Flower wrote that it was 'practically untouched by modern influences';[9] E.M Forster called it 'a neolithic civilisation'; and the classical scholar George Derwent Thomson called it a 'pre-capitalist society'.[10]

Tomás himself cautioned against comparisons between the island and his readers' usual frame of reference: 'We are

The village on the Great Blasket in 2012. The slipway and breakwater are in the bottom centre. The Congested Districts Board homes (the 'new houses') are in the upper right.

poor, simple people, living from hand to mouth ... You may understand from this that we are not to be put in comparison with the people of the great cities or of the soft and level lands.'[11] Truer words were never written.

Despite their many challenges, the islanders enjoyed a lively social life based on shared responsibility and cultural activities. Storytelling, poetry, music and dance were favourite pastimes, and community get-togethers occurred almost nightly (see Chapter 7).

Storytelling was a well-developed island art form. A great storyteller was called a *seanachaí*, and there were many on the Great Blasket. Stories were handed down from generation to generation and refined along the way. This was all great fun and a welcome respite from the hard work of the day. Music was played on the fiddle, the melodeon and the Jew's harp. Songs included traditional tunes as well as tunes composed by island poet Seán Ó Duinnshléibhe. All the while, the furious movement of the dancers' feet would raise a cloud of dust from the floor.

During the first half of the twentieth century, three islanders with only a rudimentary education wrote, and managed to have published, autobiographical accounts of their lives on the Great Blasket. These books included *Allagar na hInise* and *An tOileánach* by Tomás, *Fiche Bliain ag Fás* (*Twenty Years A-Growing*) by Muiris Ó Súilleabháin; and *Peig* and *Machtnamh Seana Mhná* (*An Old Woman's Reflections*), as dictated by Peig Sayers to her son, Mícheál Ó Guithín. Blasket author Muiris Mac Conghail wrote that these books came along at a critical time, when the Irish language was 'hovering between life and death'.[12]

This unusual literary outpouring was the consequence of a series of unique circumstances. Because of its reputation for a pure form of Irish language and culture, the Great Blasket attracted a series of well-educated 'cultural visitors' just after the turn of the twentieth century. The visitors' interest in the island was prompted, in part, by the Celtic Revival (see Chapter 8) and a growing sense of Irish nationalism. The island became a Mecca for scholars seeking to experience the living Irish language and the associated island culture. These pilgrims were fascinated by the simple way of life they observed and the stories they heard. They appreciated the Blasket lifestyle as an unspoiled manifestation of authentic Irish identity. Eventually, these visitors encouraged several islanders to write down their folktales and life experiences; and they provided considerable help and encouragement in the process (see Chapters 9 and 10).

The publication of these five masterworks between 1928 and 1939 has been referred to as the 'literary flowering' of the Great Blasket. This period also marks a significant cultural milestone in Ireland's evolution from an oral folklore tradition to a written medium. Sadly, this transition also marked the decline of the centuries-old tradition of storytelling.

Tomás was the first islander to publish a book, *Allagar na hInise*. In a figurative sense, it was Tomás who put the Blaskets on the map. Scholar Seán Ó Tuama wrote that he was the pioneer, the precursor.[13] He paved the way for the others who soon followed in his footsteps. American scholar Thomas Shea aptly referred to Tomás as the 'godfather' of Blasket literature.[14] It is Tomás who automatically comes to mind when the Great Blasket is mentioned. His classic books, *Allagar na hInise* and *An tOileánach*, have been read throughout Ireland and beyond (see Chapter 11). Paradoxically, these books are widely celebrated because they were written in Irish but have been read primarily in English.

Eventually, eleven other native Blasket authors made their own contributions to the 'Blasket library'.[15] In all, over eighty books have been written about the Blaskets and, largely because of their popularity, the island has been immortalised as archetypal of the rural way of life in Ireland. These books romanticised the island, presenting it as almost idyllic in its simplicity and cultural purity, but the island's distinctive way of life proved transitory. The practical problems related to the island's isolation persisted. In addition, the modern world was encroaching, and emigration from the Great Blasket was accelerating.

The island's peak population of about 176 was reached in 1916. A gradual exodus accelerated after the First World War as American legal restrictions on immigration eased. Other popular destinations included Dublin and London. Islanders

(L–r): Four published Blasket authors, Seán Ó Criomhthain, his wife Eibhlís
(Ní Shúilleabháin) Uí Chriomhthain, Tomás Ó Criomhthain and Muiris
Ó Súilleabháin, in the mid-1930s.

who emigrated often wrote home extolling the advantages
of their new lives. With greater exposure to a substantially
better life, islanders in their late teens and early twenties were
increasingly inclined to embark for new environs. By 1946, the
population was down to only forty-five as emigration to the
mainland and America took its toll.

Many former islanders settled in Springfield, about 100
miles west of Boston, Massachusetts, the first islanders arriving
sometime in the mid-nineteenth century. Thereafter, the path
of least resistance for those seeking their fortune was to follow
other islanders who had become established there. Eventually
about two dozen former islanders were in residence. Small
Blasket communities also sprang up in nearby Holyoke and
Chicopee, as well as in Hartford, Connecticut.

The process of emigration was fairly easy. The price of
passage to America was only about £5. Departing islanders

would travel by *naomhóg* to the mainland and then hike or take a horse-drawn cart to Dingle over the *Mám Clasach* road. After a train ride to Cork, they would board a ship at Queenstown (now Cobh), near Cork city. The voyage to America took about five days. Typically, friends or family would be eagerly awaiting their arrival, and housing and employment had often been arranged in advance.

Emigrating islanders often recalled fondly their lives on the Great Blasket. Almost thirty years after moving to the mainland, Seán Ó Guithín said: 'the Island will be in my head as long as I live. There was some sort of charm about it.'[16] At the age of ninety, over seventy-four years after his departure from the island at the age of sixteen, Mike Carney said: 'I just can't get the island out of me. I think about it every day and still dream about it at night ... I am an islandman at heart, and I will be until the day I die.'[17]

The remoteness of the Great Blasket provided the island with some level of insulation from the major national and international events that were unfolding during the late nineteenth and early twentieth centuries (see *A Comparative Timetable*, page 326). Essentially, the day-to-day challenges of island life continued much the same while Ireland and the world were undergoing dramatic changes. News of current events was brought to the island via sporadic newspapers and by word of mouth.

Sometimes the wider world would intrude. There were debates, for example, about possible British conscription during the First World War. An occasional wartime shipwreck or sinking near the island would bring a temporary bonanza of salvageable goods. During the First World War, the body of a crew member of the RMS *Lusitania* washed up after the ship was sunk by the Germans in 1915. In the Second World War, a German plane made a forced landing on nearby Inishvickillane.

Over time, a long litany of historic off-island events would have an impact on the Great Blasket. Yet it was a combination of powerful economic, social and political factors unique to this small island community that ultimately led to its decline.

As the momentous events of the early twentieth century began to change the nation and the world, the delicate equilibrium on the Great Blasket began to break down. Eventual Irish independence from Great Britain was somewhat of a hollow achievement for the islanders, because it roughly coincided with the early stages of the island's demise.

Ultimately, the deterioration of fishing along with the growing exposure of the islanders to a vision of a better life elsewhere signalled the end of the island community. The lure of a higher standard of living off the island persuaded many islanders to emigrate to America and the Irish mainland.

Women, especially, chose a different way of life when the opportunity presented itself, leaving the island at a faster rate than men. Marriages became increasingly rare. As Dáithí de Mórdha of the Blasket Centre said, 'generations of young people left [the island], leaving the majority of the island's population as either old couples or middle-aged bachelors.'[18] Some of the older men just didn't have the physical strength to row a *naomhóg*.

A major blow to the island was the closing of the national school on 1 January 1941 for lack of enrolment – only five students remained. Thereafter, island families with school-age children were forced to move to the mainland, send their children to live with relatives on the mainland while attending school, or emigrate.

By the end of the Second World War, the island community was in fully fledged collapse. Just fifteen homes were occupied. The female population was only about 30 per cent of the total. By the middle of the twentieth century, the island had reached a point at which it was no longer functioning effectively.

Ten years after Tomás' death in 1937, life on the Great Blasket took a decisive turn for the worse, from which it would never recover. The catalyst was the sudden death of 24-year-old Seán Ó Ceárna on 10 January 1947 from treatable meningitis. Because of bad weather, he died without medical or spiritual assistance. This was a blunt reminder to the islanders of their utter vulnerability.

On 26 January 1947, Seán's older brother, Mike Carney, then living in Dublin, wrote a letter to Taoiseach Éamon de Valera complaining about government inaction that, he felt, had led to this tragedy. He focused on poor communications and transportation, and reluctantly suggested the relocation of the remaining islanders from the Great Blasket. But the government was unresponsive, contending that that the problems were short-term in nature.

Three months later, on 22 April 1947, in the midst of horrendous weather, the islanders sent a dramatic telegram to de Valera expressing the islanders' sheer desperation: 'STORMBOUND DISTRESS. SEND FOOD. NOTHING TO EAT. BLASKETS.'[19]

The next day, the *Irish Press* published a front page story drawing the public's attention to the plight of the islanders.[20] Soon thereafter, a boat with emergency food and, according to legend, some strong drink arrived to alleviate the immediate need.

De Valera himself visited the Great Blasket on 14 July 1947. The front page of *The Kerryman* proclaimed 'BLASKET ISLANDERS GREET AN TAOISEACH.'[21] The islanders asked the Taoiseach to be relocated to the mainland. He said he would do his best to lighten the islander's hardships, but he made no specific promises.

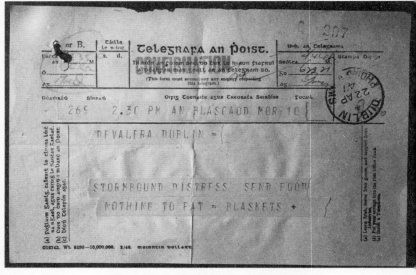

The telegram pleading for help, 22 April 1947.

Years of bureaucratic study and indecision followed. In 1948, de Valera was voted out of office for three years when his Fianna Fáil party lost its majority in the Dáil. An Interdepartmental Committee was appointed to study the matter. The islanders grew increasingly disenchanted with the government's inability to bring the matter to closure.

On 18 September 1952, the *Irish Independent* published an article entitled 'Islanders Plead for New Life on the Mainland.' Four islanders said that for many years they had been asking successive governments to house them on the mainland. 'All we received are empty promises.'[22]

After five years of investigations, reports, consultation and meetings, the government made the decision to evacuate the Great Blasket. The evacuation began with a group of twenty-two souls on 17 November 1953. In the end, only nine houses were occupied, four of them by only one person.

Taoiseach Éamon de Valera on the Great Blasket in 1947 talking to Máire
(Ní Chatháin) Uí Ghuithín and Seán Tom Ó Ceárna, Mike Carney's father
(scratching his head).

The abandoned homes on the Great Blasket gradually
began to deteriorate. The roofs and the whitewashed exteriors
went first, leaving only the remnants of the bare stone walls

Photograph of the evacuation that appeared on the front page of *The Kerryman* on 17 November 1953.

standing. The newer concrete houses built by the Congested Districts Board in the early 1900s better tolerated the ravages of time.

In 1985, Micheál Ó Cinnéide, a long-time friend of the Great Blasket who was then living in New York City, happened to notice an advertisement in the *Wall Street Journal* offering the island for sale.[23] Fearing that private development would destroy the island, Blasket advocates banded together to create the Blasket Foundation (*Fundúireacht an Bhlascaoid*). In turn, the foundation urged the government to designate the island as a national park. The fruits of their efforts include the construction of the Blasket Centre in Dunquin and the

The Blasket Centre looks out over Blasket Sound to the island.

acquisition by the government of most of the land on the Great Blasket. The ruins of the old village are now being preserved and basic visitor facilities are being built. The Blasket Centre opened in 1993 and now provides about 50,000 visitors a year with a keen insight into life on the island and its legacy through a series of multimedia exhibits.

As for the future, the Irish government is investing in the preservation of the ruins of the island village. In a fitting tribute to Tomás, the island home that he built himself was restored by the government in 2017. Regrettably, the proposal for the creation of a national park is still pending.

Today, almost sixty-five years after the evacuation, modern-day cultural visitors can take a power boat across Blasket Sound to the island, when weather conditions allow. About 10,000 visitors a year wander among the ruins, struggling to envision the island life so vividly described by Tomás in his literary masterworks. The only sounds they hear are the brisk wind off the Atlantic and the faint echoes of the past.

3. The Ó Criomhthain Family

The opening paragraph of *The Islandman* is certainly provocative. Tomás wrote: 'I can recall being at my mother's breast, for I was four years old before I was weaned.' Just two pages later, he wrote that he 'had a fancy' that he should still be nursing when he was six years old. He further wrote: 'I am "the scrapings of the pot", the last of the litter ... I was a spoilt child too.' He admitted to being 'not easy to rear' and said, 'Nobody expected me at all when I came their way.'[1] Apparently he was a surprise baby.

This bold introductory narrative immediately captures the reader's attention and sets the stage for the colourful account of Tomás' life that follows. Tomás was no doubt using the age-old storyteller's ploy of a mildly shocking beginning that was intended to draw the reader into his story. This is a technique that he probably learned in countless evening gatherings in crowded and smoky homes on the Great Blasket as he gradually became one of the island's expert storytellers.

Tomás' life story is compelling. The reader is about to embark on a journey through an extraordinary life lived in a spectacular setting.

The very first sentence of *The Islandman* indicates that Tomás was born on 21 December 1856, St Thomas' Day. The records of Ballyferriter parish, however, show that Tomás was baptised on 29 April 1855, some twenty months earlier. Unfortunately, there is no official governmental record of his birth. Civil registration of births in Ireland did not begin until 1864.

After extensive research, Blasket scholar Breandán Ó Conaire concluded that Tomás was actually born on 21 December 1854.[2] In his view, Tomás was most likely correct about being born on St Thomas' Day. He was probably named for the saint on whose feast day he was born. But, according to Ó Conaire, Tomás was probably born two years earlier than he indicated.

As for the four-month gap between his birth and his baptism, Dáithí de Mórdha advises that this was not uncommon for babies born on the island during the winter. They were formally baptised the following spring when the trip across Blasket Sound to St Vincent's Church in Ballyferriter would have been safer. In the interim, his parents may have given him an informal 'lay baptism' (a *sub conditione* baptism) shortly after his birth. Tomás refers to this practice in a story included in his *Seanchas ón Oileán Tiar* (see Chapter 11).

Tomás' error here was probably just an innocent mistake. Years later, he and his family were much more likely to remember accurately the day of his birth rather than the exact year. But this error was carried forward. Seán Ó Coileáin pointed out that Tomás used the incorrect birth date in *An tOileánach* to calculate his age at various milestone events in his life, such as starting school, getting married and even beginning to receive his old-age pension. And the perpetuation of this inaccuracy doesn't stop there. Most references in the literature, and even the date on his headstone in the cemetery at Baile an Teampaill, are most likely erroneous. In this biography, Tomás' corrected age at key dates is provided.

As to Tomás' surname, another anomaly arises. While he is commonly referred to as Tomás Ó Criomhthain, his father's and his grandfather's surname was Mac Criomhthain. Some official records continue the 'Mac' prefix in referring to some of Tomás' siblings. It appears that the family was transitioning from 'Mac' to 'Ó' over time.

Tomás' paternal grandparents were Conchúr Mac Criomhthain and Cáit Ní Chonchúir, previously of Marhin (*Márthain*) near Ballyferriter. The family were probably descended from the Mac Criomhthain family, a branch of the powerful O'Sullivan clan. These families were among the long-time leaders of the barony over on the Iveragh Peninsula (*Uíbh Ráthach*) located to the south of Dingle Bay (see the map on page xvi).

The migration of the Mac Criomhthains from Iveragh may have been as a consequence of being on the losing side of the Cromwellian or the Williamite conflict with the British during the seventeenth century. The losers in such conflicts were typically dispossessed of their holdings. In fact, there is a record of 'Mac Crohans' forfeiting Iveragh property to the Crown during this period. This forfeiture may have included a castle located outside Cahersiveen that was once owned by a Conchúr Mac Criomhthain, a man of the same name as Tomás' paternal grandfather, but who lived about 200 years earlier. Some of the Mac Criomhthains were pardoned, and others fled to Europe and elsewhere in Ireland, perhaps to Marhin. Unfortunately, it is impossible to verify this sequence of events.

The Mac Criomhthains eventually moved again, this time from Marhin to Ballyickeen (*Baile Ícín*) in Dunquin around 1811, possibly because of an eviction. The couple had at least four children: Tomás' father Domhnall (born 1808) and daughters Eibhlís (1811), Máire (1815) and Cáit (1818).

Tomás' father Domhnall 'married into the island': he married an island woman and moved to the Great Blasket. His bride was Cáit Ní Shé, who was probably born in 1811.[3] There

The Blasket Islandman

Excerpt from Griffith's Valuation Survey, 1850. The Ó Criomhthain house is fifth entry from the top.

is no conclusive information on Cáit's parents. The marriage of Domhnall and Cáit was apparently not 'arranged,' as was the custom (see Chapter 5). Tomás wrote, 'They were both willing to take one another. They hadn't the way some couples have that makes you want to take a stick to them to make them marry!'[4] They were wed on 26 January 1837.

The Ó Criomhthain family is listed in Griffith's Valuation Survey in 1850 as leasing a house and lands on the Great Blasket from Edward Hussey, a land agent, with a value of £1 12s 0d.

Tomás' parents were in their forties when he was born. Tomás remembered his father as a 'middle-sized man, stout and strong'; and his mother as 'a flourishing woman, as tall as a peeler [policeman], strong, vigorous, and lively, with bright, shining hair'.[5]

Tomás had a seemingly happy childhood in a very crowded home. As the youngest child, he received plenty of attention. He lauded his mother for her hard work (see below), but he may have been a little intimidated by her in his youth. He was worried, for example, about her possible reaction when his clothes inadvertently got soaked. He admired his father, whom he regarded as highly skilled. He described sharing many boyhood milestones with his father, including his first pair of trousers, his first big fishing catch, his first trip to Dingle and his first pair of boots. He also shared a touching story about his father's help in recovering his lost puppy, Oscar (see Chapter 4).

Eventually, Tomás and his own family lived with his parents in this home for about ten years after his marriage in 1878 (see Chapter 5) until their deaths (see below). He was very grateful to his parents for their help in raising his children and, in turn, he helped to support them in their old age.

Tomás' father died in the spring of 1888 at the age of about eighty. He had been working in his son's new potato field right up to his death; one day he simply declined to go to the field to work and expired shortly thereafter. Tomás wrote that he had predicted his own death, saying, 'I shan't see a potato come up in that field.' Tomás wrote: 'That left more of the world's trouble on poor Tomás; and that wasn't the end of my troubles either.'[6]

Shortly thereafter, in early 1889, Tomás' mother passed away peacefully at the age of about seventy-eight after a brief illness. Her brother and Tomás' Uncle Diarmuid (see below) had stayed up with her all night and announced her passing, calling out: 'She's in the next world.' Tomás wrote: 'So ended the two who put the sound of the Gaelic language in my ears the first day. The blessing of God be with their souls.'[7]

The Ó Criomhthains' house was on the north side of the lower village (*Bun an Bhaile*), just above the White Strand

Photo taken in August 1897 as part of Charles R. Browne's study of the human skull. Tomás is probably the man in the middle, and he would have been about forty-three years old. This would be the earliest known photo of 'the islandman'.

(see map on facing page). Oddly, their single door faced north, while virtually all others on the island faced south. Opposite their house was the home of Tomás 'Maol' Ó Ceárna (see below). Tomás wrote that these two houses were just a yard apart – so close to each other that either housewife could have scalded the other with boiling water from her own doorstep.[8] According to Blasket historians Joan and Ray Stagles, these houses were probably 'the survivors of two short parallel rows of houses' shown on an Ordnance Survey map of 1840 and situated in street configuration.[9]

Tomás referred to his family's ancestral home with open disdain, calling it a 'hovel'. The total living area was only about 28 square metres (300 square feet). Tomás wrote that his parents 'settled down in a little cabin to live on the produce of the sea, and they had a bit of land, too'. He wrote: 'I was cradled in one

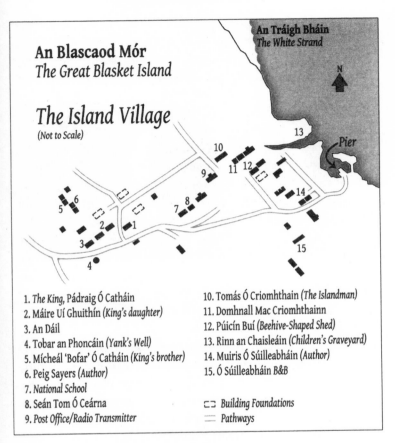

An Blascaod Mór
The Great Blasket Island

The Island Village
(Not to Scale)

An Tráigh Bháin
The White Strand

N

13

Pier

10

9   11 12

14

5   6

7   8

2   1

3

4

15

1. *The King*, Pádraig Ó Catháin
2. Máire Uí Ghuithín (*King's daughter*)
3. An Dáil
4. Tobar an Phoncáin (*Yank's Well*)
5. Mícheál 'Bofar' Ó Catháin (*King's brother*)
6. Peig Sayers (*Author*)
7. *National School*
8. Seán Tom Ó Ceárna
9. Post Office/Radio Transmitter

10. Tomás Ó Criomhthain (*The Islandman*)
11. Domhnall Mac Criomhthainn
12. Púicín Buí (*Beehive-Shaped Shed*)
13. Rinn an Chaisleáin (*Children's Graveyard*)
14. Muiris Ó Súilleabháin (*Author*)
15. Ó Súilleabháin B&B

⊏⊐ *Building Foundations*
= *Pathways*

The village on the Great Blasket. Tomás' childhood home is number 11 (Domhnall Mac Criomhthain). The home he built for his family is number 10 (Tomás Ó Criomhthain).

of the medium-sized houses. It was a little cramped house, but what there was of it was kept neat.' He described his home as 'roofed with rushes from the hill. Often the hens would nest in the thatch and lay a dozen eggs there ... There used to be two cows in the house, the hens and their eggs, an ass, and the rest of us.' He says that in such a house there would often be 'two or three dogs' and 'a cat with a couple of kittens' and a 'pet lamb or two'.[10] In many homes, there was a loft to provide more sleeping space. Fortunately, the farm animals were eventually moved to an adjacent shed, or byre, which vastly improved living conditions.

The Ó Criomhthain family was of modest means, even by Blasket standards. Tomás wrote that his father Domhnall was 'a marvellous fisherman and a great man for work. He was a stonemason and boat's captain, and handy at every trade. He often did a hand's turn for other folk.'[11] There may have been some exaggeration with respect to his alleged work for others, probably attributable to a son's natural admiration for his father (see Chapter 14). Tomás wrote that his mother too had a great capacity for hard work. One morning she fetched six creels (wicker baskets) of turf from on top of the hill on her back before he was awake. By the end of the day, she had brought down twenty creels. Tomás wrote that his father caught 5,000 fish that week.

Yet, despite all his parents' diligent efforts, the Ó Criomhthain home was among the smaller houses on the island and it was in poor condition. They struggled to get by, as did most island families. Tomás mentioned, for example, his father's need for money to buy a simple luxury item like tobacco. No doubt Domhnall and Cáit did the best they could for their family under the circumstances.

Tomás' parents had eight children over a span of sixteen years: Eibhlís (1837), Seán (1840), Máire (1841) Pádraig (1844), Cáit (1846), Eibhlín (1849), Nóra (1852) and finally Tomás (1854). Tomás' mother was a quiet matriarch of the clan, raising her own children and also taking on responsibility for temporarily raising one child of her daughter Máire and two children of her son Pádraig while their parents spent time in America.

Over the years, Tomás saw his many siblings grow up, leave home and pursue their respective lives. As he looked back on his youth he yearned for the 'good old days' when the Ó Criomhthain household was a bustling and cheerful place:

> You see how soon we [the siblings] were scattered! The merriment, the jokes, the fun that never ceased – before meals, at meals, and after meals – it was all gone now, and not a sound was to be heard ... but the voice of the old hag opposite and the droning of Bald Tom [see below].[12]

There is scant information about Tomás' two oldest siblings, Eibhlís and Seán. They appear to have died very young, well before Tomás was born. Over the years, four of his remaining siblings emigrated to America: Máire, Eibhlín, Nóra and Pádraig. Two of them, Máire and Pádraig, later returned to the island. Only Cáit and Tomás lived their entire lives in West Kerry.[13]

Máire (Ní Chriomhthain) Uí Shúilleabháin

Tomás' sister Máire, referred to in *The Islandman* as 'Maura', was baptised on 5 September 1841. As the eldest surviving girl in a big family, the care of the younger children frequently fell to her. Tomás wrote of her kindness to him as a boy; she often took him to play on the White Strand. When the national school opened in 1864, it was Máire who was sent to find Tomás on the first day of school. Tomás described her as 'a fine vigorous woman'.[14]

In her late teens, Máire went to work in the house of Pádraig Mhártain Ó Catháin, the then King of the island. On 18 February 1862, at the age of twenty, she married Ó Catháin's oldest son and her second cousin, Máirtín Ó Catháin. He was also the grand-uncle of the eventual third King of the island

and Tomás' close friend, Pádraig Peats Mhici Ó Catháin. Tomás wrote that Máirtín was looking for a spouse who knew what work was and was able to do it. This was certainly a less than romantic basis for a relationship, but it was on such considerations that marriages were arranged. Tomás wrote that the impoverished Ó Criomhthain family could not afford a dowry.

Tomás wrote that Máire's husband Máirtín died one year after their wedding. Actually, he died about four years thereafter, about a year after the birth of their only child, Pádraig, baptised on 17 December 1865. In a reversal of fortune, Máire was soon forced to move out of the Ó Catháin house and back with her parents when one of her deceased husband's brothers returned home. The Ó Catháins needed the space. Subsequently, the Ó Catháins refused to recognise her son's (and their grandson's) property rights as an Ó Catháin heir.[15]

Outraged, Máire decided to emigrate to America, primarily to raise the money to bring a lawsuit to secure her son's financial position. Her young son Pádraig stayed back on the island with Máire's parents. Máire appears to have sailed on the SS *City of Boston*, arriving in New York on 2 July 1866. She anglicised her name as Mary Kane and lived on Lyman Street in Holyoke, just north of Springfield. Where she worked is unknown, but she sent home money for ship's passage to America for her younger siblings Eibhlín and Nóra, and probably Pádraig too.

After three years in America, Máire returned to the Great Blasket with the tidy sum of £100 in savings. She promptly brought a lawsuit against the Ó Catháins. Tomás wrote that the suit was successful and, thereafter, Ó Catháin 'wasn't worth much'. Despite the lawsuit, Máire seemed to remain on fairly good terms with the Ó Catháin family.[16]

Máire married a second time on 9 February 1872, ten years after her first marriage. Her new husband was Mícheál Mhicil

Ó Súilleabháin, the son of the island poet of the same name. Tomás wrote that Mícheál was a good fisherman and that they 'built a tiny little new house for themselves and jogged along like anybody else'.[17] The couple had five children: Seán (born 1873), Cáit (1878), Eibhlín (1880), Eibhlís (1882) and Nóra (1884).

Máire enjoyed a long life, dying on 1 December 1923 at the age of eighty-two. Island poet Mícheál Ó Guithín wrote in his diary: 'Today the Lord's messenger came for Máire Chriomhthain.'[18]

Pádraig Ó Criomhthain

Tomás' brother Pádraig was baptised on 21 April 1844. He is referred to in *The Islandman* as Pats. At the appropriate age, Pádraig took up fishing with their father, Domhnall. This was very helpful to the family because they each brought home one share of the day's catch. Tomás wrote that Pádraig was 'a tall, spare man, who had a passion for work'.[19]

Pádraig married Siobhán Ní Chéitinn (Junie Keating), the daughter of a weaver from Dunquin, at the age of twenty-seven on 14 February 1871. They had two sons: Pádraig, baptised on 3 March 1872, and Seán, baptised on 12 April 1874. Tomás wrote that Siobhán died when the second boy was only three months old.[20]

Shortly after his wife's passing, perhaps about 1875, Pádraig emigrated to America, although the details of his passage cannot be confirmed. This was about five years after the emigration of his younger sisters Eibhlín and Nóra (see below). Tomás wrote: 'Not long afterwards [after the death of his wife] the bee stung my brother Pats, and before anybody knew where he was, he was half-way across to America, leaving the two young ones to my mother.'[21]

In America, Pádraig anglicised his name as Patrick Crohan. His stay was surprisingly short. Tomás wrote: 'Before we knew, Pats came in at the door, back from America, with nothing but his clothes, and poor clothes at that ... We expected that he'd stay to keep us company for the rest of his life.'[22] But that was not to be:

> The very next spring came a call from across the water for himself and his two children [perhaps from one of his sisters]. He answered the call at once. He took up the little one, who could only just walk, in his arms, and kept him there till he got across. The other boy was strong enough. Pats started in to pay their way and his own, working hard every day, and he spent ten years thus.[23]

Local records suggest that they lived on Adams Street in Holyoke, where Pádraig worked as a labourer. Raising two young lads must have been a major challenge for Pádraig as a single father.[24]

In yet another surprising turn of events, Pádraig returned to the Great Blasket a second time, 'a while' after his parents' deaths in 1888 and 1889; he had had a somewhat longer stay in America than Tomás' estimate. Tomás was surprised at this second return because his two boys were grown up by this time.

Tomás wrote that when Pádraig returned 'there wasn't a red farthing in his pocket'; he had spent all his money on his sons and whatever little was left over on drink. His return passage was paid for by two friends. Tomás was disappointed in Pádraig's sons, who, he said, never 'asked after him since'. It is possible that there was some domestic difficulty during Pádraig's second stay in America that resulted in an estrangement from his boys. In a possibly related development, Pádraig swore off drinking upon his return to the island. Tomás wrote: 'Pats never tasted a drop after he had left America, for he had bought his sense.'[25]

Tomás, aged about seventy-seven, in 1931. Photo by George Chambers.

Pádraig was living with his older sister Máire (Ní Chriomhthain) Uí Shúilleabháin (see above) and her family at the time of the 1901 Census. Perhaps after Tomás' wife died in 1904, Pádraig moved in with him, and he is listed as living there in the 1911 Census. Tomás wrote: 'I couldn't send the only brother I had adrift after he had come back from America.'[26] He always looked up to his older brother.

The brothers kept each other company and even retrofitted an old *naomhóg*. They partnered in fishing for mackerel and in lobstering, both of which Tomás described in detail (see Chapter 7). They were the only crew who harvested lobsters at night and were very successful. Tomás bragged that because they worked under the cover of darkness, nobody knew that they were fishing. The enterprising duo of seniors even salvaged some timber on Beginish. Tomás proudly reported that they earned £12 for this effort. Of course, Pádraig began to receive his old-age pension at the age of seventy.

Pádraig's elder son anglicised his name as Patrick. He married another 'come-over' named Julia on 3 September 1895 at Sacred Heart Church in Springfield. They lived at 37 Essex Street and had two children: John (1896) and Mary (1898). Patrick worked for the Boston & Maine Railroad and belonged to the Ancient Order of Hibernians. He died of pneumonia on 19 March 1914 at the age of about forty-two.

According to Tomás, nobody knew what happened to Pádraig's younger son, Seán. But research shows that he anglicised his name as John and lived in Holyoke and Springfield. There is no record of a marriage. He worked at the H.B. Smith Company and he too was a member of the Ancient Order of Hibernians. At some point, he relocated to New Britain and later to Hartford, both in Connecticut. He died in Hartford on 22 May 1914 at the age of about forty, just two months after his older brother Patrick.

Meanwhile, back on the Great Blasket, when Tomás' son Thomas T. Crohan came home from America for an extended visit in 1920 (see Chapter 13), Pádraig moved out of Tomás' house and was 'received into a house in Dunquin'.[27] He was in his eighties when his brother finished writing *An tOileánach* in the late 1920s, but the exact year of his death is unknown.

Cáit (Ní Chriomhthain) Uí Ghuithín

Tomás' sister Cáit, referred to in *The Islandman* as Kate, was baptised on 18 October 1846. She may have attended school, but only for a short while. Cáit took on considerable responsibility early in life. Her mother put her in charge of rearing her sister Máire's son Pádraig (see above). Tomás wrote that 'She was the pertest of them all [his sisters], and the one I liked best.'[28]

Cáit married Pádraig 'Pats Heamish' Ó Guithín on 27 February 1865. According to Tomás, her husband was a good fisherman who had once considered joining the army. He was a hard worker, but he wasn't very handy.

Unfortunately, Pats Heamish tended to drink too much on his trips to market in Dingle. Tomás accompanied him on one such trip and described his misbehaviour in detail: 'the drink got the upper hand of him entirely that day and made him a complete scatterbrain of him.' On another occasion, he was arrested on a trip to Dingle to purchase Christmas provisions. He was released and returned home with nothing for his children. Tomás wrote of poor Cáit coming to their mother for a drop of whiskey – a hair of the dog – to help her husband recover from the ravages of that excursion.[29]

The couple had ten children. Their first child and their last two apparently died at or shortly after birth. Four of the couple's children eventually emigrated to America, probably to Springfield. The other three remained on the island, including Cáit, who married Seán Ó Súilleabháin on 23 January 1894 and gave birth to island author Muiris Ó Súilleabháin in 1904.

Pats Heamish died at about fifty years of age in 1901. In Cáit's later years, her son Pádraig Ó Guithín and his wife Gobnait, a renowned Blasket storyteller, lived with her. She passed away in late 1918 at about seventy-two. Tomás rued that she collected her old-age pension for only three months, although she should have received payments for about two years.[30]

Eibhlín Nic Chriomhthain/Ellen Hanifan

Tomás' sister Eibhlín, or Eileen as she is referred to in *The Islandman*, was baptised on 2 August 1849. She attended the national school after it opened in 1864. Eibhlín took Tomás for the traditional tour of village homes when he got his first pair of 'breeches' (see Chapter 4). On another occasion, Eibhlín sent Tomás to get a cup of water after the teacher fainted during a visit from a school inspector (see Chapter 4). Tomás wrote that Eibhlín didn't recognise him when he returned from Dingle sporting his first pair of boots.

Eibhlín and her younger sister Nora emigrated to America at roughly the same time. Their older sister Máire paid for their ship's passage and made sure they were well situated before she returned home to the island as planned (see above). Eibhlín arrived in New York on 7 October 1869 on the SS *England*. She was twenty years old.

Eibhlín anglicised her name to Ellen and settled in Chicopee Falls, where she worked in a cotton mill. On 20 October 1872, she married fellow come-over Maurice Hanifan at St Patrick's Church. The couple had only one child, Mary, born on 17

September 1873. In the 1880 US Census, Ellen is recorded as 'widowed'. The date and cause of Maurice's death are unknown. Eibhlín died in late August 1931 at the age of about eighty-two, over fifty years after her husband's death.

Nóra (Ní Chriomhthain) Hixon/Hickson

Tomás' sister Nóra (Nora in *The Islandman*), was baptised as 'Honora Crohin' on 12 July 1852. She attended the national school, starting at about age twelve. Tomás wrote that Nóra was the family's favourite child before his birth and that his surprise arrival eventually resulted in some mild tension between them. He wrote that 'Nora's nose was put out of joint' by the situation.[31]

Tomás recalled that Nóra brought him home by the hand after his first pair of trousers got soaking wet in the course of a fishing adventure (see Chapter 4). He thought his mother would 'kill' him and Nóra coaxed him along, assuring him that she wouldn't. Nóra brought Tomás to school on his very first day. On another occasion, Nóra teased him into 'snivelling' in fear when his mother waded out to Woman's Island (*Oileáin Ban*) to gather 'shore food' on a Good Friday and was temporarily stranded by a rising tide. Nóra also got 'a good talking-to' from their mother when Tomás told his first lie. He falsely told his mother that he had asked Nóra to undo the buttons on his first pair of trousers when he needed to relieve himself and that she hadn't done so.[32]

Nóra appears to have emigrated to America at about eighteen. She was perhaps a bit young for this adventure, but her older sister Eibhlín was waiting for her. She arrived in New York on 10 May 1870 on the SS *Pennsylvania*, about seven months after Eibhlín (see above). Her older sister Máire paid for her trip and helped her to acclimatise.

Nóra went by her baptismal name 'Honora' and settled in Chicopee Falls. She married James Hickson from Garfinny, Dingle on 1 January 1877 at St Patrick's Church. Honora eventually became an American citizen.

The couple lived at 5 West Main Street in Chicopee Falls. James worked in building maintenance while Honora raised their brood of seven children. James died from cancer after a long illness on 12 April 1894 at the age of thirty-seven, leaving Honora to raise their children, then aged from one to fifteen years. Honora lived another forty-two years. She died after a brief illness on 8 December 1936 at the age of eighty-four.

Uncle Diarmuid 'The Rake' Ó Sé

Diarmuid (Diarmid) Ó Sé was Tomás' maternal uncle, and he is frequently referenced in his writing. Diarmuid was very close to Tomás, frequently acting as a kind of mentor. Tomás used numerous whimsical nicknames for Diarmuid, including 'Diarmid the Rake', 'Wild Diarmid', 'Windy Diarmid', 'Mad Diarmid' and even 'Sunshine Diarmid'. These nicknames seem to be terms of endearment, reflecting the affection that Tomás felt for his uncle.

Diarmuid was born around 1830. He married Siobhán Ní Cheárna on 13 February 1858. Sadly, his bride passed away just a few years later, perhaps from complications related to childbirth. Diarmuid married again on 20 February 1862, to Máire 'Moll' Ní Ghuithín from Inishvickillane. Diarmuid had two children with Siobhán and another nine with Máire. The family was hit hard by emigration. Only two of Diarmuid's children were living on the Great Blasket at the time of the 1911 census.

Tomás was entertained by Diarmuid's many adventures, although he voiced an occasional note of disapproval. Leslie

Matson observed that Diarmuid was boisterous, rash, rowdy, courageous and sometimes a little belligerent. In *An tOileánach*, Tomás described his several trips with Diarmuid to Dingle to sell fish and livestock. With cash in hand, these expeditions invariably culminated in a session of drinking and song. In *Seanchas ón Oileán Tiar*, Robin Flower relayed colourful stories that Tomás told him about Diarmuid, including a rabbit-hunting expedition to Inis na Bró which led to a temporary marooning on that island, and a trip to the Tiaracht hunting for birds when Tomás nearly lost his finger.

Diarmuid also had a kind heart. He did not hesitate to undertake a dangerous mission to hunt a seal when a slice of its flesh was needed to heal a nasty wound in Tomás leg (see Chapter 4). On another occasion, Diarmuid sat up all night with Tomás' dying mother, his sister, so that her exhausted family could get some rest (see above).

Tomás wrote that, although he had often described his uncle as a 'rake', a flamboyant character, he was actually 'no rake, but just the opposite'. He probably meant that Diarmuid could feel deep emotion, especially when circumstances went against him, and that he could face his troubles stoically. Diarmuid experienced multiple woes. Several of his children died very young, at least one from tuberculosis.

One of Diarmuid's sons stumbled and cracked his skull on a rock. Diarmuid and Tomás went to the mainland to get help. The son was treated, but never fully recovered. Diarmuid later told Tomás that his beloved son was 'half out of his wits'.[33] Diarmuid and Tomás then took the boy to the hospital in Dingle. The son returned to the island, but he was never the same. About three months later, he went missing. His clothes and boots were found under a rock near Black Head (*Ceann Dubh*) at the far western end of the island. It was apparent that the boy had committed suicide. Tomás broke the bad news to

Diarmuid, who was heartbroken. Three weeks later, the son's body was found floating at sea and buried in the unconsecrated burial ground at Castle Point.

In yet another tragedy, Diarmuid's son Seán 'Maol' Ó Sé drowned while on a lobstering expedition near Inis na Bró in 1923. His partner that day, Pádraig Ó Dálaigh, had disembarked at the island while Seán Maol waited for him offshore in their *naomhóg*. An unexpected squall came up and flipped the *naomhóg* upside down. Unfortunately, Seán Maol disappeared beneath the surface, and his body was never recovered.

Diarmuid, who comforted Tomás during his many times of trouble, was distraught as a result of these several crises in his life. In a reversal of roles, it was now Tomás' turn to console his uncle Diarmuid.

Tomás' neighbours in the island's lower village had a significant impact on his life and on his writing. Two families included outspoken and colourful personalities who helped Tomás to illustrate his life story in vivid terms.

The Ó Ceárna Family

The Ó Criomhthains' immediate neighbours, Tomás 'Maol' or 'Bald Tom' Ó Ceárna and his wife Eibhlín (Ní Ghuithín) Uí Ceárna, 'the old hag' or 'the grey woman', lived just a few feet away from their house. Tomás wrote disparagingly that Tomás Maol was a 'fumbler on the hill and in the field' and that 'I never saw a man more unhandy at his work'. He wrote that his father 'used to tighten up everything for him', including his thatch, and loaned him whatever tools were needed for his work. But Tomás also wrote that he was 'a thoroughly decent man' and 'he had the brains of the seven seers in his head'. Eibhlín was 'a little, undersized, untidy-haired babbler with a sallow face ... a gossip, always hither and thither'. She was an 'untidy worker' and a poor housekeeper. Despite it all, he wrote in *An tOileánach*, 'she had a generous heart',[34] although this sentiment was probably added by An Seabhac in the editing process to tone down Tomás' criticism.

Tomás referred to their son, Pádraig Thomáis, as 'a stunted, spiritless loon'. He couldn't work as a fisherman because of his tendency to get seasick. As to their daughter Máire, Eibhlín twice tried to make a marriage match between her and Tomás, but Tomás' mother successfully quashed those notions (see Chapter 5).[35]

Around 1874, Eibhlín fell seriously ill, and Tomás was called upon to help fetch the priest. Two days later she died. Tomás helped retrieve a coffin and the supplies for the wake. About six years later, Tomás Maol took sick. Again, Tomás was asked to go for the priest. His long-time neighbour and his tutor in the ways of storytelling (see Chapter 8) died the next day.[36]

The Ó Duinnshléibhe Family

The Ó Duinnshléibhe home was located two houses down the hill from Tomás, with the Seán Mhíchíl Ó Ceárna home between them. When Tomás was a boy, it was the home of Eoghain Ó Duinnshléibhe and his wife, Máire Ní Bheoláin. The couple had five children, including the infamous Seán Eoghain Ó Duinnshléibhe, who was born about 1859. There are extensive references to Seán Eoghain in Tomás' writing under a variety of nicknames including 'Tadgh', 'Tadgh the Joker', 'Seán an Ghrinn' (Seán of Fun), 'Seán na gCleas' (Seán of the Tricks), 'Heenan' after a well-known fighter and 'Seán Fada' (Long John).

Seán Eoghain was a larger-than-life character and a major presence on the island. Robin Flower described him as a

Seán Eoghain Ó Duinnshléibhe.

magnificent figure, tall and vigorous. He wrote that Tomás frequently compared Seán Eoghain's voice to '*Barrabua na Féinne*', the triumphal horn of the Fianna. Seán Eoghain gained considerable local fame as a member of the crew of *Beauty*, the winning entry of the Great Blasket in a legendary canoe race in Ventry in about 1880 (see Chapter 7).

In January 1879, Seán Eoghain married Eilís Ní Chriomhthain from Coumeenoole. The couple had two sons. But Eilís died when their second child was just an infant. On 26

Máire 'Méiní' (Ní Shé) Ui Dhuinnshléibhe, the Blasket nurse.

April 1896, some seventeen years after his first marriage, Seán Eoghain eloped with Máire Ní Shé from Dunquin, nicknamed 'Méiní', who was about twenty years old, a little over half his age of thirty-seven. Méiní had been born in 1876 in Chicopee Falls, Massachusetts to emigrants from West Kerry. Her father died when she was about two, and she moved back to Dunquin. She returned to America at about sixteen, living in Chicopee and Hartford. She returned to Dunquin for the second time three years later because of work-related health issues.

Méiní's mother was delighted about her homecoming, and efforts to find her a husband began. She was both humiliated and furious when she found out about Méiní's elopement. After a period of estrangement, Máire reached out to Méiní, and the rift was gradually healed. The new couple subsequently had two children of their own. Méiní later became skilled at midwifery and assisted at virtually every Blasket birth for about thirty-six years. She was also a skilled storyteller in her own right.

Under the nickname 'Tadgh', Seán Eoghain was the main character in a series of humorous incidents recounted in *Allagar na hInise*, several involving his headstrong donkeys. On one occasion, Seán Eoghain was bringing a half-blind donkey home when it ran off as they approached the village. Seán Eoghain and others chased after him. The courageous Méiní tried to head off the animal by standing directly in its path. But the donkey jumped right over her. Tomás wrote, 'If ever there was ever a circus day to beat it on this Island, I don't remember it.'[37] Overall, however, Seán Eoghain was less than pleased with Tomás' humorous depiction of himself (see Chapter 14).

Seán Eoghain was very argumentative and had a tendency to blame others for even the slightest misfortune. But his loud and intimidating voice was worse than his bite. At times, he was very helpful to people. He even had a flair for poetry.

Seán Eoghain died on 4 March 1932. Soon thereafter, Méiní moved back across Blasket Sound to Dunquin. She lived on for some thirty-five years after her husband's death, dying on 23 April 1967 at the age of ninety-one.

This group of neighbours contributed significantly to Tomás' writing: they broadened his knowledge of the island's storytelling tradition and their lives provided ample material for Tomás' various descriptions of island life.

4. Coming of Age on the Great Blasket

Whatever the trials and tribulations of everyday life on the Great Blasket, its children were fairly oblivious of them as they romped around their island playground. Growing up on the island was full of fun and adventure. And so it was with Tomás, who would have been known on the island by the patronymic Tomás Dhomhnaill. His youth involved plenty of island exploration along with eight or so years of schooling and a series of typical milestone 'firsts'.

As a child, Tomás was apparently small for his age and, by his own admission, he was not the most handsome person on the island. He wrote 'what ruined me was that I was 'an old cow's calf, for the rest of the litter [his siblings] were good-looking enough.'[1]

Like many young boys growing up in the west of Ireland, Tomás wore a grey 'petticoat' of undressed wool (*cóta cabhlach*) throughout his early years.[2] This attire was intended to disguise the boys as girls so as to deceive the mythical fairies who were reputed to carry off only boys.

Tomás' father made him his first pair of trousers or 'breeches' when he was eight years old. This was a major milestone in every boy's life. Tomás wrote that he was so excited that he was 'like a puppy dog unable to stand still'. As was the custom, he visited all the island houses, escorted by his sister Eibhlín, to show off his new breeches. At each house, he was given a penny or twopence as a token of esteem, and he came home delighted

A typical Blasket boy wearing his *cóta cabhlach*. Photo taken by John Millington Synge in 1905.

with a haul of three shillings. Even though Tomás felt that his mother suffered 'more trouble' with him than did his father, he gave his father the three shillings. After all, Tomás wrote, his father made his new breeches, and he needed the money to buy a supply of tobacco.[3]

A short while later, there was a minor crisis when Tomás had an 'accident' in his new breeches. He couldn't undo the buttons in time to relieve himself. His father had to make a few minor adjustments. Over time, Tomás wore a hole in the bottom that his mother patched. On another occasion, Tomás got his breeches soaked when he fell overboard while catching a six-foot-long conger eel. He was afraid his mother would be upset, but his father covered for him, praising him for his first big catch.[4]

One morning, Tomás' sister Máire took him to the White Strand, where they spotted a school of porpoises just offshore. As many as ten boats deployed their nets, driving the porpoises up on the beach. A bloody scramble ensued as the porpoises were killed. This was a boon for the islanders. Tomás wrote that the yield provided sustenance for a 'year and a day' and that 'There was no risk of me forgetting that day even if I should live to be a hundred.'[5]

One St Patrick's Day, Tomás was catching crabs with his father. A crab grabbed his thumb and index finger and wouldn't let go. Tomás was screaming at the top of his lungs. His father smashed the crab with a rock, and his finger was released. He bled quite a bit, but his father was pleased that he didn't faint. His mother treated his wound and soon he was as good as new.

As he matured, Tomás was expected to help with the family chores. Once, he helped carry a load of fish from the slipway back to their house, an arduous task. Tomás wrote: 'That was the first time, I think, that I ceased to be a spoilt darling, for my sides were sore that day from carrying the fish home in a bag on my back ... My father said that I carried more than a thousand [fish] home.'[6]

Tomás' reward for his effort was his first trip to Dingle. His first cousin, Jerry Ó Sé, also went along, but Jerry was seasick and crying for most of the trip. Tomás, on the other hand, survived the trip with his stomach intact. He admitted to bursting with laughter at the sight of his poor cousin heaving overboard. He wrote that the captain was very pleased with how he handled the open sea. Tomás was impressed by the line of buildings along the coast as they sailed by Ventry, as well as by the busy streets and the array of shops when they arrived in Dingle.

Just before they returned home, Tomás' father searched his son's pockets and counted the money he had earned in various minor ventures. He exclaimed, 'you're only a shilling short of the price of a pair of boots.' Tomás' paternal aunt promptly spoke up and gave him another shilling. Tomás reported he was 'wild with delight.' He wrote that on his return to the island, the cliff over the slipway was lined with people. He said they barely recognised him because of his new boots, which he called his 'shining glory'.[7] He was a proud young man indeed.

Tomás also described in detail his epic battle with an enormous mottled cow seal down along the shore. After raining down blow after blow on the seal, he thought she was dead. But the seal sprang back to life, taking a bite out of his leg. Despite blood flowing out of his calf 'in torrents' he finally finished the seal off with a mighty whack on the head with a stone. But he was still in fear of losing his leg. Fortunately, his Uncle Diarmuid came along and brought him home. In accordance with a traditional remedy, the leg was patched with a piece of flesh from a different seal heroically secured by his Uncle Diarmuid and another islander. Tomás said that he was grateful to them until the day they died. His leg was as good as new just a week later. As for Tomás' cow seal, Diarmuid said that he was 'astounded' because he had never seen a dead seal that size before.[8]

At some point in his youth, Tomás' learned how to swim. He does not describe his swimming lessons, but he boasts, 'I was a good swimmer in those days.'[9] This was exceptional because most islanders could not swim. This skill would serve Tomás well in later life (see Chapter 7).

Tomás wrote that one of his earliest recollections of his childhood is of 31 August 1863, when Dr David Moriarty, the Bishop of Kerry, visited the Great Blasket.[10] He was accompanied by Thomas O'Hagan, Lord Chancellor of Ireland, and probably Fr Patrick Mangan from Ballyferriter parish. Tomás wrote that it was the only time he could remember a bishop coming to the island. Mass was celebrated, and several children received the sacrament of confirmation.

At the time of the visit, there were still a few children attending the Protestant mission school, the 'Souper School'. Fr Mangan had denounced his Blasket parishioners who had the temerity to send their children to this non-Catholic school.

Bishop Moriarty and Lord O'Hagan were both strong believers in the national school system, and they found the lack of an effective school on the Great Blasket deplorable. Lord O'Hagan wrote a cheque for £25 on the spot to help finance the establishment of a national school.

The new school opened for instruction on 1 February 1864, St Bridget's Day. Tomás wrote that when he heard that the teacher had landed on the island, he was 'anything but pleased'[11] because he had just reached the age when he could hunt and fish on his own. He was about ten years old. Tomás wrote that his mother told him he started school in about 1866, but he actually started in 1864.

The student body of the national school in the early 1930s.

The national school was a one-room building located in the middle of the village. The number of students ranged from nineteen to thirty-one during Tomás' first year. The students were divided into two sections, younger children on the right and older children on the left. There was a blackboard on the wall facing each group. The teacher divided his or her time between age groups. Much later, from 1907 to 1934, there were two teachers.

Tomás wrote that his sisters started school on the day it opened. As for Tomás, he had a case of the first-day jitters, and his mother kindly allowed him to delay his attendance until the second day. He was amazed by all the new sights: the books, the blackboards and the papers. Also on that momentous day, he heard the English language spoken for the very first time when the teacher told her students: 'Home now, abhaile anois.' Tomás wrote: 'these words opened my eyes because I didn't understand their meaning.' He wrote that he was beside himself with wonder.[12]

English was the official medium of instruction, but at the outset, none of the children had any knowledge of English. The teacher and the school inspector were forced to communicate with the pupils in Irish. The parish priest wrote that teaching the children with 'English books is of course as difficult as teaching them Chinese.'[13] He argued for the gradual introduction of English, but to no avail. It was not until 1918 that Irish was adopted as the official medium of instruction at the island school, although it had been used informally for many years.

Tomás wrote extensively about his interaction at school with his close friend Peats Mhicí Ó Catháin. While they started school at the same time, Peats Mhicí was about two years younger. In *An tOileánach*, Tomás continuously referred to his friend as 'the King', even though he was not named King of the island until after the turn of the century. Tomás had a high regard for Peats Mhicí and he soon came to appreciate their mutual feelings of friendship:

> I had finished examining them all [the illustrations on the wall] when the King came in, and I was delighted to see him. His place was waiting for him and he made his way to the seat beside me, and from the way I saw him thrusting through the others, so as to be next to me, I realised that he was as fond of me as I was of him.[14]

The boys' first teacher was Áine 'Neans' Ní Dhonnchadha (Anne 'Nancy' O'Donoghue) from just outside Dingle, who taught on the island for four years. Áine was most likely raised in an Irish-speaking home, and her fluency in Irish would have been important in facilitating the difficult introduction of her students to English. Tomás wrote that he was initially puzzled by the teacher's efforts:

> I nudged Pats Micky, who was sitting by me on the stool ... I asked him in a whisper what was the rigmarole the teacher was talking to the girls round the blackboard.
>
> 'Damned if I know,' says he, 'but I fancy it's a sort of talk nobody will ever understand here.[15]

Áine left her teaching post on the island on 22 February 1868. Tomás wrote: 'the teacher was summoned home at Shrovetide to be married.' The school was closed for a fortnight while a replacement teacher was hired. It reopened on 16 March 1868 with Áine's sister, Cáit Ní Dhonnchadha (Kate O'Donoghue) as the new teacher. Tomás described his new teacher as a 'fine, comely girl'.[16]

In assessing his educational progress, Tomás expressed some frustration with his friend Peats Mhicí's fidgeting, which he felt was interfering with his advancement. He also took some pride in the appetite of the island children for learning:

> School again on Monday [Cáit's first day as the teacher], you may be sure, and we were all of us at our posts. Sure enough the King found his place next to me ... The teacher had new little books to distribute. She kept the blackboard going, too, and she was amazed that there was hardly anything she put on the board that one or other of us couldn't explain, so she had to make it harder. The Island children took great delight in this new employ, and, that being so, they had a natural gift for learning. Some of us had the spirit of a King: all of them had the spirit of the sea and the great ocean in them. The breeze blowing from the shore was in their ears every morning of their lives, scouring their brains and driving the dust

out of their skulls. Though I had a King in the making to sit by me whom the hammers of a smelting mill couldn't drive from my side – whatever it was that made him take an interest in me – he kept me from going ahead, for he was always glancing restlessly this way and that. That's the chief fault I had to find with him, for he was always distracting me just when I was beginning to make some progress. We got on very well, but we were always glad to see Saturday come to set us free to go romping off wherever we wanted.[17]

During Cáit's tenure, there were more dreaded visits from a school inspector. Leslie Matson wrote that the school inspectors were primarily interested in the students' progress in English, but they were struggling. For the students, these visits were a learning experience as they were exposed to well-dressed government officials and strange new phenomena such as eyeglasses. Tomás described the novelty of the event:

'Holy Mary!' said the King to me in a whisper, 'he's got four eyes.'

'He has', said I, 'and a light to match in them.'

'I've never seen a man like him,' said he.

Whenever he turned his head, there was a glitter in his eyes. At last the whole crowd burst out laughing – all the big ones, and the young ones were screeching for fear. The teacher nearly fainted with shame, and the inspector was beside himself with rage.

'There'll be murder done' said the King again under his breath to me. 'I wonder now did anyone ever see another man with four eyes?'

That was the first person wearing spectacles that the children ever saw.

The inspector gave the teacher a good talking-to, in a jargon that neither I nor anyone else in the school understood, and when he'd finished his speech, he seized his bag and went out of the door, and on board the boat that was waiting for him, and never came back to the Blasket again.[18]

Obviously, Tomás and Peats Mhicí and were typical schoolchildren with a tendency to make light of authority figures when the opportunity presented itself.

Tomás made a particular point of how much he valued his time with Peats Mhicí:

> Friday came, and when the day was over and we were getting ready to go home, she told us not to come back till Monday. Most of them were delighted at this announcement, but I wasn't over-pleased, for I'd rather have come back, not for any passion for learning, I suppose, but because I liked being with my chum the King.[19]

Cáit spent less than a year on the island before she too left to get married. Tomás wrote that 'the school was closed for a time until a thin lath of a master called Robert Smith came. He wasn't very nice to the rabble of scholars he found.' Smith only lasted about three months and fled for the mainland. Thereafter, the school was closed for nearly a year. Tomás made a stark self-assessment of his educational progress to that point: 'I hadn't mastered English or near it.'[20]

Their next teacher was Mícheál Ó hAiniféin (Michael Hannifin), an 'old war veteran', who stayed for six years, departing in 1876. His wife was Siobhán (Ní Scannláin) Uí hAiniféin from Dunquin, who walked with a crutch. Tomás wrote that Mícheál had 'pitted skin' and a 'sickly aspect' and that Siobhán had three legs. He said they were 'a wretched pair', but they seemed to get on well with the students.[21]

Tomás and Peats Mhicí were selected to act as school 'monitors' from February to March 1876, standing in as substitute teachers when Ó hAiniféin was ill. This would have been after they had 'graduated'. This temporary assignment appears to be an affirmation of their relative proficiency in English. According to Tomás:

> This was the last teacher I had [Ó hAiniféin], and the King, too … It was ill health that drove him out at last. He started for Cork, but he died on the way, poor fellow, near Tralee. There was little learning in him that we hadn't picked up before he went …
>
> As the teacher was in bad health, the fright the inspector gave him made him ill, though the school was open every day. He said that he would be eternally grateful to me if I would take his place in the school, with the King to help me …
>
> The King and I were a couple of teachers for a month, and – keep it dark – we were a pretty poor couple, for, whatever we might have done, the misfortune and the mischief kept us from doing it.[22]

The frequent turnover of teachers reflected the unattractive nature of the position. The island's remote location and the adverse living conditions made it difficult to recruit and retain teachers, so there were frequent disruptions to the school's operation.

According to Leslie Matson, 'Tomás on his own showing was keener to learn than Peats.' He was an excellent student. At one point during Cáit's tenure, a visiting school inspector awarded Tomás a shilling as the best 'scholar' in his class. He was very pleased with the recognition. His father was delighted when Tomás presented him with the shilling, and he promptly invested it in 'a fine lump of tobacco'. Tomás was nicknamed 'Domhnall's scholar' as a kind of tribute to his father and an acknowledgement of his son's academic success.[23]

Tomás probably attended school for about eight years.[24] He wrote that he left school about the time his brother Pádraig emigrated to America, when his family needed help at home. He would have been about eighteen, around 1872. At that point, Tomás was able to speak, read and write in English to at least some degree.

In the very last paragraph of *An tOileánach*, Tomás expresses his appreciation to his mother for the sacrifices she made so that he could get an education:

> My mother used to go carrying turf when I was eighteen years of age. She did it that I might go to school, for rarely did we get a chance of schooling. I hope in God that she and my father will inherit the Blessed Kingdom.[25]

These words were a genuine tribute to his mother as well as an expression of his understanding of the importance of his schooling later in his life.

In *An tOileánach*, Tomás related two wonderful stories of his boyhood adventures with his friend Peats Mhicí. These stories illustrate the boundless joy of boys growing up on an island and investigating the mysteries of the natural world around them. The first involves a highly successful fishing adventure that highlights their ingenuity:

> On Monday – since there was no school – the King [Peats Mhicí] ran in to me pretty early in the morning ...
> The King's business with me was to take me fishing from the rocks if we could get a crab for bait ...

Out of the door we went to hunt for crabs, but we had no luck at all.

'There's nothing in these little holes,' said the King. 'We'd better take our clothes off and go under the water in some place where we're likely to get them.'

No sooner said than we were stripped to the pelt and diving under and coming up again both of us. I went into a hole as deep as myself, and when I got my foot into the hole there was a crab there ... I thrust my foot down into the hole again, and what do you think! I fetched him up on one of my big toes. He was a huge male crab, and, usually, if one of those is in a hole, his mate is along with him. I put my foot down again and found the other one ...

The King came to me with all his clothes buttoned up.

'Come along,' said he, 'we've got plenty of bait for the day. You have two fine crabs, and so have I.' ...

We went westwards to Dunleavy's Point ... Rockfish were biting freely, and every now and again we pulled up a fine fish and put it behind us ... We had forty rockfish – twenty apiece.[26]

The second story is similar, but this time their quarry is rabbits:

Off we went, the two of us. He stuffed the ferret down his chest ... When we came near the rabbits, we found a warren. The King pulled out his ferret, tied a string to her and sent her in. Then he stretched a net over each of the holes in the warren. Soon a rabbit rushed out and the net caught him at once ...

That was no sooner done than another rabbit dashed out at another hole ... The ferret didn't come back until she'd sent out the last of them to us ... Seven fine rabbits had been hunted out of the hole to us by the ferret and caught in the nets ... Off we went to another hunting ground some distance away ... he put the ferret into one hole after another till we had a dozen rabbits apiece when we came home with the stars shining over us.[27]

These stories illustrate the exciting and carefree days of youth on the Great Blasket. Tomás and Peats Mhicí were best friends growing up together and learning important life lessons that would serve them well in the future. To these two friends, it was all great fun.

Interestingly, Tomás presents himself in these stories as the bolder of the two lads, perhaps owing to his two-year age advantage over Peats Mhicí. He didn't hesitate to take a brash and self-assured approach to given situations. In later years, Tomás would continue to demonstrate a willingness to be his own man. He was different from the other islanders and he knew it.

At some point during his boyhood, Tomás' father brought him a dog from Dingle. Tomás named his new pet Oscar, after the son of Oisín, the mythical Irish poet and Fianna warrior. One day, Tomás was cutting turf up on the hill. Oscar was with him. Apparently, Oscar caught the scent of rabbits and disappeared into a hole beneath a flagstone overhang. Tomás was terrified that he had lost him and that his father would be furious. He fished down deep into the hole and was able to pull Oscar out with a rabbit's leg clenched in his mouth. But as soon as he was free, Oscar dived straight back down the hole. This time, Tomás couldn't reach him. He went home quite upset. His father comforted him, saying, 'I believe that Oscar would never have gone back into the hole if he hadn't scented another rabbit there – possibly two or even three of them.'

Early the next morning, Tomás went off to the hill in search of Oscar. The first thing he saw was Oscar running toward him.

Youngsters of the Great Blasket frolic on the White Strand in the 1920s.

He wrote, 'you'd have thought that he hadn't seen me for half a year when he caught sight of me.' His father was standing on the flagstone, having extracted Oscar by digging where he thought the end of the hole might be. Sure enough, out came Oscar, along with 'five of the finest rabbits that were ever taken out of a single hole'.[28]

This heart-warming story indicates that Tomás' father had great affection for his son, buying him a pet, comforting him when it seemed lost and then getting up early the next morning to try to retrieve him. As for Tomás, he was concerned that he had disappointed his father by not properly managing his pet. But he was certainly thrilled with the happy ending that reunited him with Oscar and simultaneously provided the family with a supply of fresh rabbit meat.

And such were the joys of a Blasket youth.

5. Marriage and Family

As was the custom in many communities throughout Ireland at the time, virtually all marriages on the Great Blasket were arranged. A marriage 'match' was usually suggested by the parents or a relative of the prospective bride or groom. The match could be rejected by either of the two principals, but there was a certain pressure to get married and start a family. This approach seems insensitive in the context of modern concepts of romantic love, but there was general acceptance of the practice in those days.

Many weddings were held at Shrovetide, the period just before Lent. This led to a certain frenzy of activity as matches were proposed so that the wedding could be held before the artificial deadline. There was no real opportunity for courtship. Island poet Mícheál Ó Guithín wrote, 'People are very fidgety during Shrovetide.'[1] This is not surprising.

Tomás' first mention of his interaction with island girls in the original manuscript of *An tOileánach* involves a seemingly harmless story about Tomás and his friend Peats Mhicí, the future King, when they were probably in their teens. The lads were caught naked by three girls after a dip in a pool of water on the day they were catching crabs to be used as bait for fishing (see Chapter 4):

> When I reached the bottom of this well the King was facing me from the other side and the pair of us naked.

When we turned around, what did we find but three big lumps of girls looking straight at us.

The King became embarrassed a lot quicker than I did, and he turned towards the sea with his back to them, trying to hide from them. I remained standing exactly as I was when I entered this world and it occurred to me that there was no reason for me to take fright rather than them.

I hid a certain member of my body with my hands and remained standing firmly without a budge to spite them. Two of them backed off but there were never three women who didn't have a bold one in their number. It was the same here, because there was one big skinny yellow skinned one who didn't back away at all. We weren't far apart and what do you think but she said 'You should have been dry ages ago.'

I replied that there was only one side of me dry yet and that I would have to turn my backside to the sun for another while. 'And since you didn't happen to see anything unusual on this side of me, maybe it would be different if I turned my backside towards you,' I said.

'I would have thought that both sides of you would be dry a long time ago' says she.

'If I had that slippery yellow skin you have it wouldn't take half the time,' says I to her. It was only then that she moved off toward the others.

The King returned with his clothes on.

'Are you not dressed yet?' says he.

'No. Where's my hurry? Don't I have the sun and its heat' says I.

'Were you not embarrassed in front of the women and you stark naked?'

'What were they at? They weren't embarrassed and it was them who should have been. And you weren't too brave in front of them. It's a wonder they didn't chase you off to the hill,' I said to him.

The big girl who was giving me the cheek saw a baptism before she ever saw a wedding. And, of course, the signs were on her with her display that day.[2]

This vignette was deleted from the manuscript of *An tOileánach* by An Seabhac when he edited it for publication (see Chapter 10). He apparently considered aspects of this story too risqué for the Irish audience at the time, probably because of the nudity and the out-of-wedlock pregnancy. The story was later restored to the text by Tomás' grandson Pádraig Ua Maoileoin in his more complete 1973 edition (see Chapter 11).

As a young man, Tomás seemed to be relatively popular with the girls of the island, and he engaged in some mild flirting typical of young adulthood. Tomás hints that the island girls were attracted to him. On one occasion, he was cutting turf up on the hill when a group of six girls driving cows home set upon him, pulling his ear, snatching his spade from his hands and trying to knock him down. He said these girls were 'next door to being half wild'. It seems, however, that this was not an entirely unpleasant experience for Tomás.

Not long thereafter, the same group of girls was on him again, 'playing all sorts of mad tricks'. This time he decided to have some fun with them for the rest of the evening:

There wasn't one of the six, if I had given her the wink, that wouldn't have gone with me ready and willing for the knot there's no untying [marriage]; but, whoever I had my eye on in those days [see below], it wasn't any one of those six. Never mind – it would do me no great harm to have a bit of fun with them, and I had it all right ... It's long I remembered that afternoon; I remember it still.[3]

Tomás also engaged in the usual evening socialising. After the customary session of stories, song and dance (see Chapter 7), the adults would leave the young people to themselves for a time. Then the boys would escort the girls home.

Eventually, Tomás realised that he was getting a bit too old for this kind of playfulness and that marriage was looming on his horizon: 'it came into my head that the best thing I could do was to get one of the kind for a wife for myself – and it was high time, too!'[4]

It would have been natural for Tomás to think about emigrating to America or elsewhere when he reached his late teens. Two of his siblings (Máire and Pádraig) spent some in Holyoke, Massachusetts and two others (Eibhlín and Nóra) made a permanent move to nearby Chicopee. Many of his island peers also chose to pursue the promise of the new world.

Tomás appears to have taken a dim view of emigration, once referring to America derisively as 'the land of sweat'. He also wrote that his sister Máire learned to live like a rabbit in America. He wrote of his aversion to the thought of an American ganger (foreman) watching over the workers.[5] On 28 October 1921 he wrote in his diary:

> A Yank has returned from America who has been there for only a year – Muiris Chuainí – and there were two others in Dunquin with him. Whatever kind of place America is, it is better to be at sea at night than to be there it would appear.[6]

Whatever appeal America had for others, Tomás was a true man of the Great Blasket at heart. America was just not for him.

Tomás' first brush with marriage involved Máire Ní Chearna, the daughter of his neighbours across the way, Tomás

Maol and 'the old hag' (see Chapter 3). Tomás was never attracted to Máire, whom he described as having inherited her mother's 'wild hair'. When Tomás was only about fourteen, 'the old hag' offered to 'give him this girl for a wife when he's two years older'. Tomás wrote: 'I felt at once that that promise would bring me more harm than good' and that the very thought of it 'plunged me into despair'.[7] Eventually, the still unmarried Máire emigrated to America. After a five-year stay, she made a dramatic return to the island, probably in the mid-1870s. She appeared so well off that she was not recognised at first. She wore a glittering gold chain and brought with her a stash of money, a bottle of whiskey and a purse of gold. Her return was celebrated in drink and song. Nevertheless, Tomás wrote, 'after she had spent five years in the land of sweat, she was uglier than ever.'[8]

But 'the old hag' was still on the prowl for a husband for her daughter. And she desperately wanted Máire to remain on the island. For her part, Máire was intent on living on the mainland. Undaunted, 'the old hag' again hinted at a match with Tomás to his mother as Shrovetide approached. She unabashedly pointed out the money that Máire had brought back from America. Fortunately for Tomás, his mother put an end to the idea, saying, 'Our boy's young yet.' She suggested he might emigrate to America, but this was probably just a convenient excuse.

Finally, a suitable husband for Máire was found in Dunquin. Her father bought a small piece of land and a couple of cows for the newlyweds. Tomás attended the wedding, where he must have felt a sense of relief. Máire eventually had four children and spent the rest of her life on the farm.[9]

Tomás' second marriage possibility was much more serious and had long-term implications. This time, Tomás was in love. And the feeling was mutual. The object of his affection was Cáit Ní Dhálaigh of Inishvickillane. Cáit was born on the Great Blasket on 23 December 1860. She was the first daughter of Muiris Ó Dálaigh, originally from Baile an Ghleanna, Dunquin, and Blasket islander Cáit (Ní Ghuithín) Uí Dhálaigh. Tomás knew Cáit from childhood because the Ó Dálaigh family then lived near the Ó Criomhthains on the Great Blasket. They would have attended the national school together for a time.

Around 1873, when Cáit would have been thirteen, the Ó Dálaighs moved to the isolated island of Inishvickillane, where they were the only inhabitants, and where they led a rather stark and lonely existence. The family had five sons and five daughters. Tomás wrote of four of the girls, who were sitting at the hearth one day, 'they were as easy on the eye as any four women you might find in Ireland.' He admitted that 'before long, one of the daughters and I were making up to one another.'[10] Curiously, Tomás did not identify Cáit by name.

Tomás and Cáit's relationship continued through the mid-1870s, facilitated by Tomás' fishing trips to Inishvickillane with his Uncle Diarmuid (see Chapter 3). The Ó Dálaighs, who were noted for their hospitality, made them feel quite welcome. Tomás had a particularly high regard for Muiris, the family patriarch.

Cáit was a gifted singer, and Tomás was known to have a 'pleasant' singing voice as well. Singing was a central part of their time together. They were constantly flirting with one another. Once, Cáit made sure Tomás had plenty of rabbits to bring home, hoping to ingratiate herself with his family. He was impressed with her cleverness. Tomás wrote that she 'was dearer to me at that time than any other woman in Ireland'.[11]

Tomás also shared a detailed story about an extended trip to Dingle with Cáit. The Ó Dálaigh family raised pigs, and they wanted to bring two of them to market. Tomás had two pigs of his own that were ready for sale, and he offered to take all four pigs to Dingle. He and his Uncle Diarmuid picked up Cáit and her mother, along with their pigs, from Inishvickillane. After a fine send-off involving whiskey provided by Cáit's father, they spent the first night of their trip on the Great Blasket. The next day, the four set off for Dingle with their cargo of swine. There were some humorous problems transporting the pigs over *Mám Clasach*, the road from Dunquin to Ventry, and eventually to Dingle. The pigs had tender feet and couldn't handle the long walk on the rocky road. They finally had to secure a horse-drawn cart to carry the squealing animals. When they finally got to Dingle, one of the pigs escaped and plunged into the harbour, and Tomás had to dive into the water to rescue it.

The pigs were finally sold. The buyer conveniently owned a pub, where the four celebrated, and the drink flowed freely. Tomás sang the first song, followed by Cáit. Tomás responded with more songs, and the two women sang four of their own. This merriment went on for three days and three nights. Tomás slipped away briefly to buy himself a new pair of braces, outwitting the shop woman in the process. He was very shrewd when it came to money matters.

Then it was time to head for home. When they reached the Great Blasket, Diarmuid decided to go on to Inishvickillane with the women. He suggested that Tomás go along with him. He probably didn't take much persuading. Tomás and Diarmuid then spent another two days on Inishvickillane before they finally returned home. It was certainly a trip to remember. Cáit said to Tomás: 'this is a day of our life, and we shan't always be in the way of a day like it.'[12] In his writing, Tomás fondly recounted his time visiting Inishvickillane. So great was the joy he felt on that remote island during his time with Cáit that he once referred to it as *Tír na nÓg*, the otherworld 'land of youth'.[13]

Diarmuid, an eyewitness to this flourishing romance, took the initiative and proposed a marriage match with Cáit to Tomás' parents, first raising the idea just before Christmas 1877. Diarmuid said 'this girl from the Inish had excellent stuff in her.' Of his own feelings, Tomás wrote, 'for to speak the truth, that's where I myself would have made my choice at that time.' But Diarmuid's efforts at persuasion were going nowhere with Tomás' parents. Sensing that they were not receptive, Tomás wrote: 'I had to take him by the shoulder and run him out through the door.'[14]

Shortly thereafter, Diarmuid was at it again. He told Tomás' parents, 'I've got a proposal for you from the best girl that ever broke bread, the finest and handsomest girl every way.' This time, Tomás' parents seemed to go along with the idea. At the end of the evening, Diarmuid was pleased with the conversation and 'fancied that the bargain had been sealed'.[15]

But when Tomás' eldest sister Máire (Ní Chriomhthain) Uí Shúilleabháin got wind of the situation, she had other thoughts. She immediately intervened, saying that the marriage would be unwise for Tomás and his parents, and pointing out that the Ó Dálaigh family would not be close if their parents needed help. This rationale would have made sense to Tomás' parents, who were understandably concerned about their well-being during their old age. Máire's involvement appears to have been decisive and Tomás acquiesced. There would be no match with Cáit.

Tomás described his profound sorrow at the prospect of losing Cáit:

> I wasn't too cheerful, and no wonder, for I was leaving behind me the merriest days I had ever known, and, into

the bargain, I was turning my back on the girl I liked best in the whole blessed world right then.[16]

Tomás reluctantly moved on from Cáit; and Cáit, having been spurned, emigrated to America. Her parents expected that they would never see her again. A few years later, however, she returned home, still unmarried, and now in poor health. In 1885, seven years after Tomás' marriage to Máire Ní Chatháin (see below), the unfortunate Cáit died of tuberculosis. There was a large funeral, which Tomás attended and described in detail, but without much emotion.[17]

With Shrovetide 1878 approaching, Tomás' sister Máire finally succeeded in making a match for her brother. She persuaded Tomás to marry Máire Ní Catháin, the niece of her deceased first husband, Máirtín Ó Catháin. This match was surprising because of the lawsuit she had won against the prospective bride's family. Perhaps the match helped to put that dispute to rest. Another appealing aspect of the match was that the bride was the younger sister of Tomás' lifelong friend, Pats Mhicí Ó Catháin, the future island King (see Chapters 4 and 7).

Describing the proposed match, Tomás wrote:

> She [Tomás' sister Máire] had herself marked down an excellent, knowledgeable girl, whose people lived in the village, so that they could lend us a hand when we needed it, and she went on to explain the whole affair to us, like a woman reciting a litany, till she had the whole lot of us as tame as a cat ...
>
> The girl she had such high praise for – and she deserved it – was a sister to the man who is King of the Blasket to-day – though he hadn't got the title of King in those days [1878] or for long after [he wouldn't become King until sometime between 1900 and 1905].[18]

There was a sense of urgency in the air. Several Blasket couples were getting married at Shrovetide in that particular year, and there seemed to be a certain amount of pressure to go along with the crowd.

It is apparent that Tomás was almost a bystander in this matchmaking process. His immediate family effectively made one of the most important decisions of his life for him. And their motivation was largely self-serving. Only his Uncle Diarmuid advocated on behalf of his true feelings. Mícheál de Mórdha wrote: 'Although Tomás knew his own mind well, he had nonetheless to yield to his family's will and accept the match that was made for him.'[19] Tomás' personal interests were subordinate to what was perceived as being in the family's best interests. He followed a course of action that reflected his respect for his parents as well as the traditional matchmaking approach to marriage.

With respect to his bride, Máire, Tomás was less than fully enchanted, at least at the outset. He made no reference to any romantic feelings he might have had for her in his writing. This is in contrast with the affection he obviously felt for Cáit, although even with her he was less than fully explicit. Tomás mentioned Máire's name only once, and that was in his announcement of the marriage (see below).

This episode was a defining moment in Tomás' life. One could conclude that he never really got over the loss of Cáit. In the unabridged translation of *An tOileánach*, entitled *The Islander*, Tomás comments on the decision of a Blasket girl to call off an arranged marriage at the last minute. He wrote:

> I was closely related to the girl, and I wouldn't be the one to blame her for what she did, because 'life is only worth living when you have the freedom to choose,' as someone said long ago, and there's a great deal of truth in that saying.[20]

As Thomas Shea observed of Tomás, 'Fifty years later, he still wishes that he had had the freedom to choose.' And if he had, Tomás would clearly have chosen Cáit.[21]

Tomás and Máire Ní Catháin were married on 5 February 1878. There was no time for courtship. He was twenty-three years old and she was almost exactly nineteen, having been baptised on 8 February 1859. Tomás described his wedding day as follows:

> A week from that day [when the match was made] we were married – Tomás Crohan and Maura Keane – in the last week of Shrove in the year 1878. There never was a day like it in Ballyferriter. There were four public-houses there, and we spent some time in all of them until it was very late in the day. The town was packed with people, for there were a lot of other couples being married ...
>
> We had to leave Ballyferriter at last, just when the fun was at its height, but since the great sea was before us, and there were a lot of us to take across, we had to go.[22]

Tomás wrote that once the wedding party was safely back on the island, the festivities continued through the night until high noon the next day, with plenty of food and drink to fuel the merriment.

One very poignant detail of his wedding was related by Tomás in the original manuscript of *An tOileánach*. During the festivities, Tomás sang an old Irish love song, '*Caisleán Uí Néill*' ('O'Neill's Castle'). He was particularly proud of his rendition of the song, writing: 'Everyone was bewitched by the song and the way it had been sung.'[23] The lyrics tell of a crestfallen girl lamenting the loss of a lover who has left her:

Marriage and Family

Caisleán Uí Néill

('O'Neill's Castle') – An Excerpt

Céad slán don oíche aréir,
's é mo léan gan í anocht ina tús
Leis an mbuachaillín spéiriúil
A bhréagadh mé seal ar a ghlúin
Chuir tú orm an t-éileamh,
a mhíle grá bán, ach ní leatsa mo rún
Mar céad faroar géar,
ta na sléibhte 'dhul idir mé 's tú.

A hundred farewells to last night
and my sorrow it's not starting anew
With the handsome young fellow
who beguiled me awhile on his knee
You placed your claim on me,
O my fair love, but I'm not meant for you
For a hundred sharp sorrows,
the mountains lie between you and me.

'S tá an gairdín seo in' fhásach,
A ghrá geal, 's ta mise liom féin
'S tá gach pabhsae a' fás ann
níos breáchta ná a bhfaca tú riamh
Níor cluineadh ceol cláirsí
'dhul 'niar an tsráid seo ná ceol binn
*   na n-éan*
Ó d'éalaigh mo ghrá uaim,
an chraobh álainn, go Caisleán
*   Uí Neill.*

This garden is growing wild,
My bright love, and I am alone
And every flower is growing,
Fairer than you ever saw
No harpsong was heard along this road,
Nor the sweet songs of birds

Since he left me, my love,
That fair scion, for Caisleán Uí Néill.[24]

In his editing of the original manuscript of *An tOileánach* (see Chapter 10), An Seabhac evidently saw the potential for a negative reaction to Tomás' awkward handling of this situation. Accordingly, he simply omitted this element of the wedding story. Over forty years later, Tomás' grandson, Pádraig Ua Maoileoin, in his expanded version of *An tOileánach* (see Chapter 11), restored the story of the song, apparently out of respect for Tomás' voice.

Tomás' intent in singing this particular song at his wedding remains a mystery. There are differing opinions on his motivation. He may have selected it as a lament for his loss of Cáit – an expression in music of his deepest personal feelings about his arranged marriage to Máire. If this interpretation is accurate, it was certainly insensitive to his bride Máire, who may have been cringing in the audience. On the other hand, Blasket scholar Seán Ó Coileáin feels he may have chosen it simply because it is a beautiful piece of music.[25]

Cathal Ó Háinle suggests yet another intriguing explanation. Perhaps Tomás didn't sing this song at the wedding at all and simply included this episode to the manuscript four decades later when he was writing *An tOileánach* to better illustrate his love for Cáit. It could have been a storyteller's ploy for relating what he regarded as an underlying essential truth, even if it was not historically accurate.[26]

In any event, Tomás began married life with Máire. He wrote that he underwent a metamorphosis on his wedding day:

> Till that day I had known little of the world's responsibilities, but from that time on they came upon me. Everything I had to do with changed from that day. Marriage makes a great change in a man's life. His disposition and his view of all sorts of things alters, and, above all, it whets his appetite to be up and doing in life. As the phrase goes, I used to fancy, up till then, that food was sent from Heaven to us.[27]

The new couple lived with Tomás' parents in their modest house in the lower village. Over the years, the old house was once again filled with the lively sounds of a growing family. Tomás wrote that his father was a great help to him as he was raising his family. As for Máire, she seems to have been a quiet woman who focused primarily on raising her children and doing her household work.

Oddly, Tomás makes almost no mention of Máire in *An tOileánach* from their wedding day in 1878 to her death in 1904, a period of twenty-six years. The few references he makes during this period are in the context of the family's many sorrows (see Chapter 6). He wrote of the 'sore trouble' that Máire felt as several of her children experienced sickness and death and that her 'heart broke for them'.[28]

Tomás' near silence about Máire may be a reflection of his general inclination to avoid discussion of his personal feelings. Perhaps he was simply reluctant to display emotional vulnerability. On the other hand, it may be that his silence spoke volumes.

Tomás devotes only a single short paragraph in *An tOileánach* to Máire's passing (see Chapter 6). His account of her death deals primarily with the impact of her death on him. He referred to her almost impersonally as 'the poor mother', not as his wife. He wrote that Máire 'was taken from me' and called her his 'comrade' rather than expressing his thoughts in more personal and affectionate terms.[29] There are some notable exceptions to this general approach, including his lengthy description of his interaction with Cáit and his more detailed discussion of the premature deaths of three of his children, Pádraig, Domhnall and Cáit.

It seems that Tomás' relationship with Máire was at least muted. After all, it was an arranged marriage that occurred almost on the spur of the moment, with no opportunity for their relationship to blossom. In such a situation, both parties might eventually tend to focus more on their children than on their relationship with each other. The couple certainly had plenty of troubles that might challenge a marriage, including the tragic deaths of so many of their young children. In this context, Tomás' reported singing of '*Caisleán Uí Néill*' (see above) may have been indicative of a less than perfect foundation for a marriage.

The only hint of possible marital discord over the years involved a trip that Tomás and a group of other islanders took to the Iveragh Peninsula to sell a load of fish. Tomás reported that three attractive Cahersiveen women were flirting with three of the Blasket men, apparently excluding Tomás. One of the women was tall and had red hair. She beckoned: 'Come along, Blashket man, won't you have a drink?' She ripped the vest off one of the men as they ran back to their lodgings.

Tomás relays this curious story in a swaggering manner as if it was a great adventure. But the tale apparently did not sit well back on the island. One of the three men, unnamed in the narrative, was in particular trouble with his spouse; and according to Tomás, 'the rest of us didn't get off with whole skins either.' The island women were reluctant to let their men travel to Cahersiveen for quite some time. Tomás wrote: 'Idle talk sometimes causes great scandal.'[30] But it is unlikely that this situation had any lasting impact, if any, on Tomás' marriage.

Tomás wrote *An tOileánach* when he was an elderly man. He was looking back over the broad arc of his lifetime and reminiscing. Either consciously or unconsciously, he chose to approach his discussion of Cáit and Máire in very different ways. This was long after the end of his relationship with Cáit, his marriage to Máire and the deaths of both. Yet Tomás' feelings for Cáit seem to have persisted. As he aged, his fond memories of Cáit and their courting days together were frozen at a happy time in his youth and they never faded. It may be that Tomás chose to express these sentiments in his autobiography, however obliquely, as a way of disclosing his true feelings. It seems that Tomás was devoted to Máire, but that he had truly loved Cáit, at least for a time. An Seabhac, who knew Tomás and his wife well, wrote that Máire was a 'lovely, kind, loyal woman' and that she 'managed to gain his heart as they grew in love and in relationship together'.[31]

Like most of the islanders, Tomás and Máire had a large family. In *An tOileánach*, he wrote that they had ten children. In fact, they had twelve. He may have overlooked two who

CENSUS OF IRELAND, 1901.

(Two Examples of the mode of filling up this Table are given on the other side.)

FORM A.

No. on Form B. *18*

...RN of the MEMBERS of this FAMILY and their VISITORS, BOARDERS, SERVANTS, &c., who slept or abode in this House on the night of SUNDAY, the 31st of MARCH, 1901.

NAME and SURNAME.		RELATION to Head of Family.	RELIGIOUS PROFESSION.	EDUCATION.	AGE.		SEX.	RANK, PROFESSION, OR OCCUPATION.	MARRIAGE.	WHERE BORN.	IRISH LANGUAGE.	If Deaf and Dumb
Christian Name.	Surname.				Ages of Males	Ages of Females						
Tomas	Crohan	Head of Family	Roman Catholic	Read & Write	44	–	M	Farmer & Fisherman	Married	Co Kerry	Irish & English	–
Mary	Crohan	Wife	do	Cannot Read	40	–	F		Married	do	Irish	–
Patrick	Crohan	Son	do	Read & Write	18	–	M	Fisherman	not Married	do	Irish & English	–
Ellen	Crohan	Daughter	do	Read & Write	16	–	F	scholar	not Married	do	Irish & English	–
Tomas	Crohan	Son	do	Read & Write	14	–	M	scholar	not Married	do	Irish & English	–
Kate	Crohan	Daughter	do	Read & Write	12	–	F	scholar	not Married	do	Irish & English	–
Daniel	Crohan	Son	do	Read & Write	10	–	M	scholar	not Married	do	Irish	–
Maurice	Crohan	Son	do	Cannot Read	5	–	M	scholar	not Married	do	Irish	–
John	Crohan	Son	do	Cannot Read	3	–	M	scholar	not Married	do	Irish	–

I hereby certify, as required by the Act 63 Vic., cap. 6, s. 6 (1), that the
...rgoing Return is correct, according to the best of my knowledge and belief.

Joseph M. Mulloohyclon (Signature of Enumerator.)

I believe the foregoing to be a true Return.

Thomas Crohan (Signature of Head of Family).

The 1901 Census return for the Ó Criomhthain family signed by 'Thomas Crohan' and listing himself, his wife and seven children. His occupation is given as farmer and fisherman. English is used throughout.

died in childbirth or early infancy. The Ó Criomhthain brood included: Seán I (born 1879), Pádraig (1880), Eibhlín (1883), Tomás (1885), Cáit (1887), Máire I (1890), Domhnall (1892), Mícheál I (1894), Muiris (1896), Seán II (1898), Mícheál II (1900) and Máire II (1901). Island families would often name a newborn after a child who had died earlier, reflecting a superstition that God would not take two children of the same name. This resulted in three instances of Ó Criomhthain children with identical first names (Seán, Mícheál and Máire), identified above by Roman numerals indicating their birth order.[32]

The Ó Criomhthain children were enrolled in the national school for various periods of time, depending on illness and competing family demands. According to the school's register, the number of years they attended were: Pádraig (four),

Tomás in 1924 outside the new house he built. The White Strand is in the distance.

Eibhlín (seven), Tomás (eight), Cáit (five), Domhnall (seven), Muiris (eight), and Seán II (eight).

Tomás was a thoughtful and generous father. Years later, Seán Ó Criomhthain remembered the excitement in the house whenever his father returned from Dingle. He always brought home a treat for each of his children.

According to Tomás, the Ó Criomhthain home was medium-sized relative to the other houses on the island. With his expanding family, Tomás set out to improve the situation: 'Some ten years after my marriage I built a new house.' When he started building the house, about 1888, he was about thirty-four years old and had four living children. Many more were to follow. The new house was about twice the size of the old house, but with such a large family, more space was a necessity, not a luxury. Tomás was proud of his efforts. He wrote: 'if

Sketch by Ida Mary Streeter Flower of the lower village where Tomás lived. The tiny figures in the lower right depict Tomás and Robin Flower chatting.

King George [of England] were to spend a month's holiday in it, it isn't from the ugliness of the house that he would take his death.'

Tomás' new house was located only a very short distance to the north of his old house in the lower village, no 'farther than the breadth of a street'. It overlooked the White Strand. Unlike his old house, his new home faced south, like most of the other island homes.

Tomás wrote that he learned all the skills that were necessary for island life from his father. He was a stonemason and a carpenter; he designed and built his new home singlehanded over a long period of time, working around the fishing seasons. 'Nobody handed so much as a stone or a lump of mortar to me all the time I was at work on it, and I roofed it myself.'[33] This seems unusual because collaborative work was commonplace on the island. Nevertheless, Tomás' stonework was very precise, exhibiting great craftsmanship. He was particularly proud of the felt roof, the first on the island. This was a big improvement over the thatched roofs, where the hens nested, resulting in irritating droppings.

Tomás and his family moved to the new house in early spring 1893. He had apparently completed the house sometime much earlier. The delay in moving to the new house is unexplained, but it may have been because his wife was pregnant or his children were sick. By the time they moved, Tomás and Máire had six children living at home. The family certainly needed the extra space. Subsequently, Pádraig Thomáis Ó Ceárna, the son of Tomás Maol and 'the old hag', moved into Tomás' former house, with their then vacant house possibly being used as an outhouse. Tomás expanded his new house, adding another room sometime between 1901 and 1911.[34]

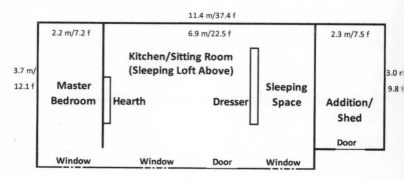

Schematic of the interior of Tomás' new house (m = metres; f = feet). The total living space is about 59 square metres (635 square feet). The ceiling height is about 2.3 metres (7.5 feet). The shed is about 7 square metres (75 square feet). All measurements are interior and are not drawn to scale.[35]

Tomás had many mouths to feed. Island families generally managed to get by on just two simple meals a day, morning and evening. The menu typically consisted of fish, potatoes and milk. Sometimes there would be bread made from flour or Indian meal. Holidays were generally celebrated with lamb. Rabbits added variety to the diet. Vegetables grown on the island were eaten in season. Tomás wrote that food, particularly meat, was more plentiful in later years, but noted that the earlier islanders who survived on a 'starvation diet are still alive and kicking'. He wrote that the Great Blasket was 'the healthiest island in Ireland'.[36]

Like all other island families, the Ó Criomhthains subsisted primarily on fishing. Following in his father's footsteps, Tomás was also a jack of all trades, supplementing his income as a stonemason and a carpenter, salvaging shipwrecks, raising livestock, hunting rabbits, gannets, otters and seals as well as a little planting. His son Seán said that Tomás cut the fabric for garments for his neighbours from his own patterns. He was skilled at tailoring and weaving and he also made panniers (baskets). Finally, he taught carpentry. As Seán said, 'Idleness never struck him.'[37] This kind of diversification in sustaining the family was a way of life on the Great Blasket. Visitor and mentor Brian Ó Ceallaigh wrote that Tomás once told him, 'You can't live on the scenery' when he wanted him to write about the natural beauty of the island, 'which he seemed to drink in'.[38]

Throughout his life, Tomás focused on what he called 'profitable work'. He worried, for example, about the poet Seán Ó Duinnshléibhe interrupting him as he was cutting turf to ask him to transcribe folktales (see Chapters 7 and 8). He was also distressed when distracted by a group of playful girls (see above). In later life, he worried that his writing got in the way of other obligations. All these situations reveal a man who was very concerned about managing his time and who felt slightly guilty when he was not on task.

Tomás rues the family's occasional free-spending ways when times were good. He wrote: 'If we had been as careful of the pounds in those days as we have been for some years past, it is my belief that poverty wouldn't have come upon us so soon.'[39]

Fishing was a very difficult way of life. The working hours were very long and the results unpredictable. Tomás wrote that he had two cows and he raised pigs, but there is no mention of him raising sheep, though many other islanders did so. And, of course, the family grew vegetables. Around 1888, Tomás began growing potatoes on a dormant section of his land. He was disappointed with the output, but he expanded the plot the next year, applying the lessons he had learned and having much better results.[40]

In the first decade of the twentieth century, the Congested Districts Board built new gravel roads on the island, a new slipway and five 'new houses' at Slinneán Bán at the top of the village. Tomás was employed on these projects and his skill as a stonemason must have been indispensable. According to *The Islander*, the first foreman on the job, Seán Ó Corcráin, stayed with Tomás for seven months. Tomás wrote that he got paid £5 for his work on the slipway.

At one point, the second foreman became frustrated by the work of the islanders and told Tomás, in English, 'Those are the four stupidest men I ever saw ... and I'll have to discharge them.' Tomás responded that if the Board wanted the homes completed, the English-speaking foreman would have to be discharged because he couldn't make himself understood. He couldn't communicate with his men, who spoke only Irish. Tomás said, 'I fancy he realised that it was with him the fault lay.' In what may have been an exaggeration, Tomás claimed that he had to finish the houses himself. He proudly reported that he worked seven days a week and that his pay was two shillings a day.[41]

In addition to his work for the Congested Districts Board, Tomás is known to have worked as a stonemason for other islanders. As late as 1919, he collaborated with Domhnall Ó Cinnéide on the construction of a tiny house for Tomás 'Bell' Ó Duinnshléibhe high up in the village. This was the smallest house on the island.

Also in his later years, Tomás, was compensated for tutoring cultural visitors, such as Carl Marstrander, Robin Flower and Brian Ó Ceallaigh, in the Irish language (see Chapters 9 and 10). How much income this generated is unknown, but it certainly wasn't enough to support his family. Tomás also mentions gifts of money, tobacco and clothing from Robin Flower and others during this period.

Finally, there was of course the business of writing. Tomás was eventually a published author and in his old age he made a respectable amount of money from his writing, particularly his books. Tomás probably didn't get paid much, if anything, for his numerous articles in periodicals; but he enjoyed the recognition they brought him.

In the aggregate, Tomás' income was probably slightly above average for an island family. But he was very concerned about his finances throughout his life.

6. Tragedy Stalks the Ó Criomhthain Family

The Great Blasket was a dangerous place to live. Threats to human life lurked everywhere. Infant mortality was high, and deaths from complications in childbirth were not uncommon. Diseases such as measles, whooping cough, tuberculosis, meningitis and typhoid fever could all be fatal. There were also accidents – falls from cliffs, drownings and fishing mishaps. Hygiene was poor and access to proper medical attention was problematic. Yet the islanders' indomitable faith in God gave them a stoical view of the dangers they faced.

Emigration involved a figurative death when a son or daughter left for America or elsewhere – in most cases never to return. In a nod to the likely implication, the traditional going-away party held the night before departure was called an 'American wake'. The next morning, all the islanders would bid farewell to those departing at the island slipway. Most of them would never be seen again.

Tomás' family experienced an inordinate number of deaths, even for the island. Their litany of premature deaths is truly dreadful. Of Tomás and Máire's twelve children, five didn't live to the age of ten (Seán I, Mícheál I, Máire I, Mícheál II and Máire II). Another four died before the age of thirty-five (Domhnall, Pádraig, Muiris and Cáit). Their son Tomás emigrated to America. And the destiny of Eibhlín remains a mystery. Only two of Tomás' children lived what might be regarded as a normal lifespan and outlived their father (Tomás and Seán II).

Tomás' wife Máire died at the age of forty-five in 1904 after a very difficult life. Tomás himself lived the longest of the entire family, dying at the age of eighty-two. He had outlived ten of his children and his wife.

All these deaths must have had a profound impact on Tomás. Brian Ó Ceallaigh wrote:

> The life for a Blasket man is not a sheltered one. There are cliffs for man and beast to fall over, the sea to drown in. Tomás has had such tragedies in his own life, and he looks on men and things seriously.[1]

In *An tOileánach,* Tomás wrote about Seán I's death in a fall off a cliff, Domhnall's drowning, and the deaths of his wife Máire and their daughter Cáit. He reported but didn't elaborate on the deaths of several children from disease. He doesn't even identify several of his children by name as they die. While he demonstrates sensitivity to each situation, he moves on quickly to the next segment of his narrative without a significant outpouring of emotion. He seems intent on facing each tragedy with courage and dignity. There is little mourning beyond the usual island wake and mainland burial. As Tomás wrote several times in different ways, 'the dead don't feed the living'.[2]

Tomás did, however, seek solace from his Uncle Diarmuid after the death of some of his children. He also went through a difficult period of adjustment after his wife's death. Méiní (Ní Shé) Uí Dhuinnshléibhe, the Blasket nurse, said: 'Tomás Criomhthain got his share of misfortune in this life if anyone ever got it. But God gave his help to the poor unfortunate man to carry his cross, and carry it he did.'[3]

**The Ó Criomhthain Family: a chronicle of tragedies
in order of death[4]**

Name	Relationship to Tomás	Cause of Death	Born	Died	Age at Death
Séan I	Son	Fell from cliff	1879	1887	8
Micheál I	Son	Whooping cough	1894	1898	4
Máire I	Daughter	Whooping cough	1890	1898	8
Micheál II	Son	Childbirth/infancy	1900	1900	0
Máire	*Wife*	*Following childbirth*	*1859*	*1904*	*c. 45*
Máire II	Daughter	Measles	1901	1905	4
Domhnall	Son	Drowned	1892	1909	17
Pádraig	Son	Tuberculosis	1880	1913	32
Muiris	Son	Unknown	1896	1915	20
Cáit	Daughter	Tuberculosis	1887	1922	34
Tomás		*Probable Stroke*	*1854*	*1937*	*82*
Eibhlín	Daughter	Unknown	1883	Unknown	Unknown
Tomás	Son	Natural causes	1885	1954	69
Seán II	Son	Truck accident (hit-and-run)	1898	1975	77

Under these difficult circumstances, one might expect signs of depression in Tomás' writing, but his reaction to these tragedies comes across more as stoicism. Yet suffering so many deaths in his family must have influenced his outlook on life, and this may account, in part, for the sombre tone of some of his writing.

The first tragedy of Tomás and Máire's married life occurred when their son Seán I, then about eight years old, lost his footing on a cliff and fell over 100 feet to his death. Seán, identified in the narrative only as Tomás' firstborn son, and his boyhood friend Mícheál Ó Catháin, the King's eldest son, were out for a day's adventure together on 6 July 1887. Tomás gave this sad account of the event:

At the time when young birds come and are beginning to mature, the lads used to go after them. My eldest boy [Seán I] and the King's son [Mícheál] planned to go to a place where they were likely to get a young gull – for one of those would often live among the chickens in a house for a year and more.

The two went together after the nests to bring a pair or so of the birds home with them. They were in a bad place, and, as my boy was laying hold of the young gull, it flew up and he fell down the cliff, out on the sea, God save the hearers! He remained afloat on the surface for a long time until a canoe [*naomhóg*] going after lobsters came up and took him aboard ...

We had only one comfort – there was no wound or blemish anywhere on his body, though it was a steep fall from the cliff. We must endure it and be content! It was a great solace to me that he could be brought ashore and not left to the mercy of the sea.[5]

Tomás' general attitude of acceptance and resignation demonstrates his capacity for managing grief. Perhaps he thought this was the kind of terrible calamity that might happen once or maybe twice in a lifetime. The very next day, he was back to the business of trapping lobsters: 'we, too, had to put out our oars again and drive on.' But much more sorrow was to follow. At one point, expressing his frustration, Tomás wrote: 'From that time on they [his children] went as quickly as they came.'[6]

Eleven years later, in 1898, an epidemic of whooping cough swept the island. Without proper medical attention, two of Tomás' children, Máire I and Mícheál I, perished, aged eight and four respectively. Tomás wrote that he spent three months sitting up caring for his sick children, but 'I got nothing for the

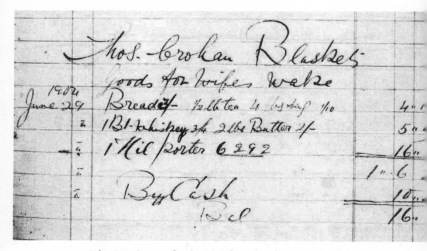

John Long's entry for the sale of supplies for Tomás' wife's wake.

time I spent, only the two best of them were carried off. That was another discouragement for us, God help us.'[7]

As for this string of deaths, Tomás wrote: 'Such was the fate of my children. May God's blessing be with them ... and with the poor woman whose heart broke for them [his wife Máire].'[8] Next came the death of his son Michael II two years later in 1900, at birth or shortly thereafter.

Gradually, the health and morale of Tomás' wife Máire began to fail. After all, she had endured the deaths of four of her children and the fifth, a toddler, was very sick. Tomás wrote: 'the sorrow of it [the recent deaths] never left the mother for good or ill, and from that time forth she began to fail, for she was not to live long, and never lasted to be old.'[9]

Máire died in late June 1904 at the age of about forty-five after twenty-six years of marriage. Tomás confessed: 'I was completely upset and muddled after that.'[10]

The ledger of John Long, a grocer and purveyor of spirits in Dingle, contains an entry for 29 June 1904 detailing the purchase of food and drink for Máire's wake. Máire was buried in Ventry, her family's ancestral home. Tomás was in despair. He wrote eloquently:

> [W]hen comrades part, the one that remains can but blunder along only too often, and so it was with me ... My low spirits did not leave me soon this time, though I was always struggling to shake them off day by day, and, Heaven knows, I had but poor success in it. Something would always be coming across me to wake my trouble again.[11]

Máire's last-born child was Máire II, who lived only about four years, dying of measles in 1905, not long after her mother's death. Four years later, in April 1909, Tomás' son Tomás emigrated to America following an 'American wake' (see Chapter 13). And the parade of Ó Criomhthain family tragedies marched on.

The best-known tragedy to hit the Ó Criomhthain family was the drowning of Tomás' son Domhnall. Little is known about the lad except that he attended the national school for seven years. The story of his death at the age of about seventeen has been well documented by several writers, most prominently by Mícheál Ó Dubhshláine in his book *A Dark Day on the Blaskets*.

Island visitor Eibhlín Nic Niocaill was a brilliant scholar and a student at the School of Irish Learning in Dublin. A member of the Gaelic League, she wrote several articles that appeared in its periodical, *An Claidheamh Soluis*. There was some speculation that she was the girlfriend of Patrick Pearse, the Irish patriot, newspaperman and eventual martyr for Ireland. Nic Niocaill visited the Great Blasket for an extended period in the summer of 1909, when she was twenty-four. She was

Eibhlín Nic Niocaill on her graduation from the Royal University, now
University College Dublin.

very popular on the island and enthusiastically participated in the social life of the community. Nic Niocaill frequently gave swimming lessons to the island children, a significant contribution because few islanders knew how to swim.

On the morning of Friday, 13 August 1909 – Friday the thirteenth – Nic Niocaill visited the King's daughter, Máire (Ní Catháin) Uí Guithín, to admire her new baby. Earlier that day, Tomás' son Domhnall had disclosed to Máire his love for Nic Niocaill. But this was probably just a one-sided boyish infatuation.

That afternoon, Nic Niocaill was teaching Tomás' 22-year-old daughter Cáit to swim off the White Strand. The King's daughter, Cáit an Rí, was with them, although she was not swimming that day. The water was fairly calm. But suddenly, there was panic in the water as a wave hit Cáit Ní Chriomhthain. She lost her footing and swallowed some water. She grabbed Nic Niocaill, and there was much thrashing about. The tide was going out. Soon the two were near exhaustion. Cáit an Rí splashed into the water, trying to help. She got close, but couldn't reach them.

Meanwhile, Domhnall was working in a field just above the strand. Méiní (Ní Shé) Uí Dhuinnshléibhe, a witness to the drama, said that as soon as Domhnall saw what was happening, he ran to the strand as fast as he could. He told his cousin Cáit an Rí not to go out any further, which probably saved her life. In turn, she urged him not to waste time taking off his heavy hobnail boots. He dived into the water in a desperate attempt to rescue the two struggling swimmers.

Nic Niocaill and Domhnall were eventually brought to shore, but efforts to revive them failed. According to Leslie Matson, Méiní later recalled some disagreement in the heat of the moment about the level of effort expended on saving Nic Niocaill over Domhnall.

Tomás' son Domhnall Ó Criomhthain with his cousin Cáit (Ní Chatháin) Uí Chathasa, one of the King's daughters.

Cáit Ní Chriomhthain nearly drowned too. She was found floating under a foot of water. When she was brought ashore by Peats Tom Ó Ceárna, it was thought that she too was dead. Nevertheless, the onlookers began to massage her body, and soon they realised that she was slowly regaining consciousness. As for Cáit an Rí, she was badly shaken by the whole incident.

Tomás had been out fishing and arrived on the scene just after the two bodies had been recovered. He suddenly realised that one of them was his son Domhnall. He recognised the distinctive pattern of the hobnails on the soles of his boots; nails that he himself had pounded in. He immediately let out an almost inhuman wail of sorrow and horror that could be heard throughout the nearby island village. According to Seán Ó Criomhthain, he kissed Domhnall on the mouth and Nic Niocaill on the hand. Seán recalled that Tomás said:

> I leave everything else for the God of Glory to lay out the road for you both to the Kingdom of Heaven and to give me the grace of patience to carry this cross.[12]

Nic Niocaill's body was brought to the King's house, where she had been staying; Domhnall's body was carried home; and Cáit Ní Chriomhthain was taken to the King's daughter Máire's house to recover. She was very weak and was confined to bed for several days. Two wakes were held on the island. A telegram advising Nic Niocaill's parents of an accident was sent from Ventry.

The bodies were transported across Blasket Sound on Sunday 15 August. The sad procession of twenty *naomhóga* in the form of a cross was led by the King's *naomhóg* carrying Nic Niocaill's coffin. The news had spread, and the convoy of mourners was greeted in Dunquin by a throng of people from all over West Kerry and beyond. Antiquarian Thomas H. Mason, who happened to be in Dunquin, said 'The funeral procession of currachs across the Sound ... reminded me of a funeral that I saw in Venice where black gondolas take the place of the mourning coaches.'[13]

Domhnall was buried in the old cemetery in Baile an Teampaill, Dunquin. Tomás wrote that the funeral was the largest ever seen in Dunquin. The legend is that Patrick Pearse himself attended, although it is more likely that he attended Nic Niocaill's funeral in Dublin.

Nic Niocaill's body was placed in St Gobnet's church overnight. Tomás and Cáit an Rí were taken to meet briefly with her grieving parents. Nic Niocaill's body was taken to Dingle by carriage the next morning and then to Dublin by train. She was buried in Glasnevin Cemetery. Pearse wrote an obituary that appeared in *An Claidheamh Soluis*.

Tomás wrote of the double drowning with a tone of resignation:

> If it was for her [Nic Niocaill] he died, it could not be helped. It was God's will.
>
> I think that if it hadn't been for my Uncle Diarmid, I should never have recovered from this trouble at all. I had God's help, too, for the daughter [Cáit] who had been in the sea was never expected at first to come round either, since she was still at her last breath ... Diarmid used to come in every day and night, making little of our despondent talk, reminding us of troubles far worse than ours.[14]

In recognition of Domhnall's bravery and Tomás' loss, Eibhlín's mother sent Tomás an undetermined sum of money every week for the remainder of his life. Tomás wrote: 'The lady's family were very kind to me for years afterwards.'[15] Seán Ó Criomhthain wrote later that the incident took a toll on his father's health and that it took him a long time to recover:

> Tomás was happy at this time. There was nothing wanting in his life … He often said afterwards that 'the blow was three times worse because he fell from the top of the ladder, instead of the middle.'[16]

This was Tomás' own account of the aftermath:

> Well, after all this anguish, I was trying to pull myself together. It was imprinted on my mind that there was no cure for these things but to meet them with endurance as best I could, and I kept trying to get through a while more of life – one year good and two that turned out ill.[17]

The drownings were reported extensively in newspapers throughout Ireland. For his heroic efforts in saving Cáit Ní Chriomhthain, Peats Tom Ó Ceárna was awarded a bronze medal and a certificate from the Royal Humane Society signed by King Edward VII, dated 15 October 1909. Peats Tom wore it proudly on special occasions.

The Gaelic League undertook a fundraiser among Irish speakers, possibly on the initiative of Patrick Pearse. A photo of Eibhlín was given to each contributor. Tomás wrote a letter expressing his appreciation for the gifts:

> I would like to thank them [the contributors] seven thousand times and to say that I will remember for ever what they have done for me. All my dead son did was to do the same as would befit any Gael, the same as every single man in this island would do.[18]

An Blasgaod Mór,
Andiu an 20ad Lá d'Iúl.

Do Stiopán Bairéad.

A Cara.

Ag seo admáil go bfuaireas ó Lámaid Fíonáin Mhic Coluim aon púnt ficead, oċt is leat-ṗaol, mar ḃronntanas ó luċt na Gaediltge. Tá orm mo ṡeaċt míle buideaċas a ġaḃáil leo agus a ráb leo go mbeib cuimne agam go deo ar a nbeóṙnadar dom. Níor ḃein mo ṁac-sa a fuair bás aċt an rud ba dual do Ġaedeal agus an rud do ḃéanfad gaċ uile fear san oileán so.

Tá súil le Dia agam go n-eireógaib liḃ san obair ṁór atá roim láṁa agaib agus geallaim-se dib go ndéanfad-sa agus muintir an Oileáin ár gcion féin cun̄ au Gaedilg do coimeád beó brioġṁar in ár mearg-na annso.

Mise agus meas agam oraib,
TOMÁS Ó CRIOMHTHAIN.

Tomás' thank-you letter for the contributions following his son Domhnall's drowning.[19]

The letter appeared in *An Claidheamh Soluis* on 30 July 1910, about a year after the drownings. This was probably the first time a piece written by Tomás was published.

Domhnall's sacrifice of his life in an attempt to save Nic Niocaill became an island legend. Both of the victims were eventually honoured by the Gaelic League. Eighty years after the drowning, a stone was erected in Domhnall's honour in the graveyard at Baile an Teampaill. It was unveiled by Seán Pheats Tom Ó Ceárna, whose father had been decorated years earlier for the rescue of Cáit Ní Chriomhthain. Cáit's son Pádraig Ua Maoileoin read a poem in honour of his uncle Domhnall.

Coincidently, a few years after the double drowning, Tomás was involved in a drowning rescue himself. Around 1911, Peig Sayers' young son Mícheál fell into the water near the slipway.

He was saved by Tomás and the lad's older brother Muiris. Mícheál later emigrated to America very briefly, but returned to the island, where he became the last island poet.

Unfortunately, this long succession of tragedies was not yet over. On 29 June 1913, Tomás' son Pádraig died at the age of thirty-two from tuberculosis in the Dingle workhouse, which was serving as a hospital at the time.[20]

Mystery surrounds the fate of Tomás' two other children. Eibhlín was born on 2 August 1883 and enrolled in the national school on 21 November 1891. Her attendance was excellent until 1898, when she attended for only about four months. She was removed from the rolls at the end of the school year, when she would have been about fifteen. This was the same year her siblings Máire I and Mícheál I died from whooping cough. It is possible that Eibhlín too was ill, but she is listed as living at home in the 1901 Census. She is not listed in the 1911 Census. There are two logical explanations: she died, perhaps from disease between 1901 and 1911; or she left for America sometime after 1901. But there is limited and conflicting evidence. Tomás called his daughter Cáit 'the daughter [singular] I had'[21] when she died in 1922 (see below), implying that Eibhlín had passed away earlier. Leslie Matson, on the other hand, wrote that Eibhlín had emigrated to America.

Muiris was born on 3 July 1896. He attended the national school for nine years from 1904 to 1912. He apparently died in 1915, when he would have been nineteen. No conclusive information on his cause or location of his death is available.

The last tragedy to afflict Tomás was the death of his daughter Cáit, who passed away from tuberculosis in 1922 at the age of thirty-five. Appallingly, two of her young children and her father-in-law died in the same year. Her death was particularly difficult for Tomás (see Chapter 13).

	Name and Surname	Relation to Head of Family	Religious Profession	Education	Age	Sex	Rank, Profession, or Occupation	Marriage	Where Born	Irish Language
1	Thomas Corhan	Head of Family	Roman Catholic	Read and Write	64	–	Farmer	Widower	Co Kerry	Irish and English
2	— Crohan	Son	Roman Catholic	Read and Write	28	–	Fisherman	Single	Co Kerry	Irish and English
3	— Crohan	Son	Roman Catholic	Read and Write	16	–	Scholar	Single	Co Kerry	Irish and English
4	John Crohan	Son	Roman Catholic	Read and Write	13	–	Scholar	Single	Co Kerry	Irish and English
5	— Crohan	Brother	Roman Catholic	Cannot read	72	–	Fisherman	Widower	Co Kerry	Irish

The 1911 Census return for the Ó Criomhthain family, signed by 'Tomás Ó Criomhthain' (not 'Thomas Crohan') and listing himself, three children and Tomás' brother Pádraig now living at his home.

Tomás faced all this heartache with an outward toughness. He typically described all these deaths in a matter-of-fact tone and continued with his narrative, although there is some indication of a period of adjustment after each death. Tomás' grandson, author Pádraig Ua Maoileoin, said:

> I was told he [Tomás] was very hard and tough in his youth ... [The Ó Criomhthains were] like iron in body and soul. It was difficult to make them cry, or shed a tear. It was difficult to imagine them mourning someone's death.[22]

Tomás may have been reserved about his losses, but they were great. Escaping their impact entirely would have been impossible, even for a hardened islandman as seemingly resilient as Tomás.

Tragedy Stalks the Ó Criomhthain Family

Unfortunately, this series of family tragedies continued even after Tomás' death in 1937. Thirty-eight years later, in 1975, his sole surviving child, Seán, then seventy-seven, was killed when he was struck by a pick-up truck (see Chapter 13). With that death, the long string of calamities that had beset the Ó Criomhthain family had finally come to an end.

7. A Blasket Life

Tomás' writing provides a wide-ranging overview of life on the Great Blasket as it was during his lifetime. He details an extraordinary life, full of beauty, hardship, adventure, danger, celebration and sorrow. His personal portrait of the island community is an important feature of the rich tapestry that comprises the literature of the Celtic Revival.

Tomás was first and foremost a fisherman. He learned the trade from his father, and he started fishing for a living after the completion of his schooling in the mid-1870s. He fished well into his sixties, a span of about forty-five years. In turn, he passed the trade down to his sons. Throughout his writing, there are detailed accounts of Tomás' fishing, lobstering and seal hunting.

The primary catch for Blasket fishermen was mackerel, but according to Tomás, the Great Blasket was actually 'the last place where the mackerel fishing started'.[1] He explained that a new type of fishing net was donated to the islanders, and since they were unfamiliar with the use of these nets, they naively sold them to fishermen in Ballyferriter. They then watched in dismay as the Ballyferriter fishermen caught substantially more fish with the new nets. The islanders were forced to go to Dingle and buy new nets to replace those they had sold. They had outsmarted themselves.

Tomás told of a memorable day in his young adulthood when he and two others were headed up the hill to cut turf.

Tomás in middle age, about 1910.

They noticed a large school of mackerel shoaling, gathering near the surface, just offshore. Tomás took pride in their quick reaction to the situation. The trio recruited two old men to help them. Then they rushed a *naomhóg* out to a seine boat that had deployed its net and was full of fish to the point of overflowing. They filled the *naomhóg* several times with an impressive catch of about 8,000 fish, 'every one of them as long as your arm'.[2]

On another occasion, Tomás set out on his first seal hunt with an unnamed uncle. He was one of two younger members of an eight-man crew. They set off for a dangerous cave on the far western end of the island. Two of the older men, including his uncle, dived into the water with safety ropes tied around their waists and carrying clubs to kill the seals. The two lads were assigned to pull the seals up and on board. Suddenly his uncle's rope broke. Thinking quickly, Tomás, who was a swimmer, dived into the water and 'by God's grace' rescued his uncle, who couldn't swim. He wrote that he nearly drowned himself in the effort. Nevertheless, the seal venture was quite successful with a yield of eight seals, one for each man on board.[3]

Tomás described the introduction of the islanders to a new type of fishing vessel under unusual circumstances, around 1880:

> At that time there wasn't a single canoe [*naomhóg*] here or any of the gear to suit them, only big [seine] boats that were always managed by a crew of eight. Each boat carried a big, heavy seine net, with stones tied to the bottom of the net to sink it, and corks on the upper rope to keep the top of the net on the surface. There were little boats, too, used by old men and young lads for line fishing, and they would often be full of the sort of fish that is caught that way.
>
> Somebody said one day that two of the Islanders had gone to a fair in Dingle, and that they had bought a canoe from a man when they were drunk. Before long we saw her coming, and we marvelled at her.[4]

Mackerel was fished from seine boats and later from *naomhóga* with a three-man crew and six nets. Tomás described the process:

> They had two seasons each year, one in May and another in November. Strangers [visitors] came to buy fish and used to sell it out fresh to England in boxes that held a hundred fish each ... Come September they use it in a

different way, the fish is cut and gutted, they cure it with salt and fill many barrels with the cured fish ... and they are dispatched off to England ... to be eventually shipped to the [United] States.[5]

Also in the 1880s, the islanders discovered that lobsters, abundant in Blasket Sound, could generate a handsome profit. Tomás wrote about the beginning of lobstering as a business venture:

> The things I had seen them throwing into the sea were pots to catch lobsters. The Blasket people were as strange to that sort of fishing tackle as any bank clerk at that time. Not much of the year had gone before there were four Dingle canoes fishing lobsters round the Blasket after this fashion. The Dingle fishermen took hundreds of pounds worth of lobsters from the waters round the Island before we had any notion how to make a shilling out of them. They fetched a pound the dozen, and, to make the story better, the dozen was easy got ...
>
> Next year off went the [island] crews, racing one another to get canoes ... I went off like the rest to get one, and Pats Heamish [Tomás' brother-in-law] went with me. We took another good fellow with us. I found a canoe easily enough ... and for eight pounds we brought it away with us ... We rubbed through the season ... and we had ten pounds apiece after paying for the canoe ...
>
> A few years went by like this, and the fishers didn't want for shillings, as the [buyer's] boats came to our very threshold with yellow gold on board to pay for the catch, however big the haul might be.[6]

Lobstering subsequently became a steady source of income from March to the end of August. Each man had about two dozen lobster pots that were hauled up four times daily. Tomás summarised the economics of lobstering:

> At every shift of the [lobster] pots you would get a dozen lobsters, and that meant a dozen shillings: those twelve shillings bought a half-sack of flour, and eight shillings a half-sack of meal, and so with everything else. A poor man could live easily enough in those days.[7]

Tomás shared a story about a surprise adventure one calm moonlit night just off the White Strand. A crew of fishermen found a huge sea creature in their fishing net. Suddenly, it went berserk, dragging their *naomhóg* a mile out to sea. The islanders were frightened and desperate not to lose their net. They gradually worked their way back to the island slipway where they finally killed the beast. Tomás wrote that it was 'as big as the whole harbour basin' and that its liver alone provided the island with oil for light for five years. Tomás didn't identify the creature, but it may have been a basking shark or a small whale. Tomás wrote: 'There's many a danger lying in wait for those that follow the sea.'[8]

In the early 1890s, a group of islanders took the two large seine boats they had at the time to market in Dingle with a cargo of fish, pigs, wool and sheep. Overnight, the boats were confiscated by 'police' because the islanders were significantly in arrears on their rent. From that point forward, the islanders had no choice but to use *naomhóga* for fishing. These were smaller vessels and normally operated with a crew of three. The islanders quickly adapted. Tomás wrote: 'We had to take to the canoes then and do our best to fish the sea with them by day and night – lobsters by day from May day to August, and mackerel by night, every night that came fine when the fish were there.'[9]

Living from the sea produced inconsistent results. Tomás, for example, wrote that 1878 'or about that' was a fine year for fish. Later, he wrote that 1887 was not a good year for lobstering because of bad weather; but fishing for pollock was excellent that year.[10] Tomás repeatedly gauged whether a given year was good or bad by the profitability of the fishing.

Unfortunately, the islanders eventually discovered that even their small *naomhóga* were not beyond the reach of the bailiffs. On 28 July 1890, the HMS *Britomart* raided the island and confiscated the islanders' only remaining vessels. This time, however, they negotiated a settlement and the *naomhóga* were returned (see below).[11]

In his later years, Tomás partnered in fishing and lobstering with his older brother and housemate, Pádraig. The two retrofitted an old *naomhóg* and generated a respectable income despite their advanced age.

In the 1890s, according to Tomás, fishing was particularly profitable:

> We had good purses of money now [after selling the catch]. There were over three thousand fish in each of our boats. We went to a house [in Dingle] for food first, and after that to the tavern. We sang half a dozen songs, and that was no marvel, for if there were poor men of our kin, they weren't us that day. We had enough to eat and to drink, and, more, there was a generous chink of money in our pockets.[12]

Tomás had a tendency to see events in a larger context. He judged that the islanders' improved financial position had given the island a rough form of home rule – Irish self-government:

> I often told the fishermen that Home Rule had come to the Irish without their knowing it, and that the first

beginning of it had been made in the Blasket now that the yellow gold of England and France was coming to our thresholds to purchase our fish, and we didn't give a curse for anybody.[13]

In 1914, Robin Flower returned to the Great Blasket and wrote that that Tomás had resumed fishing at about sixty years of age. Tomás reported that fishing continued to be relatively good at least up to 1918.[14] After the First World War, however, there were substantial fluctuations in both the price and the demand for fish. Fishing was no longer commercially viable. Tomás gives us a lesson in fishing's harsh bottom line:

> Every currach all along the coast was full to the brim with mackerel. In Árd na Caithne harbour [Smerwick] the seine nets were weighted down to the sea bottom with fish. There was never such a show or spectacle as the amount of fish on its way to Dingle. A large quantity of it was bought at a shilling a hundred. That shilling did not pay the cost of the cartage; it was sixpence short. But the man who caught the fish did not receive the shilling, nor even so much as a penny. Not a single sixpence reached the Island out of that day's fishing, although every currach there was loaded to the gunwhale.[15]

In 1921, the United States imposed a tariff on cured mackerel. The market promptly collapsed. Lobstering then became the primary means of generating an income from the sea until France prohibited imports of shellfish. The Blasket fishermen were victims of government decisions far beyond their control. In addition, fish became less plentiful in the Blasket waters, perhaps the result of overfishing. Tomás' diary entries in *Allagar na hInise* track the decline of Blasket fishing.[16] In October 1922 he wrote:

'Dingle trawlers out fishing in the bay from morning to night and coming home without even a fish to grill on the tongs! King of the Saints! Whatever has happened to the fish of the sea?' says a woman on the Blasket, after the currachs had come in three nights in a row without herring or mackerel.[17]

In the last chapter of *An tOileánach*, Tomás' reminisces about his life as a fisherman. On balance, his view of fishing as an enterprise and as a way of life is decidedly negative. He vents his frustration at the long odds of the business and the significant risks involved:

Often would we put to sea at the dawn of day when the weather was decent enough, and by the day's end our people on land would be keening [mourning for] us, so much had the weather changed for the worse. It was our business to be out in the night, and the misery of that sort of fishing is beyond telling. I count it the worst of all trades. Often and again the sea would drive over us so that we could see the land no more – a long, long night of cold like this, struggling against the sea, with often little to get, only praying from moment to moment for the help of God. It was rare, indeed, for us to get a full catch, and then often we would have to cut away the nets and let it all go with the sea. On other nights, after all the labour of the fishing, the boats would be fairly full, and we couldn't make the harbour or the land, but the swell would be rising to the green grass, the storm blowing out of the north-west, and the great waves breaking. We would have to flee then before the gale, some of us to Cuan Croumha [Crooked Creek], some to Ventry harbour, some to Dingle.[18]

Tomás himself appears to have been a proficient fisherman, although some islanders felt that he exaggerated his track record in his writing. He really had no alternative but to be a good fisherman – there was no other way to earn enough money for his large family to survive. All other income was ancillary to fishing.

Another essential element of Blasket life was harvesting the turf that was burned in home fireplaces. Families cut their own turf in bogs at the top of the island, a distance of about a mile and a half from the village. Turf was dried in the open air in a rick or stack for a month or so before being hauled home in creels. It was then stored outside the house until it was used. Cutting turf was backbreaking work that was both continuous and time-consuming.

Turf cutting was also the context for frequent conversation. When he had company while cutting turf, Tomás engaged in banter on a variety of subjects, just to break the tedium. Tomás and his neighbour and friend Seán Eoghain Ó Duinnshléibhe often cut turf together since they worked adjacent bogs. They often exchanged stories and sometimes argued good-naturedly in the intervals between their hard labour.

On one occasion, Robin Flower accompanied Tomás when he was building a rick. Every once in a while, he would stop and light his pipe. Tomás always had a poet's eye for beauty. He suddenly broke out with:

> If you were to walk all Ireland round it would come hard to you to find another place so beautiful as this. You can see the Skellig rocks and Valentia Island, the hills of Ibh Ráthach, and Dingle Bay, and Slea Head that lies farthest west into the sea of all Ireland. And away behind is Brandon Mountain, and around the corner is Cruach Mhárthain.[19]

These thoughts evolved into telling Flower detailed stories of the history of these various places. Tomás' natural tendency to put things into a broader context kicked in.

Tomás also shared several stories of being interrupted while cutting turf by the ageing island poet Seán Ó Duinnshléibhe. The poet was anxious to share and preserve his wealth of poems and stories. For his part, Tomás wanted to get on with his work, but he reluctantly humoured his elderly friend.

The islanders were the beneficiaries of multiple shipwrecks in Blasket Sound. In *An Island Community*, Mícheál de Mórda lists forty-one ships that were wrecked in the vicinity of the Blaskets.[20] These were treacherous waters indeed.

News of a shipwreck always set off a mad scramble to salvage as much of the unfortunate ship's cargo as possible. Several shipwrecks occurred when times were particularly tough on the island. Tomás wrote: 'our folk often got through a bad year with the help of storm and tempest.'[21]

On 3 April 1850, the British barque *Commerce* sprang a leak and was abandoned on the north side of the island. The ship broke up, and the islanders salvaged much of its cargo of palm oil, which they then sold. Tomás wrote that he was 'still very young' when this happened.[22] In fact, this wreck occurred about four years before his birth. He probably heard the islanders reminiscing about it when he was a young lad.

Also in 1850, the Italian brig *Caroline*, which was carrying a cargo of wheat, went aground on the White Strand. Most of the crew drowned. Tomás wrote: 'Those thousands of sacks of wheat saved the Islanders, for they lasted them and their relations for a long while.' In the aftermath, the islanders were criticised for not doing enough to save the lives of the crew. Tomás wrote that he couldn't remember the year of this event because he 'wasn't born or thought of in those days.'[23]

Tomás and his Uncle Diarmuid discovered the wreckage of an unknown ship that had foundered years earlier (1850) off Inis na Bró. They were able to salvage the remnants of its cargo of four-foot-long brass and copper bolts. They realised a tidy profit of £16.[24]

Another shipwreck yielded a load of lead-lined boxes containing an unknown brown substance. The islanders could see no useful purpose for it, so they tossed many of the boxes back into the sea. Tomás wrote that one creative islander realised that the substance could be used to dye women's petticoats. When one woman found out that her husband had discarded some of this salvage, she was furious and browbeat him soundly. The husband didn't take his mistreatment lightly and he quietly emigrated to America. Later in the narrative, Tomás reveals that the islanders eventually discovered that the puzzling brown substance was tea – 'the first that ever came to the Island.'[25]

On 12 August 1916, the British steamship *Quebra*, carrying a cargo of cotton, flour, watches, wire, brass and munitions went aground on Lóchar Rock (*Carraig a' Lóchair*). Some of the recovered goods were used on the island and the remainder were sold on the mainland. Tomás reported that 'Hundreds of pounds' worth of goods were salvaged from the wreck.'[26] On this particular occasion, Tomás was not invited to make up a salvage crew. He was about sixty-two at the time, so he may have been viewed as a potential drag on the effort. This is odd because two years later he was still working occasionally as a stonemason. He was clearly offended at having been passed over.

Tomás' neighbour, 'the old hag,' staunchly maintained that God sent these ill-fated ships to the Great Blasket in the islanders' time of need. Tomás wrote that the old folks felt that without this help, nobody would have survived.[27]

The late 1870s was a particularly difficult time on the Great Blasket (see Chapter 2). According to historian Seán Ó Dubháin, 'For three years the weather was miserable ... The summer of 1879 was one of almost constant rain and it was very cold. It was verging on famine again in many places.'[28] Tomás wrote that the British government sent three relief ships to the island with flour, yellow meal (Indian or corn meal), oatmeal and clothes.

Additional yellow meal and flour were made available to the islanders in Dingle. This led to a harrowing adventure for a group of islanders under the leadership of the King, who were pressed into service as the impromptu crew of an old hulk of a trawler. They barely made it back to the island, bailing water from the leaking ship all night to keep it afloat. The ship was towed the final distance to the island by *naomhóga* the next morning. In the meantime, the King quietly entrusted a mysterious box of bottles to Tomás for delivery to the island by horse-drawn cart and *naomhóg*. According to Tomás, both deliveries were successful:

> There were eight tons of both meal and flour in her [the trawler], a great help to the Blasket at that time. When we fell to carrying it home, you'd have thought the harbour was an ant-hill, for every man had his bag on his back ...
>
> The King didn't forget to ask after the box he'd entrusted to me when he went on the ship; and when I told him that it was waiting for him at home, safe and sound, he was mighty pleased, and forgot all the troubles of the night.[29]

The mysterious box of which the King was so protective apparently held a supply of strong drink he had bought – eight pint bottles and a naggin (a 200 ml bottle) – and he entrusted his important purchase to his close friend Tomás.

Portrait of Tomás Ó Criomhthain in 1932, aged about seventy-eight, by Harry Kernoff.

Tomás wrote that the islanders soon realised that they could not possibly consume all the yellow meal before it spoiled. Always enterprising, they found a way to further their good fortune. They decided to buy some bonhams (piglets). The idea was that the bonhams would eat the surplus meal and later be sold at a profit after fattening. Forty-two bonhams were purchased and Tomás himself bought two. He wrote that he realised a profit of £9.[30] This story was the talk of West Kerry and resulted in some resentment towards the islanders for making too much money on the donated meal. Soon, however, the islanders soon tired of tending the bonhams and they gave up raising pigs altogether.

The Blasket literature is replete with stories about skirmishes between the islanders and bailiffs, or rent collectors, involving land rent and taxes. The islanders lived a hand-to-mouth existence, and they could seldom scrape together the funds to keep up with their obligations. They were also convinced that these payments were excessive and unfair. Tension between landlords and tenants was prevalent throughout Ireland, but the islanders were among the first to flatly refuse payment. It may be that they were better able to be defiant because of the difficult logistics of collection on the island.

The Great Blasket had been owned by the Earls of Cork since the late 1500s. In turn, the property was managed by land agents such as Bess Rice and four Husseys – Clara, John, Sam and Edward. These officials were loathed by the islanders. Bailiffs would be sent to collect overdue rent and if no payment was made, they would take possession of personal property. But there was no serious threat of the islanders being evicted from their houses. As a practical matter, other people had little interest in moving into them, and no one wanted to be perceived as helping the bailiffs.

Describing the unrelenting pressure from bailiffs, Tomás wrote in *Seanchas ón Oileán Tiar*:

> A boat of these bailiffs would regularly come from Dunquin or from Ballyferriter, and they were not to be praised as neighbours ... One day they took twenty red petticoats belonging to the women, and their own wives would welcome these newly made garments, just off the needle ... There wasn't a week in the year that they wouldn't set out to the island in a boat from the mainland to take cattle and everything else they could find, and they didn't mind who the owner was. They were always relieving such a person of his possessions ... With the passing of time, the raids became less frequent and some time after that they [the islanders] did not have an easy life of it. They were short of food, and very frequently

could not pay the rent. Sometimes three years would pass before paying any rent. They were subject to high rents – two pounds per cow – and the bad weather and the wind would often destroy their crops. In the end they went six long years without paying any rent.[31]

Tomás told many intriguing and sometimes comical stories of the struggles of the islanders against the bailiffs and their attempts to foil them:

- Probably sometime in the 1870s, the bailiffs took the women by surprise while their husbands were off fishing. They were driven away by, among others, the poet Seán Ó Dhuinnshléibhe's outraged wife. As her five children were sitting at the table, part of the roof crashed down on them. They were shocked to find a bailiff up on the roof. Angrily wielding her husband's new sheep shears, she climbed up to the roof, and stuck them up to the hilt into the bailiff's backside. A spurt of blood shot down through the hole in the roof and he fell to the ground head first. Tomás, obviously proud of her actions, called her 'A stout woman and a mad woman!'[32] The bailiffs, thwarted in their mission, tended to their wounded comrade and fled the island.

- On 23 October 1879, the HMS *Goshawk* approached the island with twenty armed policemen looking to collect taxes. Tomás wrote that the men had dark uniforms and high caps with guns at the ready. The women of the island asked Tomás, a young married man at the time, to collect stones for ammunition. About thirty island women gathered on the cliff overlooking the harbour. Most of the men were away fishing. The policemen made three separate attempts to land a boat, but each time the women rained down stones, and they were repelled. One of the men was hit in the head and knocked to the ground. But they dared not fire a single shot, apparently for fear of repercussions. When the women ran out of stones, one enraged woman threatened to throw her own child down on the men. Thankfully, she was restrained by one of the other women. Tomás wrote that the ship left 'without taking a copper penny with them'.[33] But the uniformed men eventually landed a short distance to the north and circled back to the village. The official account of the incident reads that the men collected just five shillings. This was certainly a lot of effort and aggravation for the modest benefit derived. One consequence of this confrontation was that the government became aware of the desperate conditions on the island. Relief ships, including the *Goshawk*, arrived with potatoes and yellow meal the next year.

- The islanders often had advance warning of a raid by the bailiffs, who would typically only appear in good weather. They were easily visible as they crossed Blasket Sound. Tomás wrote that on one occasion, probably in the early 1880s, the islanders drove their livestock to the far west end of the island, hiding them to avoid confiscation. The frustrated bailiffs found just two old mules, which they decided not to take with them for fear of being ridiculed. Tomás wrote: 'They went home as they came – without cow, horse or sheep.'[34]

- In the early 1880s, the islanders went to Dingle in two seine boats to sell sheep, wool, pigs and fish. A celebration followed, and the islanders spent the night in town. The next morning, they were shocked to find that their boats had been impounded because they were again in arrears with their rent. When they couldn't pay the amount due, the boats were slated for auction. Tomás wrote that two friends offered him money for his share, but he declined their generosity. The islanders then had to trek all the way back to Dunquin before making the trip across Blasket Sound to the island in *naomhóga*. As for their boats, there were no bidders, and the bailiffs wound up empty-handed as the boats rotted away in a field. Discouraged, the bailiffs temporarily suspended their collection efforts. Tomás wrote that shortly thereafter, the 'middleman', the land agent, had to give up the land. A representative of the Earl of Cork himself then visited the island. The rent at the time was £2 per cow. He asked how much the islanders could afford. Someone blurted out, 'one pound per cow'. And thus a new rent was negotiated. Tomás wrote, 'We were done with bailiffs and injustice from that out ... the Islanders were well satisfied with the arrangement'[35] – for the time being anyway.

- On 28 July 1890, the HMS *Britomart*, a ship that earlier brought relief supplies to the island, returned carrying a force of 100 armed men. They easily overwhelmed the 130 or so impoverished men, women and children living on the island. The rent was seven years overdue. They quickly seized seven *naomhóga* and a yawl and towed them to Dingle, where they were held for ransom until the rent was paid. The islanders pooled their resources and a friendly Dingle merchant added to their total. The islanders then redeemed their *naomhóga* for £42, the equivalent of two years' rent. This was particularly galling for the islanders. They were convinced that the *Britomart* brought typhoid fever to the Great Blasket and several islanders died as a result. Resentment ran deep. A substantial public outcry ensued. The raid was discussed in the House of Commons in London on 31 July and again on 7 and 8 August. The upshot was a pledge from the government that Her Majesty's ships would no longer be used to collect rent.

- Tomás recalled his father and his neighbour Tomás Maol telling the story of a ship named the *Nora Creena* that raided the Great Blasket in 1910 and confiscated the islanders' fish. Tomás wrote that the islanders were delighted when the bottom fell out of the ship on its way back to Dingle and its cargo was lost to the sea. They said that the curse of the islanders was on that fated ship.[36]

After the turn of the twentieth century, raids by bailiffs became less frequent. Change was in the air. The islanders may have lost several battles, but they ultimately won the war (see below). Tomás clearly detested the bailiffs.

In the early 1900s, two systemic changes took place on the Great Blasket that had the potential to improve the islanders' economic standing dramatically. The parish priest in Ballyferriter wrote to the British government asking that its Congested Districts Board help improve the living conditions on the island. The Board ultimately agreed. A group of islanders, including Tomás, met with the priest and two representatives of the Board on the mainland. The island delegation shared the news of their meeting with the crowd awaiting their return to the island:

> We had good news, and gave it them with joy ...
>
> God's help is nearer than the door ... However hard our masters may be after us sometimes, the Great Master of all often sends them to the rightabout.[37]

Over the next fifteen or so years, the Board made several major physical improvements on the island (see Chapter 2) and undertook a comprehensive programme of land reforms. In 1907, the Board acquired the island from the Earl of Cork for the sum of £500. At that point, no rent had been collected from

A hatless Tomás in front of a byre, early 1900s.

the islanders for seven and a half years. Three years later, the Board assigned values to the island properties and instituted an instalment payment system that would eventually transfer ownership of the land to the islanders.

The ownership of the land was only one dimension of the transformation that was afoot. In a ten-year process beginning in 1907, the Board undertook the reorganisation and reallocation of the approximately 60 acres of arable land on the island. Under the new configuration, each family was assigned a combination of fertile and less fertile land that averaged about 2 acres. This change was designed to be more equitable, but this 'radical' concept generated considerable scepticism on the island.

During Spanish author Plácido Ramón Castro del Rio's visit to the Great Blasket in 1928, he and the King discussed the field reorganisation process in one of their many conversations:

> Next to the village, there is a small triangle of farmed land, split in small plots, all of them more or less of the same dimensions. Years ago, the allocation of the land was irregular. Every farmer had tiny pieces of land in different places and the farming was impossible, but the British government [the Congested Districts Board] managed to convince the farmers of the advantages of a more rational distribution. The allocation was done with great difficulty because each farmer was convinced that he was given less land than he had before ... *But thanks to the services of an old man, of great authority in the Island, who did the allocation by himself,* this improvement that actually benefited all, was finally done [italics added – see below].[38]

Tomás himself wrote that he helped the agents of the Board do the necessary surveying of the land. He described the experience in *An tOileánach*:

> Before long the officer of the Board came. He put up a tent and spent some time among us measuring and apportioning the land. It was I who held the other end of the chain for him ...

> The Board improved our holdings so that every man knows his own plot and has it fenced so that he can do his sowing in a part of it whenever he likes ...
>
> When the land was all tidily settled by the Board and every man had his own field here and there, trimly fenced, there was nothing to prevent us sowing all we wanted, and we used to do that, and more.[39]

When the new plots of land were being delineated, they had to be reshaped, and some islanders were suspicious that their new plots were smaller than their current plots. The men gathered every night in one of the houses. The ashes from the fireplace were spread on the hearth in front of the fire, the shapes of the fields drawn with a stick and compared. It took a long time for some to be convinced that a square or triangular field could be the same size as a long narrow strip of land. The new configuration was developed using a 'Gunter's chain' held by two people. Many islanders helped by holding the ends of the chain, gradually generating credibility for the process.

Simultaneously, the Board built two basic roads up the hill from the village, one upper and one lower. This layout allowed each plot of land to be reached without crossing another family's plot. In another innovation, all the plots were fenced.

Despite the initial apprehension, the outcome of this two-pronged process benefited all the island families. Seán Ó Criomhthain wrote: 'Bess and Clara [Hussey], the landlord's agents, were under the sod and young Islanders were dancing to music on their own land. That is how the wheels of this world rotate.'[40]

Tomás' involvement in this process is unclear. He wrote that he helped with the surveying, and although he is not identified by name, it is possible that he was the 'elderly man, a man of great authority in the island' referred to in the conversation between the King and Castro del Rio, who helped to lay out the plots. But there seems to be no particular reason not to name the person who played this role. Tomás may also have been involved in various negotiations with the Congested Districts Board as a member of the island's council of elders.

Tomás realised a substantial economic benefit from this process. He reported that his new rent was seventeen shillings per year, while his grandfather had paid £10. This must have seemed like a real bargain. (His circumstances got even better when he became a landowner in 1921.) In his June 1922 entry in *Island Cross-Talk*, Tomás made a simple declaration that summed up this significant advance:

> In this field you have a view towards the four quarters and what the eye will not see the ear will hear ... Tomás O'Crohan is its owner. I am Tomás and it was the Congested Districts Board that gave it to me in the division of the land.[41]

Tomás wrote that this process resulted in a renewed commitment to the cultivation of the land in the early 1920s: 'Now, when we had our gardens all ship-shape, so that neither deer nor eagle could go into them, nothing could tire us of sowing and reaping.' But, this burst of energy was short-lived:

> At this time there rose up a babbler amongst us, and his idea was to have food without sweat. He stuck his hands under his oxters [armpits]. As happens with every villainy, it wasn't long till first one and then a pair of lads did as he did, and many of them started to take their ease. This ill-conditioned rascal told them that it was the same food one would get after all, and that only horses and fools worked in this world.

First one field, then two, and then three, went to ruin, and remained fallow without a thing planted in them. The man that started this rascality went to America, and he didn't find bread growing on the hedges there. We've never been so keen on planting since as we were at first, and the walls that the Board set up to fence the fields are beginning to fall.[42]

While there were significant reforms that addressed fundamental issues of equity, the changes proved insufficient to staunch the flow of emigration from the Great Blasket. Moreover, two ironies soon emerged. First, the islanders found that the land that one owns is no easier to till than the land one rents. And second, the islanders finally achieved ownership of the land at the very time that the island as a whole began its long slide into decline.

Tomás was born into in the rich folk culture of the Great Blasket. This tight-knit island community gathered together almost every night for storytelling, music, dance and poetry. These gatherings were often held in the home of Máire Uí Cheárna, which was nicknamed the Dáil. During the summer, they were sometimes held outdoors on the White Strand or overlooking the slipway. Tomás described the gaiety on warm summer evenings:

There were four types of music there and seven different dances, all held in the Gaelic manner. There were songs sung there the finest ever sung. It was no wonder, for there was the sound of the ocean, the echo of the cliffs and the sound of the voices rising over the hill ... it was like a small Oireachtas [dance competition].[43]

As for the younger crowd, 'There was a special house in the village that the young folk, boys and girls, used to gather in and stay till midnight ... I am proud to be able to say that nothing wrong ever happened among them for the sixty-seven years that I have known it.'[44]

Storytelling was a well-developed art form on the Great Blasket. The skill was acquired over time by routine practice. Both the skill and the stories were handed down from generation to generation. The storytelling had a spontaneous quality, and everybody was welcome to get involved.

Although he provides few details, Tomás was a Blasket storyteller in the oral tradition, a *seanchaí*. It wasn't until much later in his life that he became a writer (see Chapter 8). That he was a product of this tradition is evident from the style and content of his writing. For example, he always had great admiration for the Fianna, who were adopted by the nationalist movement as inspirational figures – and they are often mentioned in his written works.

Some stories told of historical events, such as the wreck of the *Santa Maria de la Rosa* of the Spanish Armada just off the island in 1588, and the story of twenty-one drownings in a sudden storm in the mid-1850s at Sorrowful Slope (*An Leaca Dhubhach*). There were also stories about mythical Irish warriors; the Hound of Cuchulainn (*Cú Chulainn*) and Finn Mac Cool (*Fionn Mac Cumhaill*). There were scary stories about fairies and banshees. Many stories imparted a lesson or a moral.

The story of Piaras Feiritéar, a poet and Blasket hero, was an island favourite. His family had for generations leased the island from the Earls of Desmond. Ferriter was involved in an uprising against the British and he was aggressively pursued by their forces. But he was prepared for that possibility. He discovered a cave on the remote north-western side of the island where he felt no Englishman could ever find him. Seán Ó Criomhthain wrote that you needed to be agile as a cat to locate this hideout. Eventually, however, Ferriter was captured on the mainland and hanged in Killarney in 1653. According to the legend, he held a communion wafer in his mouth, and divine intervention caused the hangman's rope to break three times. This should have entitled him to a reprieve of his death sentence, but Ferriter said he didn't want to be the leavings of a rope. The fourth time, the rope held.

Another favourite story involved the great victory of the island's entry in a canoe race in Ventry. Tomás gives his version of events in *Seanchas ón Oileán Tiar*. The islanders and their *naomhóg*, named *Beauty*, were challenged by a group of Ventry men after other potential entries dropped out. The Ventry team expected an easy win.

> They got themselves ready, like the other naomhógs, and were ready to start the race when they got the signal. That was it. When they got the signal, the naomhóg set out, and in the last course of the race the Island's naomhóg was far ahead of them all. They won very comfortably, and nobody on the strand begrudged them for it because the other naomhóg was far too overconfident and pompous after they had seen the other boats pull out of the race. When the Blasket's naomhóg came ashore after winning the race, the people ran out into the water around the naomhóg, the men still in it, and picked up the boat, the naomhóg and the men, oars and ropes, out of the sea, until it was picked up by a wave.[45]

This victory was a tremendous source of pride for the islanders and was immortalised in the poem '*Beauty* Deas an Oileán' by Seán Ó Duinnshléibhe, the island poet. The island schoolchildren were required to memorise this tribute in verse.

The islanders were enthusiastic singers, and songs were a regular part of the traditional evening gatherings. Popular tunes included *An Chúilfhionn* and *Port na bPúcaí*, both haunting laments. Other songs included *Róisín Dubh* and *Jimmy Mo Mhíle Stór*.

Tomás enjoyed singing, and he is reputed to have had a good voice. He particularly liked *Cuilt an Oileáin,* a song that Ó Duinnshléibhe had written and that was later included in *Seanchas ón Oileán Tiar* (see Chapter 11). He also composed songs of his own.

Tomás chose the medium of song to expresses his feelings for his first love, Cáit Ní Dhálaigh. In an indirect expression of his sentiments, he focused primarily on her beautiful singing. Perhaps he felt it would have been indiscreet to be more explicit about his affection. Poet Máire Cruise O'Brien wrote that the story of 'Tomás' first love ... is told almost entirely in terms of songs sung when they met at fair or fireside ... All of them are intensely passionate and basically unhappy songs, as was the fashion.'[46]

As for musical instruments, the islanders played the tin whistle, the harmonica and the melodeon or squeeze-box. They even made violins out of 'wreck' wood that washed up on the island. Islander Peaidí Mhicil Ó Súilleabháin said that there was a melodeon in Tomás' house, but there is no indication that he played it.

Tomás enjoyed stepdancing, performing jigs, reels and hornpipes. He wrote that that his father could stepdance and that he gave him his first dance lessons. Sometime during his young adulthood, a dance teacher visited the island for a month and set up shop in the old Souper School. Tomás took advantage of the opportunity and paid the fee of four shillings. The teacher lodged near Tomás and he benefited from some extra lessons. He boasted that 'Before long I was a marvellous

Tomás wearing his waistcoat, probably his Sunday best, mid-1930s.

dancer.' He also claimed that he was a popular dance partner, particularly for the older women, bragging that 'I was a bit of a cool character in those days.'[47] Later, he passed this skill down to his son Seán as his father had to him.

And then there was poetry. Seán Ó Criomhthain wrote that his father composed poetry, probably refining his poetic skills under the tutelage of his literary mentor, Seán Ó Duinnshléibhe. Several of Tomás' poems were published in periodicals and various anthologies of his work (see Chapter 11).

Tomás was also intellectually curious. In his unpublished diary, island poet Mícheál Ó Guithín, Peig Sayers' son, described a session when George Thomson, Muiris Ó Súilleabháin and himself composed riddles for Tomás to solve.[48] The breadth of Tomás' interests is astonishing.

Life on the Great Blasket was lived on the edge. For the most part, the islanders stoically accepted their difficult lot in life. Despite their challenges, they managed to survive by relying on hard work, their sharp wits and a deep faith in God. Ultimately, the islanders believed that God would sustain them in difficult times and come to their rescue in moments of peril. John J.M. Ryan wrote: 'The world into which *The Islandman* leads us is a world of faith, of boundless trust in God and thankfulness for His help and protection amid the hardships and difficulties of a precarious existence.'[49]

Seán Ó Criomhthain wrote that faith was an essential element of island life:

> The first people to inhabit the Western Island [the Great Blasket] brought a great gift with them, the living faith which they had inherited from previous generations. That living faith was acquired not from reading books, but from their fathers and mothers who day and night taught it by their words and talk and prayers, and what they taught lasted as long as people lived on the Island ...
>
> There never was and never will there be a fisherman without faith. Fishermen spent their lives under God's weather, and they were often at death's door but were

saved by the grace of God. Whatever faith you profess it is strong when you are at sea because the sea has neither pity nor mercy for anyone.[50]

The islanders were Roman Catholics, the efforts by Protestant missionaries, the 'Soupers,' to convert the islanders during the mid-nineteenth century having been largely unsuccessful.

When the weather allowed the trip across Blasket Sound, the island men attended Mass on Sundays at St Gobnet's church in Dunquin. Attendance at Mass in the winter was infrequent. Tomás referred to the struggle to go to Mass as 'endless trouble'.[51] When the islanders couldn't get to Mass, they would say the rosary on the island at the same time that Mass was offered at St Gobnet's. The island women seldom made the trip to Mass and their religious practice revolved around a group recitation of the rosary led for years by Peig Sayers.

Tomás wrote that in 1920 there were thirteen Sundays in a row when the men weren't able to go to Mass. On Easter Sunday, 1921, he wrote: 'Isn't it a great gift that there are six currachs gone to God's Mass today compared with last year, when no boat ventured out any Sunday for three months.'[52]

Once each summer, the parish priest would visit the island to say Mass and hear confessions. These much-anticipated visits were referred to as the 'Stations.' Religious services were conducted in one of the houses and later in the national school. Describing the event, Tomás wrote:

> It is 'Station' day for us. God's messengers have come to visit us ...
>
> The Islanders were washed and in their Sunday best to meet them ... Two Masses were said and since they had the fine day to spend as they pleased, they were in no great hurry to leave ...

When they were standing outside on the green near the main road, with the sun shining brightly above their heads, the priests declared that the Island was a wonderful place.[53]

On Station day, a group of islanders would fetch the priest in Dunquin in the morning and return him later in the day. From his middle years onwards, Tomás was chosen to help assist the priest during his annual visit.

Tomás related several other religious-oriented vignettes:

- In *Island Cross-Talk*, Tomás wrote that on Good Friday in March 1921, he went to gather 'strand fare' with a handkerchief and a spade when the tide went out. It was a fast day for Catholics and islanders customarily didn't eat meat or eggs, drink milk or take snacks. Instead, they would prepare a special meal of seaweed (dilisk), limpets, periwinkles and barnacles. On his way to the Gravel Strand, Tomás encountered the King's son, Seán An Rí Ó Catháin: 'I hurried off from the field and faced for the shore. Who should meet me but the Crown Prince of the Blasket; he was keeping up the tradition along with everyone else.'[54] Tomás was pleased that members of the King's family set a good example in keeping up the island's religious customs.

- In *Allagar na hInise*, Tomás recalled an Easter Sunday when the islanders were bragging about the number of eggs they had eaten that morning. They did not seem inclined to travel over to St Gobnet's to attend Mass, but:

> The King came along with an air of authority ... He got five or six who were previously undecided to go out to Mass [by *naomhóg*] – the King manages to arouse religious sentiments because he has the big name.

'It is a great shame,' says the King, 'that anyone in full health should stay and not go to God's Mass on a soft calm day like today.'

I suppose that he was right in a way, but another scripture says, 'Mind your own business and do not bother anyone else. The man who rises himself will be lowered, and the man who lowers himself will be risen.'[55]

Tomás wrote little about the role of organised religion in his life, and there is no sense of any burning religious zeal. It is apparent, however, that he was a loyal Catholic: he was critical of the Protestant 'Soupers'; and he resented Mrs David Peter Thompson's negative description of the island people written in the 1840s (see Chapter 9).

Tomás made frequent references to God in his writing: it was 'By God's grace' that he was able to save his uncle from drowning during a seal hunt; he wished God's blessing on his deceased children and wife; he accepted that it was God's will that his son Domhnall drowned in the futile effort to save Eibhlín Nic Niocaill; he thanked God for sparing the life of his daughter Cáit in the same incident; and he thanked God for preserving his memory of the events of his lifetime.[56] On New Year's Day 1923 he wrote:

I am writing this at the start of the New Year in God's name, and if we spent the Old Year well, may we spend the New Year seven times better, with the support and help and love of God and of mankind. And, since our people throughout Ireland cannot understand each other, may God grant the grace of understanding to them before the year is long gone.[57]

It is not clear whether Tomás was in the habit of regular prayer. He mentioned that his father said the rosary every Sunday as he was growing up. But there is no discussion of his own prayer habits or even his personal efforts to attend Mass. In *Allagar na hInise* he described a beautiful winter day when he took a prayer book to Black Creek Point intending an interlude of contemplation. He admitted, however, to being distracted by the beauty of the scene and the sight of girls dancing and boys playing football. In the summer months, Tomás enjoyed retreating to *Tobar an Bhuailteora* (Thresher's Well), where he would stretch out and listen to the sound of the water dripping into the pool and reflect on life in general.

Tomás believed in a crude form of predestination. In a folktale he shared with Robin Flower, he said: 'There is such and such a time marked out for a man on this earth and, when his day is come, if he went into an ant's hole, death would find him there.'[58]

Loyalty to the island's values and its people were a hallmark of Tomás' character. He was generous within the limit of his resources. Peig Sayers said that he could be relied upon to lend her some flour in her time of need. He realised that, in an island community, mutual dependence was essential to survival. His sense of propriety extended to the animal kingdom. In his diary, island poet Mícheál Ó Guithín described his anger when he saw a donkey being beaten. Tomás said: 'It's a bad heart some people have.'[59]

In his old age, Tomás observed that religious fervour on the island was waning. But the examples he gives are more in the way of changing religious customs and do not seem to reflect an erosion of the islanders' basic religious beliefs. He wrote, for example, that priests get only half the respect as they did in his youth. People no longer genuflected upon meeting a priest and women were now allowed to travel in the same boat as a priest.

Summarising the islanders' spiritual life in the last chapter of *An tOileánach*, Tomás wrote:

> We were apt and willing to live, without repining, the
> life the Blessed Master made for us, often and again
> ploughing the sea with only our hope in God to bring us
> through.[60]

And so it was that the islanders carried on with their lives through formidable adversity with trust in a divine plan and a never-ending hope for a better tomorrow.

Tomás related several stories in *An tOileánach* about the islanders' apparent weakness for alcohol. Trips to market in Dingle also provided an opportunity to imbibe. Tomás shared several stories about bouts of drinking and misbehaviour with several companions, including his brother-in-law Pats Heamish and his uncles Diarmuid and Tomás Ó Sé. These episodes included celebration and song, but they also included fights, bad hangovers and at least one arrest (Pats Heamish). Some of these affairs were multi-day adventures. There were also some understandable repercussions when the men returned home in less than optimal condition.[61]

Tomás wrote about a particular lobstering expedition with his brother Pádraig, on which they came across a small steamship in Blasket Sound. They struck up a conversation with the crew and did some business, selling lobsters, crayfish and fish. Their compensation included some food and a bottle of clear liquid. Tomás proceeded to sample the contents of the strange bottle. 'When I had drunk it, I stood for a moment – so Pats told me afterward – and then fell flat in the bottom of the canoe. The poor fellow thought I was dead.'[62] Obviously, it was strong liquor of some type. Tomás was ashamed that his brother had to row the pair all the way home by himself in a gale.

Weddings were an occasion for great celebrations that began immediately after the ceremony in the pubs of Ballyferriter and continued back on the island. The observance of holidays was another opportunity for partaking of a 'drop'. Tomás, for example, described a festive Christmas Eve celebration at his sister Cáit's house and then more drinking and song on Christmas Day that went on until dawn the next day.

Wakes were a solemn occasion with traditional rituals, but they were also an opportunity to partake of porter, whiskey and tobacco. Tomás gives an extensive account of the wake of a relative in Dunquin. The mourning, drinking and smoking continued until the early hours of the morning. For his part, Tomás disapproved of drinking at wakes.[63]

Tomás always portrayed himself as a participant in these festivities, but not to the extent of his compatriots. There is certainly evidence that Tomás took 'a drop' from time to time. But there is no indication that he had a problem with alcohol. In the last chapter of *The Islandman*, as Tomás was bringing his autobiography to a conclusion, he wrote:

> If we deserved blame a little at times, it would be when a drop of drink was going round among us. The drink went to our heads the easier because we were always worn and weary, as I have described, like a tired horse, with never any rest or intermission ...
>
> It wasn't thirst for the drink that made us want to go where it was, but only the need to have a merry night instead of the misery that we knew only too well before. What the drop of drink did to us was to lift up the hearts in us.[64]

The inclusion of this explanation at the very end of the manuscript is curious. It seems that Tomás felt compelled to rationalise the islanders' reputation for hard drinking. Perhaps he was reacting to gossip that cast the islanders in a bad light, and he wanted to set the record straight. Tomás' candid explanation makes sense. The islanders were not regular drinkers, and their occasional use of alcohol in Dingle and in celebrations probably led to overindulgence.

Tobacco was another matter. Most adults on the island smoked a pipe, including many of the women. Smoking was considered an important personal and community ritual. It was not uncommon for clouds of tobacco smoke to waft over island get-togethers. Despite their relatively modest means, islanders always seemed to scrape together the money to buy tobacco. In *The Islandman*, Tomás created a striking visual image about an older couple smoking in bed:

> If the old woman was alive, the old man would stretch across to give her a light from the wisp; then the smoke from the two old pipes would drift up the chimney, and you could imagine the that the couple's bed was a steamship as they puffed away in full blast.[65]

Tomás smoked his pipe regularly almost to the very end of his life. His daughter-in-law Eibhlís, who cared for him during his decline, blamed his heavy tobacco use for his ill health.

Tomás was an enthusiastic participant in the traditional hurling matches held on the White Strand. Primitive hurley sticks were made from furze stems, and the ball was made of 'stocking wool sewn with a hempen thread.' Tomás wrote that the regular Sunday matches were intense, involving 'the hardest days any of the young people had to face.'[66]

He also describes two particular hurling matches in considerable detail. The biggest match of the year was traditionally held on Christmas Day. At Christmas 1877, Tomás and his uncle Diarmuid were on one team, and his uncle

Tom was on the other. Diarmuid's team won three games, and Tom's team was winless. Post-game feelings were running high. And sibling rivalry was at work. Diarmuid teased his brother Tom, who responded by punching him in the side of his head, knocking him out cold.

A week later, on New Year's Day, there was another match. This time, Tomás took a good swipe at the ball, and it hit his uncle Tom smack in the kneecap. He was seriously hurt and needed to be helped back to the village. Tomás' mother was worried about permanent damage. But, given their recent history, Diarmuid wasn't too sympathetic, saying 'He'll make a fine cripple.'[67] Of course, a round of drinking and song ensued. Tomás provides no information on his Uncle Tom's recovery.

The Blasket community was a pre-modern society where time more or less stood still. Beyond the island, however, the world was marching steadily onward. Tomás wrote of the islanders' wonder when they first experienced several technological marvels.

He recalled a conversation between his father and Tomás Maol one cold winter evening. The islanders had observed a strange ship passing through Blasket Sound. They saw smoke coming from the vessel and assumed that it was on fire. Seeking to help extinguish the blaze, they launched *naomhóga* and rowed furiously in pursuit of the ship. But the ship kept moving away from them without the benefit of sails or oars. It became clear that 'something was propelling it'. This was not the islanders' first exposure to a steamship, however; Tomás Maol said that he had passed on earlier reports about such ships only to be called 'Tomás the Liar'.[68] The islanders were habitual sceptics.

Tomás described a trip to Cahersiveen in the early 1880s to sell fish. A storm hit overnight and one of the seine boats, the *Black Boar*, went missing. It had apparently been washed out to sea. Tomás wrote there was a 'hue-and-cry' all over the village at this 'heavy loss'. On a later trip to Dingle, Tomás overheard that a boat had been found adrift near the Skelligs and that it was now on Valentia Island (see map on page xvi). The elated islanders realised that this was probably their missing boat and they set off to Valentia retrieve it. A local priest was entrusted to review the matter, and the boat was returned to the islanders.

While on their mission, the islanders climbed a hill on Valentia to do some reconnaissance of the sea conditions before heading home. From the top of the hill, they observed several astonishing things. On one side of the hill was a quarry with 'big diggers' (probably steam shovels) that Tomás described as a 'wondrous sight'; and on the other side, they saw Glanleam, the mansion of the Knight of Kerry. Tomás reported that 'we marvelled' at this magnificent home with its extensive gardens and statuary, and he remarked that this was the furthest they had ever been from their homes. There was excitement in the air.

Continuing on and coming up over the top of the hill, the islanders were stunned by another amazing sight:

> On the other side of the hill we saw a huge mast, with as many ropes tied to it as found in any vessel that ever sailed the seas. There were many gadgets tied to that mast; you'd have been blinded if you looked at them in the sunlight. It was the mast that carries the large cable bringing messages from Newfoundland to Ireland. A dozen experts are in charge of that mast.[69]

This passage refers to a steel communications tower that was erected by the United States Office of Coast Survey on Valentia in 1866. It was located adjacent to the Anglo-American Cable House at Telegraph Field – the European terminus of the first permanent operating transatlantic cable, which ran almost 1,700 nautical miles to the village of Heart's Content, Newfoundland, Canada. The cable, a major communications achievement, carried telegrams between the old and new worlds.

Thomas Shea points out that Tomás used his own frame of reference in describing the facility. He referred to the steel tower as a 'huge mast', the guy wires 'ropes' and the metallic attachments 'gadgets'. Shea wrote that Tomás, relating the incident forty years later, 'evokes a sense of immediacy, capturing the Islander's bewilderment and awe'. Shea suggests that this sight may even have conjured in Tomás' mind the possibility that he could communicate with a much wider audience.[70] Interestingly, this story was dropped from the original manuscript of *An tOileánach* by An Seabhac, but later restored in the unabridged version edited by Pádraig Ua Maoileoin (see Chapter 11).

From their boyhood, Tomás was very friendly with Peats Mhicí Ó Catháin. The two men shared a mutual respect that began in their days as students at the national school. They seemed naturally drawn to each other and became very close. They were also competitors in the classroom, with Tomás taking pride that he was selected for an academic award over his friend. And they shared many youthful adventures.

In 1878, the pair became brothers-in-law when Tomás married Peats Mhicí's sister, Máire Ní Chatháin. Sometime between 1900 and 1905, Peats Mhicí was designated 'King' of the Great Blasket. This was the pre-eminent leadership position on the island. Peats Mhicí was the last to serve in this capacity; no successor King was appointed after he died in 1929.

As adults, the two men played different but important roles on the island. The King was the social and political leader, while Tomás was more of an intellectual. There are multiple favourable references to the King throughout Tomás' writing. His lifelong respect and affection for Peats Mhicí is clear. In *An tOileánach*, Tomás acknowledges him as the 'chief man'[71] on the island.

Yet Tomás' grandson, Pádraig Ua Maoileoin, described some possible underlying tension: 'He [Tomás] has a very clever way of praising the King; you would hardly realise that he was indeed criticizing him, or so that is how I feel.'[72] Scholar Risteárd Ó Glaisne wrote: 'Tomás Dhónaill was an independent man, and for as much respect as he had for his friend, Peats Mhicí, he didn't like to defer too much to him'; and according to Leslie Matson, 'Tomás is not an uncritical admirer [of the King] – he even complains that the King dislikes chat when there is work to be done ...'[73]

Nevertheless, there was no doubt in Tomás' mind that Peats Mhicí was the right man for the position of King:

> So it's little wonder that when knowledgeable people came our way and thought that there ought to be someone with the style of King in the Island, they chose out the man [Peats Mhicí] fit to take the title and to carry it with credit.[74]

It is clear that Tomás understood the King's style of leadership and he expressed his view of his friend in a tongue-in-cheek manner:

> It was not long before the King popped his grand radiant head into the house. He was warmly welcomed like the nobles of times past. A chair was put under him, but he did not have time to sit down as he was in a hurry to polish off the task at hand.

The people of the house thought he was about to disclose some sort of secret, but he was not like that, and I had a certain understanding of the King's way of thinking; the likes of him do not tell their business as they pass by the house as a small child might.[75]

In his journal entry in *Island Cross-Talk* dated 'End of April 1919', Tomás wrote whimsically: 'the King heard the cuckoo today. I suppose nobody hears it except a King or a man of high rank like him.'[76] Thus, even in a casual conversation, Tomás expressed his understanding of the King's special leadership status in the island community.

In his role as 'host-in-chief' of the many cultural visitors to the island, the King would routinely refer visitors seeking to improve their knowledge of the Irish language to Tomás (see Chapter 9). He knew that Tomás was the islander best equipped to tutor the visitors. And it certainly didn't hurt that his brother-in-law realised some economic benefit at the same time, especially since Tomás was struggling to raise the King's deceased sister's children.

With respect to politics, Tomás supported Sinn Féin and the cause of an Irish republic, while his friend the King supported the Anglo-Irish Treaty and the formation of the Irish Free State (see below).

It is intriguing that Tomás and Peats Mhicí Ó Catháin, two of the most important figures in the long history of the Great Blasket, lived roughly concurrent lives. Overall, the relationship seemed to work well, probably because each intuitively understood their respective skill sets as well as their highly compatible roles on the island.

According to scholar George Thomson, Tomás and the King were the only people on the island to read newspapers regularly. The King's biweekly trips to deliver and collect the

Peats Mhici Ó Catháin, the King and postman, in front of the Dunquin post office with his mailbag.

post in Dunquin meant that he was the usual disseminator of information about current affairs. The islanders would surround him at the slipway on his return to the island to hear about breaking news. Newspapers were sometimes read aloud at the nightly gatherings. It was through this process that news about a whole series of important events reached the islanders, including Irish Home Rule, the First World War, the Easter Rising, the Irish War of Independence, the Anglo-Irish Treaty, the creation of the Irish Free State and the Irish Civil War.

Tomás was keenly interested in national and world affairs and monitored them closely. At the end of the First World War, for example, he was concerned about the Paris peace talks and the fact that US President Woodrow Wilson had returned to America again without a final resolution.

The island's remote location tended to insulate it to some extent from the influence of politics. The islanders were more focused on dealing with the serious day-to-day problems of subsistence than the larger issues confronting Ireland.

Nevertheless, the islanders regularly engaged in lively political debate.

Despite his close relationship with the King, Tomás did not hesitate to disagree with him on key political issues. Author and frequent Blasket visitor Risteárd Ó Glaisne wrote that 'the two didn't see eye to eye in politics. It's clear from the different pieces in *Allagar na hInise* that the King sided with John Redmond while Tomás and another group's sympathies were with Sinn Féin.[77] (Redmond was an Irish nationalist MP who eventually achieved the passage of the Irish Home Rule Act – which was not implemented because of the First World War.)

Leslie Matson elaborated on their political differences:

> [T]he King showed none of Tomás' enthusiasm for the cause of Sinn Féin during the period after the rising when it was crushing the Nationalist party. At the end of the Civil War period, some 'Freestaters' had dinner in his [the King's] house, a situation which Tomás, being more inclined toward the Republican side, would not have endorsed. One suspects that there was also a touch of jealousy; calling him 'Fear na Corónach' [Man of the Crown] as he does, may well have been ironic. Tomás considered himself the outstanding representative of the island people to the world of scholarship and letters; it was at his feet that scholars like Marstrander and Flower sat ... This was especially so after the publication of *Allagar na hInise* and *An tOileánach*, though the King's life was by then all but over.
>
> Tomás would never have been a popular leader as the King was – in fact he stirred up a certain animosity by some of his claims ... It would be easy to exaggerate this negative element in Tomás' feeling: after all, the King plays a pivotal part in a great number of the stories he has

to tell, and his dominant approach is one of admiration and friendship for this man whose sister, after all, he had married.[78]

Pádraig Ua Maoileoin, Tomás' grandson, even went so far as to say:

Kings are, I suppose, sympathetic to other Kings and their reign. Or at least this King [Peats Mhicí] had certain sympathies with the King of England. Of course, he was no exception at the time; even though the Rising had drastically changed the attitude of the Irish people by the time Ó Criomhthain was writing, which is felt with respect to the majority of the people in the book.[79]

In *Island Cross-Talk*, Tomás provides a chronology of the ongoing political debate on the island. In January 1922, for example, he wrote:

The crew [of a *naomhóg* that went to Dingle] were questioned about the Free State, but it was a confused enough answer they gave. People in favour of the Free State hadn't a word to say, but those against it were beside themselves with rage. The same story all over Ireland, I suppose. People thought there would be no more strife but it looks very much as if there will be now.[80]

Tomás' political views were no doubt heavily influenced by his extended interaction with the island visitors, many of whom were involved in the Celtic Revival and later in the continuing struggle for Irish independence. After all, he was writing a description of a pure and unique Irish folk culture that supported the dream of an independent Ireland.

8. Inspiration, Irish Literacy and Early Writing

The transformation of Tomás, a simple fisherman and farmer, into a renowned published author took over six decades. The process began with his innate powers of observation of people, places and events. It was advanced through his humble education at the island's national school. He developed a passion for storytelling as a young man. In middle age, he learned to read and write in Irish, largely on his own initiative. Along the way, he expanded his general knowledge by reading a range of newspapers, magazines and books. And, finally, he was inspired to write about himself and the Great Blasket by a series of island visitors, several of whom mentored him during his emergence as an author.

Robin Flower wrote that Tomás came from an oral tradition of folk songs, folktales and poetry: 'All this tradition Tomás inherits from the poets and taletellers with whom he consorted eagerly in his young days.'[1] Tomás' early interest in folklore was cultivated through his routine participation in the cultural life of the island community and his interactions with talented island storytellers, including two of his neighbours (see below).

Tomás' first published literary work was a short story entitled '*Fiach Fada Mhuintir Oileáin*' ('The Long Hunt of the Islanders'), published in 1916 when he was about sixty-two years old.

His first book, *Allagar na hInise*, was published in 1928 when he was seventy-four, and his best-known work, *An tOileánach*, a year later.

In April 1922, Tomás wrote: 'Wouldn't it delight my heart to be able to read a book of my own before I died.'[2] Before his passing, Tomás would realise his dream not just once, but three times.

Tomás' immediate neighbour in his youth was Tomás 'Maol' Ó Ceárna. As a lad, Tomás spent quite a bit of time next door as Tomás Maol shared stories from his ample memory bank of island folklore. Tomás described his neighbour as not being very handy; but he was a fount of knowledge, having immediate recall of stories as well as island facts such as key dates and islanders' ages. As an accomplished storyteller, he was always entertaining and 'excellent company'.

Tomás wrote: 'I was passionately fond of Tom's tales.'[3] Once, when he was suffering from an infected finger, he said the pain vanished as soon as Tomás Maol began to tell a story. The spell of the *seanchaí* distracted Tomás from his wound.

In *An tOileánach,* Tomás relates a version of *The Boat from Gortadoo*, a tale shared with him by Tomás Maol. Around 1818, a boat from Gorta Dubha, near Ballyferriter, came upon the scene of an abandoned ship adrift off Beiginis being looted by some men from Dunquin. The Gorta Dubha men overpowered the Dunquin men and transferred the cargo into their own boat, but they were too greedy, and the boat eventually became overloaded and sank. The Dunquin men, angry at the loss of what they saw as their booty, made no effort to save the Gorta Dubha men, who were thrashing about in the water. Twenty-one Gorta Dubha men drowned. The incident led to a long period of hostility between the two villages. Tomás wrote that the animosity ended only when there was a marriage between a woman from Gorta Dubha and a man from Dunquin.[4]

Another Tomás Maol tale involved his father. He and two other islanders were fishing one day and saw a boat that seemed to be in trouble. They climbed aboard to help, but the captain kidnapped them and cut their *naomhóg* free. The sly captain needed help sailing his boat back to Belfast, so he forced the unsuspecting islanders into service. Once in Belfast, one of the islanders escaped and allegedly walked all the way back to Dunquin, a distance of over 480 km (300 miles). The two other islanders were charged with some trumped-up offence. Their lack of English put them at a distinct disadvantage in court, but an army captain from Kerry spoke up on their behalf. Justice prevailed. They were freed and compensated for their forced labour.[5] Tomás included this version of the tale in *An tOileánach* and a slightly modified version was published as '*Fiach Fada Mhuintir Oileáin*' in *An Claidheamh Soluis* (see Chapter 11).

One can imagine the young Tomás being mesmerised by the dramatic telling of these and other stories. While he could not have appreciated it at the time, the island's oral storytelling culture was gradually being handed down to him. Tomás would certainly make the most of it. Of the impact of Tomás Maol on Tomás, Leslie Matson wrote:

> Tomás 'Maol' did not attract acclaim during his lifetime – in fact the opposite was true – but in his influence over the young Tomás Ó Criomhthain, in the enthusiasm he generated in him for the stories that were on the lips of so many in his day, he left a lasting memorial whose value no one can gainsay.[6]

Séamus Ó Duilearga of the Irish Folklore Commission referred to storytellers like Tomás Maol as 'walking libraries'. Unfortunately, the only Tomás Maol stories that have been preserved are those that were retold by Tomás in his writing.

The others are gone for ever. As Matson remarked, this is a stark reminder of what has been lost by the passing of the oral storytelling tradition. As for Tomás himself, he was gradually accumulating his own extensive knowledge of island folklore, not only from Tomás Maol, but also from the other island storytellers in almost nightly entertainment sessions.

Another neighbour and frequent work partner of Tomás, Seán Eoghain Duinnshléibhe, was reputed to be one of the finest storytellers on the island, with an extensive memory of heroic folktales. Seán Eoghain once told Robin Flower, 'It was only the other day that I had all the old tales in my mind, and I could have spent the night telling them to you without a word out of its place in any tale.'[7] Tomás and Seán Eoghan spent much time working together cutting turf, no doubt swapping stories to pass the time.

Besides absorbing the stories themselves, Tomás was also acquiring storytelling techniques. This was all an essential part of Tomás' informal training as a storyteller and future author.

Muiris Mac Conghail wrote that Seán Ó Duinnshléibhe (1812–1889), the island poet in Tomás' time, was the first person to instill in Tomás an appreciation of the importance of writing. The poet was originally from Ballynaraha (*Baile na Rátha*), Dunquin, having married into the island. His literary reputation was well established during Tomás' youth and he had considerable respect for the poet.

In *An tOileánach,* the poet teaches Tomás a lesson in the importance of committing stories and poems to writing. This was probably around the mid-1870s, when the poet was around sixty-three years old and Tomás was in his early twenties. Tomás was cutting turf at the back of the island when the poet arrived. He promptly recited 'The Black Faced Sheep' ('*Cora Odhar*'), the very first poem he had composed. The poet then sought out Tomás' help:

'The poem will be lost,' says he, 'if somebody doesn't pick it up. Have you anything in your pocket that you could write it down with?' ...

It wasn't to oblige the poet that I fished out my pencil and some paper I had in my pocket, but for fear he would turn the rough side of his tongue to me. I set about scribbling down the words as they came out of his mouth. It wasn't in the usual spelling that I wrote them, for I hadn't enough practice in it in those days.[8]

Tomás co-operated with the poet, at least partly because he didn't want to offend him and then become the butt of his satire; he had witnessed this treatment of other islanders and was anxious to avoid the same. So he found his pencil and paper and got to work. Since he was still illiterate in Irish at the time, Tomás used the English alphabet he had learned in school and his crude effort at phonetic spelling to write out the poem.

On the day after Christmas in 1877, Tomás went up the hill tending the cows. Again, he came across the poet. Tomás was wary because of his previous experience with the man; these encounters typically led to precious little work getting done. Tomás wrote that the poet asked him 'Have you got any of the "Song of the Ass"?' Tomás confessed that he had only part of this composition. Again, the poet asked if he had his pencil with him and said, 'I shall carry all the songs I ever made to the grave with me if you don't pick them up.' He was putting the onus of preserving his work squarely on Tomás. And so they began. A disgruntled Tomás reported on their session:

I promise you, friend of my heart, that by the time I had a dozen verses written down that bitter, cold evening I wished heartily that the poet was dead, for, whoever found his ways easy to deal with, it wasn't me, and before

I had the poem scribbled down on my paper it was black night.[9]

It is intriguing that in both instances the poet asked Tomás whether he had pencil and paper with him when he was working away from the village. He must have been familiar with Tomás' ability to write. And he must have been aware of Tomás' habit of writing drafts of his poetry during work breaks (see below).

Tomás, however, was less than pleased with the poet's interruptions. On one occasion, he wondered, 'was I myself fated beyond all the people in the Island to have all my time wasted by the poet? – for I never saw him frequenting any of the others, but only me.'[10] He also wrote that the poet wasn't too keen on hard work. Despite these sentiments, Tomás had a special relationship with the poet. Seán Ó Coileáin wrote that they were kindred spirits, and according to Robin Flower, 'The island poet may have made him suffer, but he taught him much.'[11]

The poet died, after a long illness, in 1889, when Tomás was about thirty-five. Robin Flower gives us a glimpse of Tomás' great sense of loss at his passing:

> And with that he [the poet] made confession of his sins and died. And with him there went a vast store of now irrecoverable tradition. It is a constant theme with Tomás that we have come too late and that Seán died too early. 'If only the things he had to tell could have been written down,' he says, 'you would have seen something. For he never forgot anything that he had heard once ... There are no tales in the Island since he died.'[12]

The poet was a very influential person in Tomás' life, and he played an essential role in his growth and development as a writer. In the process of transcribing poetry and songs from an acknowledged master, Tomás absorbed a sense of the basic elements of poetry which he would later apply in his own compositions. The poet was 'the only important creative figure he had known from within his culture in the writing up of his genesis as a writer'.[13] Tomás wrote: 'I knew his character better than anybody else though he was old in my day.'[14] In many ways, Tomás positioned himself as the poet's literary successor on the island. Tomás' track record in this role speaks for itself.

Tomás' development as an Irish-language author coincided with a resurgence of interest in Irish culture during the late nineteenth and early twentieth centuries – the so-called 'Celtic Revival'. This movement sought to reverse the decline of Irish culture, language and literature over hundreds of years of British rule. Throughout Ireland, the English language had become dominant in everyday conversation; and the number of Irish speakers had fallen precipitously from about four million to about one million as a result of the Great Famine and emigration. Tim Enright wrote that 'the Irish language had retreated to the western seaboard [of Ireland], except for pockets left here and there.'[15] The Irish language was withering away. To counteract this, the Irish language became the focus of an attempted rejuvenation.

One manifestation of this resurgence was the founding of the Gaelic League (*Conradh na Gaeilge*) in 1893 with Douglas Hyde as its first president. Forty-five years later, Hyde would be elected the first president of the Republic of Ireland. The League's objective was 'de-anglicising' Ireland. It promoted Irish culture and language as unique and intrinsically valuable. The League was intended to be apolitical. Hyde envisioned the Irish language as a 'neutral ground upon which all Irishmen might meet.'[16]

Concurrent with the Celtic Revival, various nationalist political organisations were gathering strength, leading eventually to the Easter Rising in 1916. There was obvious overlap between the two movements. Martyred Irish revolutionary leader Patrick Pearse, for example, wrote extensively in Irish and served as the editor of *An Claidheamh Soluis*, the Irish-language newspaper of the Gaelic League.

As the Celtic Revival evolved, the Great Blasket emerged as an almost idyllic model of pure Irish culture and language. The story of the island provided a compelling illustration of what it meant to be genuinely Irish. Because of its authenticity, it was considered worthy of scholarly scrutiny (see Chapter 9). As time went on, the writing of native islanders advanced its reputation. John Eastlake wrote: 'The Blasket texts have often been read as embodying the culture of Irish-speaking communities more strongly than other writing.'[17]

Tomás himself was a passionate member of the Gaelic League. He wrote: 'I've been working harder year by year [on Irish], and to-day I go harder at it than ever for the sake of the language of our country and of our ancestors.'[18]

The residents of the Great Blasket spoke Irish almost exclusively. The islanders took great pride in their particular brand of Irish, maintaining that it was pure and uncorrupted by the proliferation of English. Scholars agreed, routinely referring those who wanted to learn authentic Irish to the Great Blasket. While the islanders had command of spoken Irish, virtually all were illiterate in their native tongue. This was quite sufficient for everyday life on the island. Tomás, however, had higher ambitions.

He achieved literacy in English well before he was fully literate in Irish, having been taught to speak, read and write in English during his roughly eight-year enrolment in the national school from 1864. The quality of his letters to Robin

Flower, Brian Ó Ceallaigh, An Seabhac, his son Thomas and others suggests that his ability to write in English was passable, but not nearly as refined as his writing in Irish.

Muiris Mac Conghail wrote that Tomás' first education in reading Irish may have been in connection with the 'Souper School' that operated on the island from 1840 to 1863. The 'Soupers' taught a limited number of islanders to read in Irish, focusing on the Irish Bible. They did not, however, teach their students how to write in Irish. Tomás may have had his initial lessons in reading Irish either directly from the Soupers or from their students. If he did have lessons from the 'Soupers', Tomás makes no mention of them, perhaps because of the repeated admonitions of Fr Patrick Mangan, the parish priest, to avoid engagement with Protestants.

Instead, Tomás attributed his ability to read Irish to relatives in Dunquin. This was probably the second phase of his education in Irish, in the waning days of the nineteenth century. He wrote in *An tOileánach* that bad weather would sometimes make him a 'prisoner' on the mainland, especially in the winter. In these situations, he would stay at his cousin Neill (Ní Chriomhthain) Uí Mhuircheartaigh's house on the mainland. Neill had spent some time in America before returning to Dunquin and she had some facility in English and Irish. She married Seán Ó Muircheartaigh, who was able to read and write in Irish. Tomás wrote that the Ó Muircheartaigh children gave him lessons in reading Irish and probably some limited writing lessons as well:

> In the house where I used to stay the children were always going to school. The Irish language was being taught in the Dunquin school in those days ... The children of this house used to read tales to me all the time whenever I happened to be in their company until I got a taste for

the business and made them give me the book ... It didn't take me long to get so far that I hadn't to depend on them to read out my tale for me.[19]

Tomás confirms that he had been working on Irish since 1899 and maybe earlier. In early 1926, he wrote: 'I have been twenty-seven years hard at work on this language, and it is seventeen [actually nineteen] years since the Norseman, Marstrander, came my way.'[20] Describing Carl Marstrander's arrival in 1907, Tomás wrote: 'The King explained to him that I was the man, *for I was able to read it* [italics added] and had fine, correct Irish before ever I read it.'[21] In their first get-together, Marstrander gave Tomás the Irish-language novel *Niamh* (see Chapter 9), which he was able to read.

The third phase of his education in Irish occurred about 1908, shortly after the departure of Marstrander. Tomás wrote that 'a good Irish speaker'[22] named Tadhg Ó Ceallaigh arrived on the Great Blasket (not to be confused with later island visitor Brian Ó Ceallaigh – see Chapter 10). A travelling teacher for the Gaelic League, Ó Ceallaigh offered Irish language classes in the island school in the evenings. Tomás was a faithful student. He didn't miss a single class. He had started learning to read and write Irish about a decade earlier and he may have been interested in working specifically on his writing. Ó Ceallaigh was just the resource Tomás needed.

At about that time, Marstrander wrote to Tomás and asked him to prepare a list of every animal, bird, fish and plant on or about the Great Blasket. He asked Tomás to write the words in Irish, spelling them after 'my own fashion'.[23] Ó Ceallaigh and Tomás agreed to collaborate on the project. They spent part of each day working on the list and finished it in just a month. The material was then dispatched to Marstrander in Norway.

This 1908 list is the earliest evidence of Tomás' writing capability in both Irish and English. His compilation of this list

Excerpt from Tomás' handwritten list of Blasket flora and fauna in Irish and English developed with Tadgh Ó Ceallaigh for Carl Marstrander.

is also the very first mention in his books of his writing, other than his transcribing of poetry for Seán Ó Duinnshléibhe. This exercise enabled Tomás to improve his written Irish, giving him more confidence in his ability as a writer, which further helped to set the stage for the emergence of the budding author.

Tomás' handwriting progressed gradually over the years, as did his spelling. He wrote in Roman script until he learned Gaelic script in middle age. Over the years, he developed quite elegant penmanship, as is evident in his painstakingly crafted handwritten letters and manuscripts (see Chapter 10).

Tomás must be admired for his sustained effort over a long period to learn to read and write Irish, and he was probably the first of the islanders to achieve this milestone. He didn't achieve full literacy in Irish until around 1915, when he was in his early sixties, about three-quarters of the way through his life. To have acquired these skills under these circumstances and at his own initiative is impressive. Clearly, he was highly motivated.

Several Blasket scholars felt that Tomás was not a great oral storyteller of the stature of fellow-islander Peig Sayers. Dunquin native Joe Daly (*Seósamh Ó Dálaigh*), a folklore collector with the Irish Folklore Commission, wrote that Tomás 'was a very good writer and a very good Gaeilgeoir [Irish speaker], but that he didn't have that number of long folktales'. Leslie Matson wrote that many of his stories were in the category of 'traditional lore', tales of days long gone by and of characters and happenings of his youth or the not too distant past. Folklorist Bo Almqvist, on the other hand, said that Tomás was more interested in stories of recent people and events, which, of course, is evident in his classic works.[24]

Tomás was a pivotal figure in Ireland's transition from oral to written storytelling. Tim Enright wrote that his writing captured the moment of transition from speech to writing. Tomás wrote that he would exercise his literacy back on the island by reading stories in Irish aloud to the other islanders. In this role, he was a personification of Ireland's literary revolution. Tomás foreshadowed this unfolding transition in an ominous passage:

> Very soon I had a book or two, and people in this island were coming to listen to me reading the old tales to them, and, though they themselves had a good lot of them, they lost their taste for telling them to one another when they compared them with the style the books put on them. It would be long before I tired of reading to them, for I was red-hot to go ahead.[25]

At this point, the genie was out of the bottle. There was no turning back.

Tomás' primary frame of reference for his writing was the Great Blasket, but several factors enabled him to place everyday events in a wider context. He was by far the most widely read of the islanders, and his reading exposed him to a broad range of thinking. He was also the main Irish language contact person on the island for its many cultural visitors (see Chapter 9), and his extensive face-to-face interaction with these well-educated people inevitably served to broaden his horizons. In addition, while the islanders may have been isolated from much of Ireland, they had strong links with communities further afield, particularly Springfield, Massachusetts. Letters from kinfolk who had emigrated were read aloud, giving Tomás and his fellow islanders a window on life in America and elsewhere.

Tomás read at least portions of *Niamh* and *Scéal Séadna*, Irish-language novels by Fr Ua Laoghaire (Peter O'Leary) and probably some of the several books that Brian Ó Ceallaigh shared with him, including English translations of works by Pierre Loti of France, Knut Hamsun of Norway and Maxim Gorky of Russia (see Chapter 10).[26]

Tomás' personal 'library' eventually consisted of about sixty books and journals including *The Muses' Pageant* by W.M.L. Hutchinson, *Gods and Fighting Men* (Lady Augusta Gregory), *The Mystery Lady* (Robert W. Chambers), *The Roadmender* (Michael Fairless), *Eachtra Robinson Crúsó* (Daniel Defoe), *The Rubáiyát of Omar Khayyám* (translated by Edward FitzGerald), and an English-Irish dictionary. While not in Tomás' personal collection, there was an English version of Boccaccio's *Decameron* on the island. Whether Tomás read these books is unknown. Many probably arrived as gifts after the publication of *Allagar na hInise* and *An tOileánach* and, therefore, didn't significantly influence his writing. About a quarter of his library comprised books published after *An tOileanach*.[27]

A contemplative Tomás in 1924 at about the age of seventy in a photo by Carl Wilhelm von Sydow. This photo was the basis for the portrait of Tomás by Bert Finn (see cover).

Tomás also received the Gaelic League's newspapers and journals. He referred to the League's publication *Misneach* (known primarily as *An Claidheamh Soluis*) in entries in *Island Cross-Talk* in January and April 1922.[28] He received newspaper clippings in the post from Ó Ceallaigh (see Chapter 10); newspapers, including the *Irish Independent* and some English newspapers, such as the *Daily Sketch*, from the mainland; and books and newspapers from relatives in America and from the crews of the big lobster boats that occasionally visited the island.

This reading advanced Tomás' general knowledge well beyond that of a 'peasant'. He may have given us an insider's perspective on island life, but his outlook was influenced by his pretty extensive reading. And his ability as a writer far exceeded that of the typical islander. As Seán Ó Tuama wrote, 'O'Crohan was exposed to highly crafted and self-consciously literary works before writing *The Islandman*.'[29]

Tomás' first attempts at creative writing were probably his efforts to write poetry as a young man. His son Seán Ó Criomhthain said:

> He used to compose it [poetry] while working. When he was cutting turf and got tired – in those days the tea ... was packed in white paper pound bags. Tomás always held on to those white bags. They were very handy for him because he would put them into his pocket together with a pencil, and he composed most of his poetry when going to the strand or up the hill saving turf. He'd sit down on a little mound, have a smoke and write down the verses. He'd come home then in the evening, take out one of those big donkeys of foolscap pages, write down the verses and then send every piece he had composed to Fionán [Mac Coluim; see below].[30]

According to Seán, in the early years of the twentieth century his father was encouraged to write by two Irish-language activists associated with the Gaelic League, Fionán Mac Coluim (1875–1966) and Cormac Ó Cadhlaigh (1884–1960). While the details are unclear, it appears that they both visited Tomás on the Great Blasket in pursuit of authentic spoken Irish. At their encouragement, Tomás shared a selection of his very early writing in Irish with Ó Cadhlaigh and probably Mac Coluim, beginning before 1907.[31]

Mac Coluim went to work as an organiser (*ard-timire*) and song collector for the Gaelic League in County Kerry in 1902. He visited the Great Blasket several times over the years. Mac Coluim was later involved with *An Lóchrann*, an Irish-language periodical edited by An Seabhac. A short article by Tomás appeared in *An Lóchrann* in January 1917.[32]

Seán said that Ó Cadhlaigh, who arrived sometime after Synge's departure in 1905, was one of the first visitors he remembers coming to the Great Blasket. He is said to have visited the island at the suggestion of Mac Coluim and spent his time there collecting 'old stories and old sayings'. He also introduced Tomás to the writing of Ua Laoghaire.[33] Both Ó Cadhlaigh and Mac Coluim went on to have distinguished careers and worked to preserve Irish folklore throughout their lives.

Tomás also sent short articles he had written to An Seabhac, who was involved in several Irish-language publications over the years. Mac Coluim had told An Seabhac about Tomás' writing and this captured his attention. This would be critically important about ten years later when An Seabhac suggested that Brian Ó Ceallaigh visit the Great Blasket to improve his Irish.

Tomás was not shy about sharing his thoughts with others in Irish-language literary circles. On 8 July 1915, he wrote to Seosamh Laoide, one of the founding members of the Gaelic

League, and who had visited the island in 1907, about an Irish-language book he had read, *Tonn Tóime*. Tomás was expressing his disagreement about the meaning of the words in the title. In both English and Irish, Tomás wrote, 'small words, the pebbles of language, mattered more than did the big, imposing ones.'[34] This very perceptive observation indicates that, very early on, Tomás was thinking about writing style.

Tomás received ample encouragement in his literary endeavours throughout his life. His many achievements resulted in positive feedback that served to motivate him even more. Even when he was still at the national school, he received an academic prize from a school inspector, and his penchant for learning earned him the nickname 'Domhnall's scholar'. Pádraig Ua Maoileoin wrote that Tomás won a prize for his poetry at the Oireachtas festival sometime after the turn of the century. He was the islander most sought out by a series of distinguished visitors from Ireland and the Continent over many years (see Chapter 9). Later, he won several prizes for his writing, including one from *Fáinne an Lae,* the weekly bilingual newspaper of the Gaelic League, and a gold medal and a statue of Queen Tailte for his prose at the Tailteann Fair in 1932 (see Chapter 11). All these accolades must have reinforced his belief that he was on the right track and that he should persevere. They must have appealed to his sense of personal accomplishment.

At some point, there emerged a financial motivation for Tomás to pursue his writing. He was obviously a man of modest means. He never specifies how much money he made or accumulated, but he refers many times to his diligent efforts to earn 'yellow gold'. He was constantly focused on earning a living and worried about how to balance his writing, his reading, his work and the other tasks of daily life.

With the arrival of the cultural visitors, Tomás found that he could generate at least some income from tutoring visitors in Irish. In 1919, he wrote to Ó Ceallaigh that he was paid £1 a month by the Gaelic League for promoting the Irish language on the island and distributing books and newspapers among his neighbours. This was apparently arranged by Fionán Mac Coluim. Over time, he found that writing poetry made less money than writing prose. His writing for newspapers and journals may have generated a modest level of much-needed income in his old age.

As late as June 1923, when he was sixty-nine years old, Tomás wrote to Ó Ceallaigh asking if he could think of a plan that would generate £1 a month in income so he could concentrate on his writing. He eventually received royalties from his books after they were published in the late 1920s, but this income stream was probably modest, especially at the outset, and began late in his life.

Tomás took a great deal of personal satisfaction from seeing his writing in print. Seán Ó Criomhthain said he was always delighted when one of his articles was published in *An Claidheamh Soluis* or *An Lóchrann*. There is no doubt, however, that Tomás thought his writing would generate some income: 'I hear many an idle fellow saying that there's no use in our native tongue; but that hasn't been my experience. Only for it I should have been begging my bread!'[35]

It is not clear if and when he began to think of himself as an author rather than a fisherman and farmer. But at some point in his sixties, he could certainly have included his writing in his definition of 'productive work'.

Alan Titley said that when Tomás began to write in earnest, he also began to blossom as a person. He began to realise that he was special and he was proud of it. He became more self-assured and he didn't hesitate to boast about his many accomplishments. He understood that he had overcome enormous obstacles and that his personal literary contributions would endure, even if the community on the Great Blasket faded away. Tomás wrote: 'Since the first fire was kindled in this island none has written of his life and his world. I am proud to set down my story and the story of my neighbours.'[36]

Other forces that probably drove Tomás include his innate intellectual curiosity and his desire to achieve a kind of immortality through his writing. And he was undoubtedly motivated by the lessons he learned about the transitory nature of the oral tradition from his fellow islander Seán Ó Duinnshléibhe. Tomás' development as a published author marked Ireland's transition to a new written form of story-telling. This was no small transformation. Because of Tomás, the story of the island was preserved in a highly portable medium. The Great Blasket and Tomás himself were about to become famous throughout Ireland and beyond.

9. Influential Island Visitors

Tomás was a brilliant and highly motivated man. His efforts to achieve literacy in Irish and to broaden his general knowledge enabled him to advance from writing short magazine articles to producing full-length books. His close relationships with a series of island visitors were crucial in this process. These visitors arrived on the Great Blasket as students of the Irish language, but many of them evolved into mentors, facilitators, editors and close personal friends. Together, they enabled Tomás to take the next steps in his personal journey as a writer.

Throughout most of the nineteenth century, the physical isolation of the Great Blasket contributed to enormous social isolation. Trips to the mainland were infrequent and focused primarily on selling fish and livestock and buying supplies. There was, of course, some merriment along the way. The men of the island made the trip across Blasket Sound to Mass in Dunquin on Sundays when the weather permitted. Conversely, most of the outsiders who visited the island were bailiffs looking to collect rent or taxes or Protestant missionaries, the 'Soupers'.

Two nineteenth-century visitors, Mrs David Peter Thompson and Jeremiah Curtin, left the islanders distrustful of outsiders. Both took a dim view of the living conditions on the island and said so very publicly. Thompson's husband was one of Lord Ventry's land agents, and she was a promoter of the Protestant mission to the Great Blasket. In 1846, she wrote that island's inhabitants were 'in a state of extreme ignorance, not a single individual on the island could read, write or speak a word of English'.[1] Taking an anglocentric view of the island, she equated illiteracy in English with ignorance. After his visit in 1892, Curtin also wrote an account that portrayed the islanders as primitive. These hurtful public mischaracterisations, along with the ongoing battles with bailiffs, made the islanders wary of visitors.

At the dawn of the twentieth century, the Celtic Revival led to a growing interest in the Irish language. In turn, a phenomenon known as 'cultural tourism' emerged. Scholars were drawn to the Irish-speaking communities along Ireland's west coast in search of the authentic experience of the living Irish language. In this context, it was the remoteness of the Great Blasket as well as the purity of its spoken Irish and the richness of its cultural traditions that made the island an invaluable location for learning and research.

As the Celtic Revival was gaining momentum, Tomás' friend, Pádraig Peats Mhicí Ó Catháin, was named King of the Great Blasket sometime between 1900 and 1905. The new King had a more open approach to visitors. He assumed the role of 'host-in-chief', transporting guests to the island by *naomhóg*, introducing them around, providing lodging in his house and making connections with tour guides and translators. The new King may have felt less threatened by the visitors because of his command of English and because he was more accustomed to dealing with outsiders.

George Thomson was impressed with the genuine welcome extended by the islanders:

> The Islanders took these strangers to their hearts. They welcomed them all the more warmly because of their

own traditional respect for poetry and scholarship, and, in return for teaching them the language, they learnt from them that their island was one of the last homes of an ancient civilization which, though now on the verge of extinction, had preserved certain values which the modern world had lost.[2]

Extended visits to the Great Blasket typically went beyond learning Irish and included participation in the broad cultural life of the island, including storytelling, poetry, song and dance. The visitors found this total immersion process enormously enriching. Author Robert Kanigel wrote that what may have begun as a dispassionate effort at linguistic study and cultural observation became much more. Many visitors became enthralled with the island and they developed deep and long-lasting relationships with the islanders.

The visitors had a positive impact on the islanders as well. Breandán Ó Conaire said that the Celtic Revival effectively placed the islanders on a pedestal. Their new-found self-esteem caused a kind of psychological revolution – the islanders were no longer embarrassed by their folk culture; it had become a source of great pride.

All this had a profound influence on Tomás. He was lifelong friends with the King, who was also his brother-in-law, and because of his fluency in both English and Irish, he was the primary person on the island whom visitors sought out as they pursued their study of Irish. According to Leslie Matson, Tomás' 'command of Irish was, needless to say, exceptional, but one suspects that the initial reasons why he was recommended, by islanders and others, was that by this time he had gained a reputation among his fellows of being interested in books, and reading of all sorts, and had a reputation of being a man of scholarly, even studious, temperament.'[3]

It became common practice for the King to refer visitors who wanted to improve their Irish-language skills to Tomás. Máiréad Nic Craith wrote:

> Tomás' friends [the visitors] were interested in the language and Gaelic culture when they arrived to the Blaskets, and they didn't have any particular interest in Tomás over the other Islanders. His reputation as a writer had not been established at this point and even though scholars such as Flower and Marstrander sought him out from early on, the reason he got to know them was, moreover, due to the fact that the guesthouse belonged to his brother-in-law [the King], and they were happy for Tomás to get a few extra pennies ... It was this connection through marriage between himself and the King, as well as their longstanding friendship, that granted Tomás access to the visitors in the 'Palace' [the King's house].[4]

The King eventually built an addition to his house that doubled as a bedroom and a classroom where Tomás conducted classes in Irish for Carl Marstrander and Robin Flower. Tomás described this 'classroom', known as 'the Norseman's room' in tribute to Marstrander, as follows:

> There is a window in this Palace, which looks out to the open sea. The man himself has a table that runs across it, and he spreads his books out on it. He has a decorative chair and another chair for anyone he trusts enough at the other end of the table. There is not a saying that cannot be voiced at that table the meaning and root of which cannot be seen with your very own eyes out this window, and it is my opinion there isn't a university window in the country that could compare in presenting such a vision before the eyes of the students, it wasn't difficult for

anyone who called by to acquire precision and perfection of the language. There is not a colour ever seen by the eye, blue, green, white, purple, red or yellow, that cannot forever be seen from the window of the palace.[5]

Tomás was only too happy to oblige his students, spending hours teaching them, embracing his role as their 'master'; and he was reluctant to refuse help to anyone.

Thus began a series of island visits by scholars from many of the intellectual capitals of Europe. These visits extended over twenty-five to thirty years in the early twentieth century. Scholar Máirín Nic Eoin said that cultural tourism exposed the great richness of the language and culture of the island.[6] And the visitors exposed the islanders to a culture beyond the island in which books were a central feature. Kanigel referred to this process as a 'freakish collision between two worlds'. Of the visitors he wrote, 'It would be hard to imagine a coterie of people more brilliant, more adventurous, more deeply interesting than these.'[7] Scholar Irene Lucchitti points out that, of the four most important cultural visitors, two (Carl Marstrander and Robin Flower) were 'outsiders' and brought a broad perspective on island folklore; and two (Brian Ó Ceallaigh and An Seabhac) were 'insiders' who were actively involved in promoting the Irish language.[8] No one could have foreseen where this dynamic would lead. Neither Tomás nor the island would ever be the same.

As for Tomás, he very much appreciated the role that the visitors played on the island. In a poetic tribute to the visitors, he likened them to St Patrick, who came to Ireland with no Irish and yet had an enormous impact.

This confluence of scholars, writers and activists on the Great Blasket was essential to the development of Tomás as a writer. Without exposure to and interaction with the visitors, he would never have imagined that he was capable of writing and publishing books, and he would not have acquired the skills to do so.

John Millington Synge (Great Blasket Visit: 1905)

The first significant cultural visitor to the Great Blasket was John Millington Synge, who spent a fortnight on the island in 1905. Born on 16 April 1871, Synge was an Irish playwright, poet and author, and one of the founders of Dublin's Abbey Theatre. At the age of thirty-four, he travelled across Blasket Sound to the island in the King's *naomhóg* and stayed in the King's home. His interest was largely sociological. He brought a camera and took some of the first photographs of the island and its people.

The island made a big impression on Synge. He was particularly taken with the King's married daughter Máire Ní Chatháin. This attractive 23-year-old woman is considered by many to have been the inspiration for 'Pegeen Mike', the heroine in Synge's controversial play, *The Playboy of the Western World*. Synge was the earliest of the visitors to appreciate fully the richness of the island's culture and to write about his observations for publication.

There was, however, a negative reaction among the islanders to some of the comments Synge made in his journal *The Shanachie* in 1907 and later in his book *In Wicklow and West Kerry*. There was a suggestion that Máire may have overdone her hospitality, serving tea and bacon to Synge without being asked. And Máire herself took exception to a passage about using her apron for curtains, insisting that her curtains were made in America. Finally, there was Synge's reference to Máire's feet and ankles, which could have been embarrassing for her. The islanders felt that Synge was writing to convey a particular

John Millington Synge, the first prominent cultural visitor to the Great Blasket.

image of the island and that he misrepresented the reality of island life. All of this had an adverse impact on the islanders' feelings about Synge's visit.

There is no record of any interaction between Tomás and Synge on the island, although they must have spent some time together. One can be assured that the keenly observant and vocal Tomás was involved in the subsequent controversy over Synge's narrative. In fact, this may have been his first participation in literary criticism, giving him an insight into how the written word can be interpreted differently by different audiences and perhaps misconstrued.

Synge's writing helped put the Great Blasket on the radar of those interested in the Celtic Revival – it became more widely known among the Irish literati that the island was fertile ground for the study of native Irish culture. As for Synge, he contracted Hodgkin's disease and died in 1909 before he turned forty, only four years after his island visit.

Carl Marstrander (Great Blasket Visit: 1907)

The next significant cultural visitor to the Great Blasket was Carl Johan Sverdrup Marstrander from Norway. Born on 26 November 1883, he was twenty-four years old at the time of his visit, arriving in early August 1907, although Tomás mistakenly wrote that he visited about 1909. He stayed for about five months, leaving just before Christmas. Marstrander was a linguist with a specialty in the Irish language. His objective was to study the purest form of Irish he could find. He taught at the School of Irish Learning in Dublin beginning in 1909.

The tall Marstrander's physical appearance was quite different from that of the islanders. Seán Ó Criomhthain describes him as 'a strong, hardy and athletic man over six feet in height and [he] had little spare flesh on him but he was as healthy as a salmon'.[9] Marstrander was a champion pole vaulter, and he had

Carl Marstrander, the Norwegian visitor to the Great Blasket, pictured much later in his life.

qualified to represent Norway in the 1906 Athens Olympic Games. He is reputed to have forfeited his slot on Norway's team to pursue his interest in Irish. According to Blasket legend, he once jumped right over Tomás' house using the mast from a *naomhóg* for a pole. This story stretches credibility, but it lives on in Blasket folklore. In any event, the islanders had great respect and admiration for the man. They affectionately nicknamed him '*An Lochlannach*' – 'The Viking'.

The King acted as host and facilitator of Marstrander's visit. Tomás wrote:

> One Sunday at the beginning of July a canoe from Dunquin brought a gentleman to the Blasket. He was a tall, lean, fair-complexioned, blue-eyed man. He had only a flavouring of Irish on his tongue. He went among the people and observed them, and in the evening he asked some of them whether he could find a place to stay. They told him he could, and he arranged to lodge in the King's house ...
>
> He was asked what was the reason he didn't stay in Ballyferriter parish, and he said there was too much English mixed with their Irish, and that didn't suit him; that his business was to get the fine flower of the speech, and that he had observed that the best Irish was here ...
>
> This was Carl Marstrander ... He spent five months in the Blasket. One sitting a day we had for half that time ... [Then] He put another question to me: Was it possible for me to spend two sittings a day with him?[10]

By that time, Tomás had been learning to read and write in Irish for about ten years and had achieved a degree of proficiency; so he was the logical person to work with Marstrander, who compensated Tomás for his efforts.

Tomás genuinely liked and respected Marstrander. In turn, Marstrander recognised Tomás' unusual capabilities and recommended him as a resource to other linguistic scholars. But the two men were never in each other's company again. They maintained a correspondence for many years, although it eventually lapsed.

Marstrander imparted to Tomás an understanding that the Irish language itself was important – that it mattered in a wider cultural context. According to Tomás' grandson, Pádraig Ua Maoileoin, Marstrander awakened in the islanders a new esteem for themselves. Robert Kanigel wrote: 'Marstrander lent them stature. They were fishermen? Yes, but something in how they lived was precious and rare.'[11] Irene Lucchitti wrote that Marstrander 'aroused an awareness in Tomás that his own abilities were exceptional'.[12] Marstrander left him with a sense of his importance that would be part of the foundation for his subsequent writing.

Muiris Mac Conghail wrote that Tomás remembered Marstrander until his dying day and said of him, '*Ní fear go dtí é*' ('There wasn't a man like him').[13] Marstrander went on to have a long career as Professor of Celtic Languages at the University of Oslo. He was interned several times in a prison camp during the German occupation of Norway in the Second World War. He died on 23 December 1965 at eighty-two. At his funeral, the Irish ambassador to Norway offered an eloquent appreciation of his devoted service to the Irish language.

Robin Flower (Great Blasket Visits: 1910–1914 and various years to 1939)

Englishman Robin Ernest William Flower was the cultural visitor who would maintain the longest relationship with the

Great Blasket and its people, a span of almost thirty years from 1910 to 1939. Flower and Tomás became extremely close.

Flower was born in Leeds, England on 16 October 1881, and educated at Pembroke College, Oxford University, earning a double first in classics. In 1906, he began his long career at the British Museum in London, where he was Deputy Keeper of Manuscripts from 1929 to 1944. Early in his career, Flower began compiling a catalogue of Irish manuscripts at the museum. In 1910, he was given a grant of £15 and three weeks' leave from work to study 'Old Irish' under Carl Marstrander at the School of Irish Learning in Dublin. In turn, Marstrander encouraged Flower to travel to the Great Blasket for a first-hand experience in authentic spoken Irish. Marstrander told Flower that the island was the best place to learn Irish.

Heeding Marstrander's advice, Flower visited the island for the first time in 1910 when he was twenty-nine years old, and Tomás was about fifty-six. According to Seán Ó Criomhthain:

> Bláithín [Flower] himself packed his bags the following year ... and didn't stop nor stay until he reached the Blasket. He was given a room by the King and his daughter Cáit an Rí, a woman who, the Lord have mercy on the dead, was well able to look after him and give him plenty of Irish. He asked Cáit where Marstrander's teacher [Tomás] lived.
>
> 'If you looked out the window,' said Cáit an Rí, 'you could see the top of his chimney below the bank.'
>
> 'I must call to him,' he said.[14]

Tomás agreed to serve as Flower's 'master' in Irish, as he had for Marstrander. Flower then began the process of improving his Irish by taking dictation from Tomás in Irish to develop his vocabulary and writing. Teaching Irish to highly educated

A young Robin Flower at about the time of his first visit to the Great Blasket in 1910.

The construction of the island's slipway in 1910. Robin Flower is in the centre, hatless, shoeless and sockless, but with a big smile. Tomás is just to the right of Flower.

scholars had the corollary effect of advancing Tomás' own knowledge and appreciation of the language, eventually facilitating his early writing efforts.

Flower also shared in the communal work of the island, joining the men in their routine business and accompanying them on hunting and fishing expeditions. He even helped out on projects such as the building of the new slipway by the Congested Districts Board – and he had blisters on his hands to show for it. After he left the island in 1910, Tomás sent Flower a postcard thanking him for tobacco that he had sent and inquiring about the condition of his hands.

Flower married Ida Mary Streeter on 4 February 1911. That summer, he brought his new bride with him to the Great Blasket on a kind of honeymoon. Ida was an accomplished artist and produced several beautiful sketches illustrating the island and its homes.

Postcard from Tomás to Robin Flower inquiring about the healing of the blisters on his hands that resulted from his work on the construction of the new slipway on the island:

> From the Great Blasket
> My spirited friend, I will have to seek tidings of your condition from now on. Wasn't that a fine present you sent me from Dingle, may your hands never be empty. I should like to get an account from you as to how you are getting on. Is the mark of the pickaxe still on your hands?
> I am with great regard for you,
> Tomás Ó Criomhthain

Over the ensuing decades, Flower became a frequent visitor to the island, returning year after year with his growing family. His children even attended the national school for a time. Robert Kanigel wrote:

> Flower returned to the island in 1911; then he came again every year through 1914. In 1913, he wrote Kuno Meyer [a German scholar of Celtic studies and the first

Director of the School of Irish Learning in Dublin] that he'd had a productive time, transcribing island stories for three hours a day, hunting rabbits with the king's son, Seán. In 1914, he was on the island when word reached them that the Austrian archduke had been assassinated, setting off the Great War. It was 1925 before Flower returned, this time with his children, as he would many times more over the rest of his life.[15]

Flower himself provides a description of one dramatic reunion with Tomás, his master, in the King's house:

> But a sudden feeling comes upon you of a new presence in the room. You look up and see, leaning against the wall almost with the air of a being magically materialized out of nothing ... The face takes your attention at once and holds it. This face is dark and thin, and there look out of it two quick and living eyes, the vivid witnesses of a fine and self-sufficing intelligence. He comes toward you, and with a grave and courteous intonation, and a picked and running phrase, bids you welcome. You have indeed come home, for this is Tomás Ó Crithin, the Island poet and story-teller.[16]

As they discuss what form Flower's next lessons will take, Tomás speaks of the erosion of the Irish language and about the weakening of spirit of community in Ireland. He sits chewing seaweed. Flower's questions lead to another story. And so the conversation flows.

Flower's command of Irish grew with each succeeding year. His relationship with Tomás and the island went far beyond the study of Irish. Flower very much enjoyed being part of daily life on the Great Blasket. The island became his second home.

From 1912, Flower began to gather stories, accounts of historical events and island traditions from Tomás. Flower later found similarities between Tomás' stories and Arabian tales, Shakespeare and Chaucer, literature very much in the European tradition. A compilation of his painstaking transcription of folklore related by Tomás over the years was eventually published in 1956 as *Seanchas an Oileán Tiar* (see Chapter 11).

Tomás was also a beneficiary of these sessions. Mac Conghail wrote that 'Tomás drew on much of Flower's knowledge of Irish and other literatures to enrich his own mind. Their correspondence enabled Tomás to write on topics other than folklore, which he had already been doing for Irish language publications.'[17] Of their sessions together, Tomás wrote:

> We used to spend the time together writing. We had two sittings every day at it. He spent some time every year in my company to get every word we had written arranged in order till it was right and easy. That book [*Seanchas ón Oileán Tiar*] will tell of every disaster that befell round the Blaskets, both the little and the big.[18]

During Flower's visits, a casual conversation would sometimes take on a literary flavour, with Tomás a key participant:

> On one of my visits after a long interval ... we began to reckon up the deaths which had occurred since my last visit. The talk inevitably took the form of a recitation of the rich store of proverbs accumulated in a folk civilization on the necessity of death and the consolations of a religious faith ... At last, however, a silence fell as they waited, visibly searching their minds for a fresh inspiration. Suddenly, an old woman in the corner leaned forward and said with an air of finality:

'Cá'il an sneachta bhí comh geal anuirig?' (Where is the snow that was so bright last year?)

I sprang up in excitement and cried out: 'Ou sont les neiges d'antan?'

'Who said that?' asked the King, an expert in this lore.

'François Villon said it,' I replied.

'And who was he?' he returned. 'Was he a Connaughtman?'

'No, he lived hundreds of years ago and he said it in French, and it was a proverb of his people.'

'Well,' broke in Tomás, 'You can't better the proverb. I've always heard that the French are a clever people, and I wouldn't put it past them to have said that before we did.'[19]

Flower travelled to the Great Blasket again on 23 June 1914, and he expressed his surprise that Tomás had resumed fishing at the age of about sixty:

Oars are scarce now, for everybody is at sea now ... even Tomás has taken to the sea again. We were across in about an hour. Kate and Tomás came down to the slip to meet us. Everybody looks just the same.[20]

The relationships that developed during Flower's visits to the Great Blasket were nourished during his time in London through correspondence on a wide variety of subjects. Muiris Mac Conghail wrote:

Both the Island King, Pádraig Ó Catháin, and Tomás Ó Criomhthain were writing to Robin Flower in London from 1910, and the many visitors over the years maintained correspondence with the community in both Irish and English.[21]

Flower's exchange of letters with Tomás from 1910 to 1926 was particularly robust and helped the latter to write on a wide variety of subjects beyond folklore. They may also have influenced his literary style to some degree. *An tOileánach*, for example, was written primarily in the form of letters to Brian Ó Ceallaigh (see Chapter 10).

Flower was a very generous man, regularly sending gifts of money to the islanders, particularly in difficult times such as during the First World War. Flower trusted the King to decide how to distribute the funds equitably among the islanders. Interestingly, Tomás gave Flower a report on the King's discharge of this responsibility:

> The King has your bill [money] ... he has to go to Dingle to break it. I have no more knowledge of the matter, when I do I will let you know. I'm managing myself and I don't know anyone who is truly starving still. I suppose the King will decide based on that, I don't know ...

By the end of the week, the King had broken the bill. The money was split between the Island people and Tomás got his fair share of it ...

> Your old master got ten shillings from him, the King is always good to me. I think he gave a crown to some of them, and a pound to others, but his intention was to give more or less the same to every house.[22]

In 1930, the British Museum authorised Flower to return to the Great Blasket to make a series of gramophone (Ediphone) recordings of the island's folktales. He recorded the voices of Peig Sayers and others as they told their stories. Just a year later, on 12 June 1931, the *Irish Times* quoted Flower as suggesting that the decay in Irish folk culture was partially attributable to the very instrument he used to make a permanent record of the island masters. He said that Blasket youth found listening to the gramophone more entertaining 'than the telling of tales around the fireside'. Flower said, 'It is strangely ironical that the instrument which does most to preserve Ireland's folklore should be an agent of its decline.'[23] Whether Tomás was recorded by Flower is uncertain and no such recordings appear to have survived.

Flower's most important contribution to Tomás' legacy was his translation of *An tOileánach* into English, entitled *The Islandman* and published in 1934. While other versions of Tomás' autobiography have been published over the years in both Irish and English (see Chapter 11), it is Flower's translation that has been by far the most widely read. Flower's close personal relationship with Tomás and his familiarity with his patterns of speech and writing that were developed over many years put him in an ideal position to play the role of his translator.

Flower's deep understanding of the island is evident in his book *The Western Island*, first published in 1944. Flower told Séamus Ó Duilearga that he tried to demonstrate in this book his enormous gratitude to Tomás and the many other islanders who had such a profound impact on his life. Later that same year, Flower suffered a stroke. He wrote: 'I have temporarily lost all foreign languages and a great deal of English.'[24]

On 15 January 1946, Flower went for a walk near his home in London and didn't return. He was later found in a park, where he had collapsed. When his wife and daughter arrived on the scene, he didn't recognise them. He died the next morning at the age of sixty-four.

The *Irish Press* wrote: 'Dr Flower was one of the very greatest Gaelic scholars of our age with especial command of our literary history.'[25] Ó Duilearga said that of all the academic

Robin Flower with Tomás outside his house.

recognition bestowed on Flower, his favourite was the title of 'Bláithín,' his nickname on the Great Blasket: this 'honour from the little island kingdom was that which Robin Flower appreciated most of all'.[26] Flower's ashes were scattered around the peak at *An Dún*, his favourite place on the island. His passing came almost exactly one year before the death of young Seán Ó Ceárna on the Great Blasket set off a chain of events that would eventually lead to the evacuation of the island in 1953.

Flower played a major role in the cultural and literary emergence of the Great Blasket. Mac Conghail wrote:

> Although the Island was well known within Ireland as an important source of Irish language material, it was Flower who put the Island on the literary map and brought its culture to a wider audience. He established with some other English men, such as George Thomson, the Greek and Homeric scholar, and Kenneth Hurlstone Jackson, the Celtic scholar, a climate for the Island community in which it would be possible for the Islanders to write about their lives and the Island in their own language.[27]

Despite Flower's enormous impact on Tomás, Mac Conghail felt that he may have underestimated Tomás' literary capability. He wrote that 'Although it is quite clear that Flower had an enormous regard for Tomás Ó Criomhthain, I do not believe that he saw the potential in Tomás as a creative writer.'[28] There is no indication that Flower urged Tomás to write beyond the short articles and poems that he was submitting to various periodicals. That task was left to Brian Ó Ceallaigh (see Chapter 10).

Tomás took great pride in the fact that scholars from throughout Ireland and Europe travelled to the Great Blasket to learn Irish from him and to discuss his writing. He was delighted that he was perceived as an expert in the Irish language and that his knowledge was considered valuable.

After Tomás began to appear in print in 1916 and while he was writing *Allagar na hInise* and *An tOileánach*, a second wave of cultural visitors to the Great Blasket began. Notable people who made the journey to the island and met Tomás include, in chronological order of their visit:

Carl Wilhelm von Sydow (1878–1952)

The Swedish scholar Carl von Sydow visited the Great Blasket in 1920 and again in 1924. He had studied Irish under Carl Marstrander and was a professor at the University of Lund for many years. He was seeking to immerse himself in the Irish language and to study Irish folklore. He became particularly friendly with Tomás. Von Sydow took many photos during his stay, and they now comprise an important visual portrait of island life.

Seóirse Mac Clúin (1894–1949)

Around 1920, Fr Seóirse Mac Clúin (George Clune) a priest from County Clare, set out to assemble a compendium of the Irish idiom complete with an alphabet and an inventory of words, phrases and sentences. He felt that the best place to conduct research was the Great Blasket. And, of course, the best person to assist him was Tomás, who was about sixty-six years old at the time. Tomás reported:

> Father Clune came and spent three weeks with me. He said Mass for us every day. He came back again [the next

year], and I was a month in his company. We helped one
another, correcting all the words in 'Réilthíní Óir'. We
used to be sitting at it eight hours a day in two sessions –
four hours in the morning and four in the afternoon – for
all that month. That's the most painful month's work I
ever did, on land or sea.[29]

The result of this exercise was *Réilthíní Óir*, a work published in
1922 and comprising two volumes totalling almost 550 pages.
In the foreword, Mac Clúin expressed his gratitude to several
others for their contributions to this work. Oddly, there was
no mention of Tomás' help with the editing. Understandably,
Tomás was both hurt and upset at this oversight. Nevertheless,
Tomás greatly benefited from the exercise, with his command
of Irish becoming even stronger.

George Thomson (1903–1987)

On Sunday 26 August 1923, twenty-year-old George Derwent
Thomson arrived on the Great Blasket. Born in the London
neighbourhood of Dulwich, he was a brilliant student of the
classics at Cambridge University. He was also interested in the
Irish language. A friend suggested that he visit Robin Flower
at the British Museum, who in turn recommended that he
visit the Great Blasket. The exact date of Thomson's arrival
coincided with the first election in the new Irish Free State
after the Irish Civil War.

Thomson quickly became very friendly with islander Muiris
Ó Súilleabháin, who was about the same age. Remarkably,
Thomson is reputed to have achieved fluency in Irish in just six
weeks simply by walking around the island talking with Muiris
and others. Seán Ó Criomhthain said: 'George's command of
Irish was better than that of Muiris or anybody else among us.'[30]

George Thomson with islander Muiris Ó Súilleabháin in his Garda uniform.

While he was on the island, Thomson had the opportunity 'to sit at the feet of the "Master"'[31] (Tomás), who was just finishing *Allagar na hInise*. Tomás must have made a big

Celtic scholars Osborn Bergin of University College Dublin (left) and Daniel Binchy of the School for Celtic Studies, Dublin (right) on the Great Blasket with Tomás in the mid-1920s.

impression the scholar, who was forty-nine years his junior. The two corresponded for about a decade with Tomás sending Thomson poems that he had written.

As for Muiris, he left the island to join the Garda Síochána in March 1927. Thomson encouraged him to use *An tOileánach* as a model and to write his memoirs up to that point in his life. The result was the highly successful *Fiche Bliain ag Fás*, published in 1933. Thomson returned to the island with Muiris in 1934 to celebrate the book's success. By this time, Tomás had only three more years to live. Muiris subsequently left the Gardaí to write full time, but he was never able to match his early success. He rejoined the Gardaí, but drowned in Galway Bay in 1950. Thomson wrote an insightful book on the Great Blasket entitled *Island Home*, first published in 1987.

Thomas F. O'Rahilly (1882–1952)

Born in Listowel, County Kerry, Thomas O'Rahilly was a prolific writer and editor specialising in Irish language and history. He taught Irish at Trinity College Dublin, University College Cork and University College Dublin, and was director of the School of Celtic Studies at the Dublin Institute for Advanced Studies. Tomás wrote: 'Tomás Ó Rathaille was often in our midst, every year on his holidays. It was he who sent me most of the books I have.'[32] Years later, O'Rahilly was involved with Robin Flower in proofreading drafts of Tomás' *Seanchas ón Oileán Tiar*.

Daniel Anthony Binchy (1899–1989) and Osborn Bergin (1873–1950)

A scholar of Irish linguistics and early Irish law, Daniel Binchy studied at University College Dublin and the University of Munich, and was Ireland's ambassador to Germany from 1929 to 1932. He spent holidays in West Kerry, staying in Coumeenoole. Sometime in the mid-1920s he and his distinguished teacher and friend, Osborn Bergin, travelled to the island to meet Tomás. In his account of the visit, Binchy remarked on Tomás' 'unique mastery of the language' and his 'modesty' in connection with his accomplishments. Several years later, during Binchy's second trip to the island, Tomás expressed his frustration at the suggestion that *An tOileánach* was written in 'hard Irish'. Tomás insisted to Binchy, 'There isn't one word in it that wouldn't be understood by every child on the Island.'[33]

Marie-Louise Sjoestedt-Jonval (1900–1940)

A Swedish-born Celtic scholar, Marie-Louise Sjoestedt-Jonval was educated at the Sorbonne. She lived in Paris, where her father was a diplomat. While studying in Dublin, she met Seán 'an Chóta' Ó Ciobháin (Seán 'the Coat' Kavanagh) from Dunquin (the brother of the infamous publican, 'Kruger' Kavanagh). In the summer of 1925, they visited the Great Blasket. Then twenty-four years old, Sjoestedt-Jonval was captivated by the island, returning annually until 1929 and again in 1933 and 1936. Over these eleven years, she witnessed the publication of the first wave of Blasket books. On the island, she was affectionately known as 'Máire Francach'. ('French Máire').

Sjoestedt-Jonval spent considerable time with Tomás, as well as with Peig Sayers and her son Mícheál Ó Guithín. She later credited them for their help in her 1938 publication, *An Irish Talk – Kerry*. Like many others, she became concerned

about the erosion of the Irish language with the increasing use of English in West Kerry and even on the island. She was a strong supporter of the publication of Irish-language books, including the works of Tomás. A very perceptive scholar, she accurately predicted that when the true Irish-language classics are listed, among them would

Marie-Louise Sjoestedt-Jonval

be 'the work of peasant, fisherman and storyteller Tomás Ó Criomhthain'.[34] Unfortunately, Sjoestedt-Jonval suffered from depression, and she committed suicide in Paris on 26 December 1940 at the age of forty.

Plácido Ramon Castro del Rio (1902–1967)

A journalist and writer from the Galician region of Spain, Plácido Castro visited the Great Blasket with Robin Flower in September 1928 at the age of twenty-six. Plácido Castro wrote that Tomás, who he referred to as 'the island poet', was 'the most important character of the village'; his 'imagination is inexhaustible'; and 'When the books of the eminent Celtist are finally published, Thomas will be one of the most sounded men in Ireland, honoured by all the

Spaniard Plácido Ramon Castro del Rio, visitor to the Great Blasket in 1928.

good Irish as a loyal keeper of the people's traditions.'[35] An account of his visit was later published in Spanish and English as *A Galician in Ireland*.

George Chambers (1873–*c*.1960)

A London businessman with a flair for poetry, George Chambers first visited the Great Blasket in June 1931 (see Chapter 13). He was fifty-eight years old at the time and

Sketch of George Chambers
(artist unknown).

married with two children. On his very first day on the island,
he met twenty-year-old Eibhlís Ní Shúilleabháin. Despite their
38-year age difference, he was immediately smitten. Upon his
return to London, the pair began a correspondence that would
continue for more than three decades. Two years later, on 3
May 1933, Eibhlís married Seán Ó Criomhthain, Tomás' son
(see Chapter 13). Eibhlís cared for her father-in-law in his final
years and shared regular updates on his deteriorating condition
in her letters to Chambers, who occasionally sent Tomás gifts
of tobacco. In early 1934, Tomás sent a thank you note to
Chambers and expressed his fondness for the man. In 1936,
Chambers sent Tomás Christmas gifts. Chambers returned
to the island for a final time at the age of sixty-five in 1938,
the year after Tomás' death. He published a book of poetry
titled *The Lovely Line* which includes several poetic tributes to
Eibhlís. Chambers died at eighty-seven, not long after the last
letter sent by Eibhlís dated 28 August 1960. The letters from
Chambers to Eibhlís have not survived.

Kenneth Hurlstone Jackson (1909–1991)

Born in Surrey, England, linguist Kenneth Hurlstone Jackson arrived on the island in the company of Robin Flower on 7 June 1932. At the time he was a student at Cambridge University. Jackson was concerned about the passing of the oral tradition and the loss of invaluable folklore. He and Tomás, who was then in his late seventies, undoubtedly discussed this issue. Jackson's work was focused on preserving the stories of Peig Sayers.

Seán Ó Faoláin (1900–1991)

Seán Ó Faoláin, who was from Cork, was educated at University College Cork, the National University of Ireland and Harvard University. He travelled to the Great Blasket to visit Tomás, probably in the early 1930s. He included a summary of his brief stay in his book *An Irish Journey*, writing that he sat at Tomás' hearth. He acknowledged that Tomás was a 'famous shanachie', but he also referred to him as a 'pompous old man'. He recalled: 'I enjoyed tussling with old Tomás, and he enjoyed tussling with me,'[36] saying that they matched each other proverb for proverb. Their mutual respect was obvious. Ó Faoláin was a widely renowned author of many short stories, novels and biographies.

This parade of prominent visitors to Tomás' door over a period of about thirty years from 1905 to 1935 is extraordinary. But there were two other visitors who would have an even greater impact on Tomás. They would facilitate Ireland's impending transition from the oral tradition to the written word and help Tomás write and publish his two classic books.

10. A Published Author in the Making

Tomás became more focused on his writing when he turned sixty, around 1915. Perhaps the passing of the years led him to confront his mortality and motivated him to expand the scope of his writing before it was too late. He may have been hearing echoes of the then long-deceased island poet Seán Ó Duinnshléibhe who, in his own later years, was anxious to have his stories and poems transcribed so they would not be lost when he died.

By this time, Tomás had acquired many of the skills necessary to take the next significant step in his evolution as an author. He had spent the previous two decades or so learning to read and write in Irish. He had a working knowledge of various genres of literature. And he had some experience writing short pieces for periodicals. Now it was time to apply his skills to more substantial works. But he was hardly at the stage in life when anyone, let alone a native of the Great Blasket, was likely to bloom as the author of a series of published books.

Fortunately, Tomás was not alone in engaging in this daunting challenge. The writing and editing of his first two books, *Allagar na hInise* and *An tOileánach,* involved a collaboration of three fascinating men. Tomás, of course, was the primary author and he provided the raw material. Brian Ó Ceallaigh, an avid student of Irish, was the first to identify Tomás' potential as a writer. He convinced Tomás to commit his observations and memories to writing and provided guidance along the way. An Seabhac was responsible for refining the two manuscripts so that they were ready for publication. So close was the collaboration of this trio that they developed a kind of symbiotic relationship in the process.

Ó Ceallaigh and An Seabhac emerged at just the right time to enable Tomás to overcome his initial reluctance and to launch and complete these writing projects that would prove to be the culmination of his life's work. Their guidance and support were essential in the evolution of Tomás from a fisherman and farmer with a writing hobby into the legendary 'islandman' of Irish literature.

Brian Ó Ceallaigh (Bryan Albert O'Kelly) was born in Killarney on 13 January 1889. He arrived on the Great Blasket in April 1917 at the age of twenty-eight. His visit began almost exactly one year after the Easter Rising, and while the First World War was still raging in Europe. Like many other cultural visitors, Ó Ceallaigh was seeking to develop a greater proficiency in Irish. He stayed for about eight and a half months, returning home on New Year's Eve 1917.[1] Ó Ceallaigh was perhaps the single most important visitor to the island in relation to its literary flowering. He motivated Tomás to elevate his writing far beyond short periodical pieces.

Ó Ceallaigh's family was reasonably well off. He was educated in languages, history and law at Trinity College Dublin and the University of Paris, and he had at least some knowledge of six languages. He went on to study history at the University of Marburg in Germany, where he was rounded up and imprisoned, along with other foreign students, when Britain declared war on Germany on 4 August 1914. Hoping to secure his release, Ó Ceallaigh wrote a postcard to Kuno Meyer, the German founder of the School of Irish Learning, whom he had known in his Dublin days. Meyer was travelling

Blasket visitor and
Tomás' literary
mentor Brian
Ó Ceallaigh.

in the United States when Ó Ceallaigh's postcard arrived, but
his sister Antonie put him in touch with Sir Roger Casement,
one of the key leaders of the impending Irish republican rising.
Casement was in Germany at the time seeking to advance the
Irish cause.

Casement arranged for Ó Ceallaigh to be temporarily
paroled and brought to his hotel in Berlin, where they met
twice on 19 December 1914. Casement asked Ó Ceallaigh for
help, apparently in recruiting Irish prisoners in the Limburg
prison camp for a possible 'Irish Brigade' in the war against
Great Britain. Ó Ceallaigh declined. He felt that he was
not 'cut out' for such a role.[2] Nevertheless, Casement was
subsequently instrumental in securing Ó Ceallaigh's release

on 7 January 1915. Ó Ceallaigh then travelled to London, probably via France. A month later, on 8 February 1915, Ó Ceallaigh gave a written statement to the British government on Casement's activities. Casement was captured by the British when a German submarine landed him at Banna Strand in County Kerry on 21 April 1916, three days before the Easter Rising. He was eventually charged with treason, convicted and hanged in London on 3 August 1916. There is no indication that Ó Ceallaigh's statement was a factor in Casement's prosecution. In an effort to undermine pleas for clemency, the British alleged that Casement was gay and these claims were probably accurate. (Homosexual acts were illegal at the time.)

When Ó Ceallaigh returned to Killarney in the autumn of 1916, his mother urged him to learn the Irish language, apparently thinking that fluency in Irish would help him secure employment as a school inspector. She arranged for An Seabhac to tutor him. After five or six lessons, Ó Ceallaigh was making good progress and he was eager for more. An Seabhac was familiar with Tomás' expertise in Irish, and he urged Ó Ceallaigh to further his study of the language on the Great Blasket, giving him a note of introduction to Tomás.

Ó Ceallaigh lodged in the King's house during his stay on the island. Marstrander had brought Tomás a copy of Ua Laoghaire's novel *Niamh* in 1907, and Ó Ceallaigh brought him a copy of another Ua Laoghaire novel, *Scéal Séadna*, ten years later. Both books undoubtedly helped to stimulate Tomás' interest in writing.

Tomás and Ó Ceallaigh spent a lot of time together. Ó Ceallaigh was captivated by Tomás' broad repertoire of island lore, including stories, poems and songs. He was also interested in Tomás' keen observations on island life. Many lively conversations took place as they sat looking out of the window in the King's house. According to Máiréad Nic Craith:

> Sometimes they set to work in the King's Palace [house],
> but of course, they would often set the book aside in
> favour of chat and company ... Sometimes they would
> read *Séadhna* on a rock that they called 'gort na mara'
> [the field of the sea].[3]

Ó Ceallaigh was a quiet, shy, brooding, even mysterious
man. He may have been sickly. He seemed to be cautious and
suspicious of others. He is said to have had few real friends, but
he got along very well with both Tomás and An Seabhac.

As the months passed, Ó Ceallaigh began to realise that
Tomás had some real promise as a writer and began a gradual
process of encouraging Tomás to commit his oral folklore
material, his memories and his musings to writing. In his
preface to *Allagar na hInise*, Ó Ceallaigh (or perhaps An
Seabhac on his behalf – see Chapter 11) wrote:

> Before I went to the Blaskets Tomás used to write down
> old songs and folktales but he had no concern with what
> is normally termed literature. I urged him to write down
> pieces about himself, the Islanders, or anything else he
> wished.[4]

Ó Ceallaigh explained the genesis of Tomás' two classic books
in an article eventually published in the *Sunday Independent*
exactly one week after Tomás' passing:

> I thought it a pity that this life should die, unrecorded,
> and I felt that Tomás could make it live on paper for future
> generations. I tried therefore, to make him realise what
> interest everyday incidents which were occurring around
> us would possess for people who were accustomed to a
> more comfortable and complicated existence ...

Gradually, Tomás wrote with more firmness and continuity and more vividly, even about things that might appear dull in themselves. He was a mason as well as a fisherman by occupation, accustomed to put up a house stone by stone.

'Do the same with words as you would with stones,' I used to say to him. He liked to think that he was a mason in words.[5]

But Tomás had reservations about expanding the scope of his writing. At one point, he suggested that a description of life on the island would not attract popular interest: 'Everyone knows what life is like here.'[6] While this was true of the 150 or so residents of the Great Blasket and their off-island family and friends, Ó Ceallaigh envisioned a much wider audience. Seán Ó Criomhthain said that his father had modest expectations for where his writing might lead: 'He hadn't the slightest idea that he would ever see a book of his in print because not much was being published in Irish in Tomás' time.'[7]

One of the early results of Ó Ceallaigh's prompting was a short story describing island women singing in lilting Irish about their longing for passage money that would enable them to emigrate to America. Written at the behest of Ó Ceallaigh, this story, one of Tomás' first published works, was called '*An Guth ar Nóin*' and was published in *An Lóchrann* in December 1917. Ó Ceallaigh described it as 'beautiful'.[8]

As for Ó Ceallaigh himself, he continued to pursue his career after he left the Great Blasket. He travelled to the island several more times, apparently including a visit in 1918 when there was a discussion about Tomás writing a diary. Máiréad Nic Craith suggests that Ó Ceallaigh may have been inspired to encourage Tomás to write in this format by the 1918 publication of a diary called *Lóchrann* by Bríd Stac from Dún an Óir near Ballyferriter. Stac's framework was available to Ó Ceallaigh and, through him, to Tomás.[9]

Tomás speculated about his young friend's motivation as well as about the long-term implications of his work for his own mortality:

> I thought at first it was because he [Ó Ceallaigh] wanted to be reading the language but he kept me at it for five years. He said it would be a great pity if I were idle, like the poet Seán O'Donlevy long ago, and that I should write a couple of books while I had life in me, so as to live on after my death.[10]

Seán Ó Criomhthain wrote that Ó Ceallaigh's guidance to Tomás was simple and straightforward:

> 'Today is Monday. Write down everything you see on Monday and come again on Tuesday. Continue on and write down what you see on Tuesday. Keep going and write down everything you see every day of the week, and when you have filled a certain number of pages of foolscap put them into an envelope and send them to me in Killarney. I'll keep them safely.' Tomás continued on writing and writing a diary and from that came *An tAllagar* that we have today.[11]

In September 1918, Ó Ceallaigh wrote to Tomás asking him to start writing the diary. And he did: 'The first day of October, Tuesday, it would be a big fishing day, every canoe as full as each other.'[12] Ó Ceallaigh had successfully leveraged their friendship and applied all his powers of persuasion to convince Tomás to take his writing to the next level. He gave Tomás his own Waterman fountain pen along with a supply of ink and paper.

At the end of the first month, Tomás said he wanted to continue, even if he was slow at it. Brian had a difficult time with Tomás' Irish and Tomás would often explain himself in notes intended to clarify his language.[13]

This manuscript is a series of handwritten entries primarily on lined paper, but also on a wide assortment of other paper – whatever was available when Tomás ran out. The dating of the entries by Tomás and Ó Ceallaigh is inconsistent.

Tomás' decision to follow through on Ó Ceallaigh's encouragement was a major turning point in his life and in the history of the island. He had decided to take a huge leap of faith and commit his life experiences to writing. Tomás reported:

> He [Ó Ceallaigh] spent a year with us ... When he had gone, I used to send him a journal every day for five years. Then nothing would satisfy him but that I should write of my own life and tell him how I had passed my days ...
>
> What you're reading now [*The Islandman*], reader, is the fruit of my labours.[14]

Back on the mainland, Ó Ceallaigh achieved his goal of becoming a school inspector on 1 June 1918. But his appointment was not attributable to his knowledge of Irish, as his mother had anticipated. According to Muiris Mac Conghail, it was actually a reward for the information he had provided to the British government on the activities of Sir Roger Casement. It is seems unlikely that Ó Ceallaigh shared any information about his involvement in the Casement matter with either Tomás or An Seabhac.

Unfortunately, Ó Ceallaigh was unhappy in his new position. Then, just a year later, in June 1919, he lost his job when he failed an examination. It is unknown how he earned his living for the next few years, although he may have worked as a teacher.

In the meantime, Tomás was hard at work, as he had promised, writing entries in his diary. Each included a short vignette of island life. Tomás sent the entries to Ó Ceallaigh in batches of twelve pages of foolscap. They were dispatched via the post on a regular basis for over four years, concluding in early 1923.

At the outset, the diary may have been an elaborate way of practising Irish and staying in touch. Mac Conghail described the diary entries as 'a long distance conversation with his friend Brian.'[15] It appears that their original intent was not to write a book. Perhaps there was some thought that excerpts could be published in one of the Irish-language periodicals. After a while, it became clear to both men that a book was a possibility.

Ó Ceallaigh had some concern about the safety of the packages. He knew that during the war some of his letters had been opened by the government. To hedge this risk, he enclosed brief explanatory enclosures in his mailings. On 1 November 1922, for example, he wrote: 'To anybody opening this letter: These sheets of paper are sent for a purely literary and personal purpose.'[16]

Because they were written and sent off to Ó Ceallaigh in batches, Tomás wasn't able to consult his earlier instalments when writing subsequent segments. This only added to the challenge. Further, the diary nature of the project meant that it was a long-drawn-out undertaking. A total of over 550 entries were involved, a very impressive output under the circumstances.

While Tomás was still working on his diary, Ó Ceallaigh began thinking about yet another project. Sensing Tomás' capacity to sustain a storyline, he and An Seabhac came up with the concept of a novel set on the Great Blasket. The story involved a girl who visited the island and fell in love with a Blasket lad. Ó Ceallaigh sent the concept to Tomás, but he rejected the idea, saying that nothing like that ever happened. It would be a lie. He would only write what he regarded as true.

As an alternative, Ó Ceallaigh proposed that Tomás write his autobiography. He brought Tomás several books, including Pierre Loti's *Pêcheur d'Islande* (*An Iceland Fisherman*) and Maxim Gorky's *My Childhood* and *In the World*. Ó Ceallaigh wrote that he read extracts of these books to Tomás, presumably in English translation. Ó Ceallaigh said that Tomás preferred Gorky. Tomás himself wrote: 'I myself have read a piece of each book ... I like them well.'[17] He also read at least portions of *Growth of the Soil* by Knut Hamsun, which won the Nobel Prize for Literature in 1920.

The common thread among these books was the struggle of ordinary people living under difficult circumstances. Each had a heroic quality to them. Ó Ceallaigh wrote that 'Gorky showed Tomás that a fisherman could write a book as well as a learned man.'[18] If others could tell such stories in a compelling fashion, Tomás could too.

Tomás finished *Allagar na hInise* with an entry dated 1 March 1923. He wrote that he began writing *An tOileánach* in June 1922, but it appears that he actually started it on 4 February 1923, when he was about sixty-eight years old. He approached the book chronologically, starting with his childhood memories. As in the case of *Allagar na hInise*, segments of *An tOileánach* were sent to Ó Ceallaigh in batches, this time in the form of letters. For a time, the writing of the two works overlapped. Some of the packages from Tomás apparently contained material for both projects, and there was some confusion about which enclosures were intended for which project. Tomás, however, was clear in his mind that the two works were entirely separate. He wrote: 'The first thing I did was to situate the compass and remove the cornerstones, so that there would be no connection between the work I

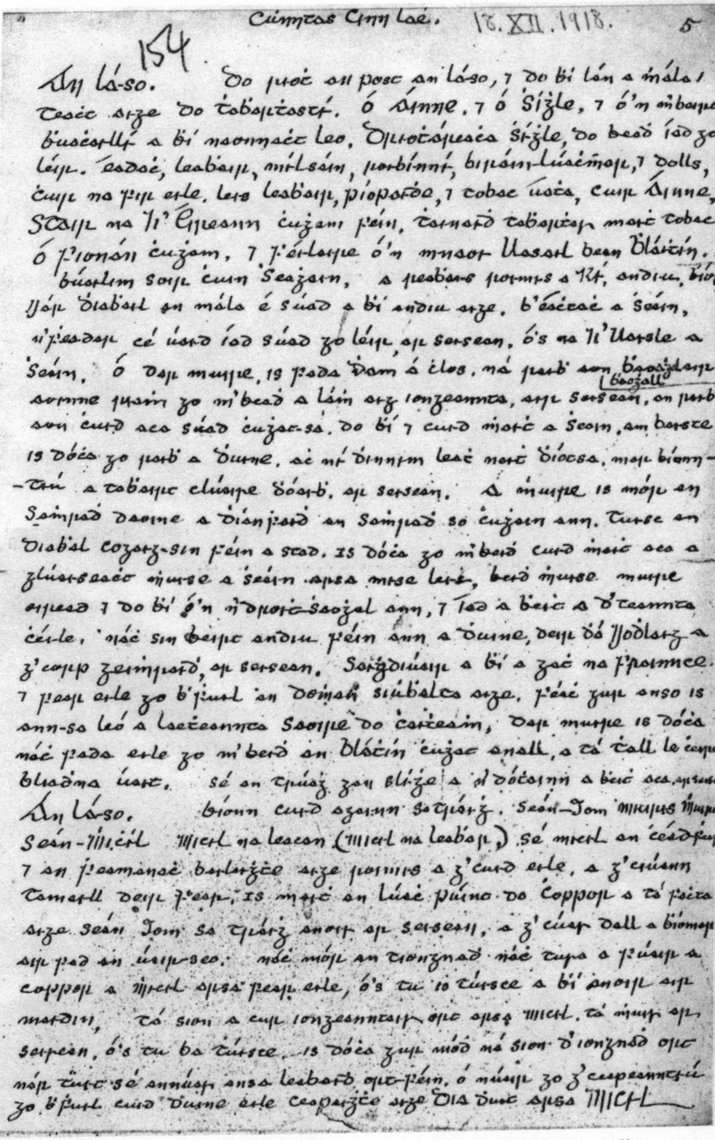
Cúntas Cinn Lae. 18.XII.1918. 5
154

Tomás' meticulously handwritten entry for 18 December 1918 in *Allagar na hInise*, dated by Ó Ceallaigh.[19]

had completed [*Allagar na hInise*] and the work I had yet to complete [*An tOileánach*].'[20]

Tomás' writing continued unabated. He completed what was effectively a first draft of *An tOileánach* in June 1924, when he stopped sending his instalments to Ó Ceallaigh. The reason for this cessation is a mystery. He sent another fifty-two pages to An Seabhac in January 1926 (Ó Ceallaigh had apparently passed responsibility for the manuscripts to An Seabhac by this time – see below). Another batch, including the first version of the concluding chapter, is dated 3 March 1926. A conclusion, added at the urging of An Seabhac, is dated 27 September 1928.

Tomás and Ó Ceallaigh had maintained their batch production process for over six years, encompassing both books. Tomás wrote in Irish, and Ó Ceallaigh would write back in English. Tomás' pattern was to write something every couple of days.

Irene Lucchitti wrote that Ó Ceallaigh engaged in a process of 'coaxing' Tomás, encouraging him and giving him general direction on content and format. Ó Ceallaigh wrote: 'I did not force him. What he cared to write about was good enough for me.'[21] But he went beyond just encouraging him. He applied a certain amount of pressure to write, always finding ways to overcome Tomás' reservations. He also fed the process with writing supplies as well as tobacco. Robert Kanigel went further, writing that Ó Ceallaigh 'practically dragged it [his writing] out of him.'[22]

Lucchitti also wrote that by sharing with Tomás books of a particular genre, Ó Ceallaigh was 'grooming' him as an author of a certain type. In effect, Ó Ceallaigh was encouraging Tomás to produce writing that was similar to the examples provided. And, of course, that is exactly what Tomás did. Seán Ó Criomhthain said:

When Tomás saw that those poor simple people [Loti and Gorky] had come out and described their own lives, 'Yerrah,' said he, 'if they're fools, I'll make a fool of myself too. I'll have a shot at it.' He took up his pen and continued writing until finally the well ran dry ... from the time he began *An tAllagar* until the time he finished *An tOileánach* I'd say he was writing for six or seven years. He also used to write essays for *An Lóchrann* and other such publications. He was all the time writing.[23]

Seán Ó Criomhthain was the only person living with Tomás while he was writing his instalments of *Allagar na hInise* and *An tOileánach*. He painted a dramatic picture of Tomás engaged in his writing after evening tea, starting at about seven or eight o'clock:

There was a table here in the corner at the right-hand side of the fire-place. Tomás would pull up the table. There was a lamp high up on the wall with a mirror on it behind the globe and two wicks, each of them as big as a light-house. Tomás would draw up to the fire. His pipe was always on the hob along with his tobacco. He'd smoke a fine blast of the pipe and then turn around, get his foolscap ready and set to work with his pen, a beautiful one which he had got from one of the visitors ...

It was a Waterman's fountain pen, and every night when finished with it he'd dry it with a piece of cloth and a bit of paper and put it away. If a butterfly or a cricket in the corner as much as touched it he'd nearly kill them. Not a hand was to be laid on the pen in case it might be damaged ...

He used to write depending on how long the house was quiet, and according as thoughts occurred to him he'd put the finishing touches to them, and he was often writing when I came home. It might be ten o'clock or half past ten and Tomás would still be on the pen.[24]

Excerpt of Tomás' original manuscript of *An tOileánach*, dated 17 September 1923 by Ó Ceallaigh.[25]

Seán said his father would write only in the evening and never when there was company. If visitors saw that he was writing, they would steer clear of his home. He remembered Tomás saying many times that 'noise doesn't suit the writer'.[26] Tomás concentrated on his writing during the winter months. He didn't do a lot of self-editing while he was writing, and he had a great memory of events. Seán said his words flowed 'like water in a river.'[27]

Tomás' grandson Pádraig Ua Maoileoin recalls life on the Great Blasket while Tomás was engaged in his writing:

> My memory of Tomás goes back a long way. I used to be in and out to the island at that time, when I was young. He died in 1937. I was going on visits from about 1925 to about 1935 or so, now and again ... It was another world on the island. The place was alive. Full of energy and high jinks and sickness and everything else ... At night he would sit down when everyone else had headed off around the island, visiting neighbours and so on. Tomás would be below with his pen describing the events of the day. He was writing *Allagar na hInise* (*Island Cross-Talk*) at the time.[28]

The eventual results of these labours were extraordinary, but the raw manuscripts were still not ready for publication. They included two long handwritten manuscripts in Irish, one a diary and the other an autobiography. Ó Ceallaigh attempted to rewrite the beginning of *An tOileánach,* but his knowledge of Irish was so weak that it was garbled and had to be further edited by An Seabhac. Remarkably, the first time Tomás saw the many instalments together was when the fully edited whole appeared in book form.

Over the years, the friendship between Tomás and Ó Ceallaigh deepened. An Seabhac wrote that Tomás loved Ó

Ceallaigh as a son. Referring to Ó Ceallaigh in a letter to Flower in December 1918, Tomás wrote that many gentlemen came to the island, but 'no one of them ever looked after Tomás but one [Ó Ceallaigh] ... He gave me the means to live and if he did may God give him the same help.'[29] The pair exchanged a series of letters on many topics. In a letter he wrote to Ó Ceallaigh in July 1921, for example, Tomás included a poem expressing his heartfelt longing for his friend:

> The nights are getting longer and the days are shortening
> On the fields of the Great Blasket.
> If only I could see Brian this year
> On the fields of the Great Blasket.
> It is very true that life is troubled
> Every year since we parted from one another
> But we will be reunited one day
> On the fields of the Great Blasket.[30]

Also in 1922, Tomás wrote to Ó Ceallaigh to express his sympathies on the death of his mother. He shared his profound sense of loss on his daughter Cáit's tragic death earlier that year (see Chapter 13) and closed this letter with 'Goodbye and eternal blessings to you, oh fine man that you are.'[31]

When the two manuscripts were still in a very rough form, the perplexing Ó Ceallaigh decided to move to the Continent. He was very unhappy and may have been experiencing health issues. The Casement matter may have been haunting him too; his report on Casement (who was highly regarded as one of the heroes of the Easter Rising) was sitting in a file in Dublin Castle and could be released at any time.

Ó Ceallaigh felt, however, that he had a personal obligation to Tomás to move his manuscripts forward to publication. Mac Conghail wrote:

Ó Ceallaigh brought the manuscript to the Irish Texts Society in London, but in view of the work involved in preparing the text for the press, they felt unable to undertake the task. He even brought the material to Paris with him, but to no avail. Finally, he went to see the Minister of Education, Eoin MacNeill, but the department did not at that time have a publications scheme in operation.[32]

Now under increasing pressure to fulfill his self-imposed commitment to Tomás, Ó Ceallaigh reached out to An Seabhac. Fortunately, his former tutor and friend agreed to take up the challenge. Of Ó Ceallaigh's departure from Ireland, An Seabhac wrote: 'Brian left in a lonely state and I never saw him again' and, tellingly, that 'Brian had to leave Ireland and I understood he would not return.'[33] Mac Conghail supposed that Ó Ceallaigh left Ireland in late 1926. His last Irish address was the Esplanade Hotel in Bray, County Wicklow.

The rest of Ó Ceallaigh's life is a mystery. Séamas Ó Duilearga, a founder of the Folklore of Ireland Society and later the director of the Irish Folklore Commission, reported that he and his travelling companion, Blasket visitor Carl von Sydow, had a chance encounter with Ó Ceallaigh in 1927 in a train station in Berlin. They had a brief conversation about the Blaskets through an open train window. Mac Conghail suggested that this conversation may have been the last contact Ó Ceallaigh had with Ireland. There is virtually no information about his years living in Europe.

Ó Ceallaigh eventually died from poliomyelitis on 28 December 1936 in Split, Yugoslavia, now Croatia, on the Adriatic Sea. He may have been under the care of the Jesuits at the time. His grave is marked only by a cross and a number. It is doubtful that Ó Ceallaigh ever saw the fruit of his efforts, the published versions of *Allagar na hInise* and *An tOileánach*, though Tomás sent copies of both to his sister for forwarding.

In an article marking his death, the *Irish Independent* wrote: 'It was a flash of insight on Mr. Kelly's part that made him realize that Tomás had a story of his own to tell and that the story would be a permanent monument of the Gaeltacht.'[34]

Coincidentally, Tomás himself would pass away just a little over two months after Ó Ceallaigh. Commenting on the almost simultaneous passing of both men in an RTÉ radio broadcast, An Seabhac said 'I felt with the coming of that news that some lonely tragedy had happened.' Clearly, he sensed the significance of the proximate deaths of two men who were very close to each other in life and who collaborated to produce two classic works of Irish literature.

Ó Ceallaigh was the principal catalyst in the publication of *Allagar na hInise* and *An tOileánach*. Others had played an important role in preparing Tomás as an emerging author, but it was Ó Ceallaigh who more or less insisted that he sit down and write in a sustained way for many years. Lucchitti wrote of Tomás' literary intimacy with Ó Ceallaigh: 'His first reader was Brian Ó Ceallaigh: he engages in writing his life, in large part at Brian's behest and, in part out of loneliness for Brian. He writes with Brian's pen and he sends his writings to Brian.'[35]

Ó Ceallaigh reminded us that Tomás had a limited worldview with which to create context for his writing:

> [Tomás] is a journalist who has never seen a Dublin Street, to whom Dingle is the distant city; he has never been in a bookshop; never seen the inside of a library; never travelled by train. The island and the island-covered sea around, are his world, in storm and calm, with the Blessed Master present, looking over it all.[36]

Seán Ó Coileáin's assessment is that Ó Ceallaigh was the first to recognise Tomás' latent ability to write creatively. Without Ó Ceallaigh's mentoring and encouragement, there would be no Tomás as we know him today. Seán Ó Criomhthain said unequivocally that it was Ó Ceallaigh who 'prompted him to write every book he wrote'.[37] Later in his life, Tomás himself wrote: 'I realize that in many ways I was blind until I met him [Ó Ceallaigh]. The help of God is often nearer than the door ... I would not have left two books behind me were it not for the man who got me working.'[38]

Pádraig 'An Seabhac' Ó Siochfhradha was born in 1883 in Burnham, outside Dingle, where his father worked as a gamekeeper for Lord Ventry. He was an organiser for the Gaelic League in the Killarney area from 1912 to 1917, and cycled all over West Kerry setting up branch chapters and promoting the Irish language. He was reputed to swoop into villages like a hawk, which is how he came by his nickname. He became a leader of the Irish Volunteers in County Kerry in 1913 and was imprisoned by the British three times for his activities. An author himself, An Seabhac's best-known books are *An Baile Seo 'Gainne'* and *Jimín Mháire Thaidhg*, both based on his West Kerry youth. He was the first president of the Folklore of Ireland Society and was involved in creating the Irish Folklore Commission. He also served as secretary to the Irish Manuscripts Commission and later as principal editor of An Gúm, the government-affiliated publisher. He served in Seanad Éireann on three occasions.

An Seabhac probably made the pilgrimage to the island several times. He said in an RTÉ interview that he first met Tomás when he was just a boy of ten or twelve years old. Tomás sent him Irish-language pieces that he had written as early as 1908. He had written to Tomás introducing Ó Ceallaigh in 1917.

At the point when Ó Ceallaigh had taken Tomás' manuscripts to the threshold of publication, he left for the Continent. He had successfully prevailed upon An Seabhac to edit the works and to arrange for them to be published. An Seabhac was well aware of Tomás' ongoing work on these projects. Ó Ceallaigh and An Seabhac met often in the early to mid-1920s in Killarney and Dingle and after 1922 in his house in Dublin. Ó Ceallaigh recalled a conversation he had with An Seabhac on Bray Strand in 1922:

> 'I have often asked myself' said 'An Seabhac' to me ... 'if a man living in a remote Gaelic-speaking district, unacquainted with the English Ireland, could write a work of literature.'
>
> 'It is done,' I said, and I told him about the work of Tomás for five years.[39]

An Seabhac later wrote that he accepted the manuscripts and the responsibility for pursuing their publication on two conditions: that Tomás agree to his role; and that he be granted permission to edit the manuscripts as he saw fit. Shortly thereafter, Tomás sent a letter to An Seabhac confirming the arrangement. Tomás was pleased that someone from the Dingle Peninsula was involved. And thus the editing commenced.

An Seabhac may have been motivated, at least in part, by the consistency of the material with the broad cultural and political agenda of the Celtic Revival. At the time, however, he had no way of knowing the literary significance of his task. As for Tomás, he most likely trusted An Seabhac based on their previous interaction. And he probably felt that giving him full editorial authority was necessary to achieve his ultimate goal of publishing his writing in book form.

An Seabhac's editing was a major challenge. Seán Ó Coileáin wrote that 'it was a feat to put it together'.[40] These manuscripts were Tomás' first attempts at authoring full-length books, and he was totally unfamiliar with the practical constraints that come with publishing a book and then bringing it to market as a commercial proposition. The manuscripts needed a considerable amount of refinement. And there were gaps to be filled.

An Seabhac's first project was Tomás' diary. He started the editing in 1926, and it was published as *Allagar na hInise* in 1928. He then began editing Tomás' autobiography in early 1928, leading to the publication of *An tOileánach* in 1929. An Seabhac fully exercised his editorial discretion in *An tOileánach,* incorporating the following types of modification into the original manuscript:[41]

- Tomás' personal spelling system was converted to more conventional spelling, and the West Kerry dialect was modified so that it would be more clearly understood by a broad audience.
- The total length of the manuscript was shortened to enhance readability, as required by the publisher. Among the deletions were repetitious descriptions of storms, near-drownings and trips to Dingle.
- Several island songs were omitted. Tomás had included them because of his perception of their centrality to island life. And he was not happy about their deletion. He wrote: 'If I had my way, I'd have included a half a dozen fine songs here and there in these writings. However, I have no choice in the matter and I have to do as I'm instructed by my esteemed editor.'[42]
- The text was modified so as to respect the perceived sensibilities of the reading public by eliminating potentially offensive material such as the tale of Tomás getting caught swimming in the nude by three girls on the White Strand, Tomás' singing of '*Caisleán Uí Néill*' at his wedding and specific words such as urine, bladder and mucus.

Commemorative stamp issued in 1983 honouring An Seabhac on the 100th anniversary of his birth.

- Some narrative was eliminated that tended to cast the islanders in a bad light, such as fights, harsh judgements about neighbours and quarrelling. James Stewart wrote that some of the material deleted made the islanders appear 'too punchy, too sexy, too sly or too slanderous'.[43] An Seabhac wanted to maintain the quasi-idyllic image of the island.

- Certain words borrowed from the English language, such as 'palace', were eliminated to retain the perception of the cultural purity of the island and its spoken Irish.

- The manuscript was separated into chapters to organise the content better and improve the flow.

- An Seabhac also asked for a new chapter from Tomás describing the island houses and island life in general. Tomás wrote: 'I may as well give some brief account of the way we managed things in this Island when I was young.'[44] His reluctance is evident in his tone.

- An Seabhac asked Tomás for a new and more robust concluding chapter (Chapter 25). The new ending has a different tone and includes Tomás' reflections on the broad span of his life as well as the famous and often-quoted passage: 'the like of us will never be again.' This more recently written chapter demonstrated his growing maturity as a writer. But he also shared his frustration with the editing process: 'Perhaps it hasn't got such a short tail on it now. If there is a sentence there that you don't like, leave it out.'[45]

An Seabhac also asked Tomás for more detail on the two loves of his life, Cáit Ní Dálaigh and his wife, Máire Ní Catháin. Tomás declined, apparently because he felt that these matters were discrete and private areas of his soul.[46]

An Seabhac carried on an extensive correspondence with Tomás during the editing process. Essentially, Tomás provided a draft manuscript and An Seabhac asked clarifying questions and performed the polishing that he thought was necessary to achieve publication. The resulting text reflected the prevailing attitudes of the day.

Monsignor Pádraig Ó Fiannachta wrote:

> I remember An Seabhac showed me in around 1963 the heap of letters he had from Tomás as answers to questions he had asked when working on the manuscript. It wasn't just spelling and meaning that worried him, it was references to people still living that he thought shouldn't be published as a courtesy.[47]

Breandán Ó Conaire described an editorial consultation with a priest that occurred on 2 November 1928 about an unidentified portion of the manuscript. He wrote that, as a result, the story was sent 'in the right direction.'[48] The nature of any editing that might have been performed is unknown.

An Seabhac's editing is controversial; some commentators feel that his work compromised the fundamental authenticity of the narrative. In her 1930 review of *An tOileánach*, Marie-Louise Sjoestedt-Jonval thanked An Seabhac for letting her review Tomás' original manuscript. She said she understood the rationale for An Seabhac's editing, but felt that too much had been sacrificed in the name of the practicalities of publication and of respectability – a kind of censorship. She wrote that some episodes 'entirely innocent in their naiveté have been ... sacrificed to pedagogic requirements and to "respectability"'.[49] Robert Kanigel, on the other hand, wrote: 'I think An Seabhac can be seen as a sagacious editor, alive to his readers' needs, helping his author better satisfy them. By no means dismissive of Tomás, he was taking him seriously, grooming him, helping to "professionalize" a novice author.'[50]

There has been some suggestion that there was some interference by the government in the final narrative. An Seabhac flatly denied this allegation: 'Every line they [the government-affiliated publisher] received from me they printed it.'[51]

Beyond the editing of the narrative, it was An Seabhac who formulated Tomás' nickname as well as the title of his autobiography, *The Islandman*. These were brilliant marketing ideas. Tomás would never have thought to call himself 'The Islandman' – he would never have been so presumptuous.

An Seabhac understood and respected the historical and cultural significance of Tomás' writing. In his introduction to *Allagar na hInise,* he wrote:

> On reading it I soon discovered its uncommon character. It riveted my attention ... In Tomás's writing there is truth, baldly expressed, an account without ornament and a completely accurate picture of a community of people ... which only a member of that community could fully understand.

> This book is a voice from the Gaeltacht itself ... Tomás is of the Gaeltacht. He knows nothing else in the wide world. He never put a foot outside Corcaguiney [the Dingle Peninsula] ...
>
> The reader must imagine that small, lonely island, the most western habitation in Europe ...
>
> To them Ireland is a distant country. Springfield or Holyoke, Mass. is more of a capital city for them than any in the land of their birth.
>
> Tomás O'Crohan belongs to that community, at one with them in almost everything, except the uncommon gift he possesses of being able to commit his thoughts and reflections to the permanence of writing. He is an old man now, seventy-two years of age.[52]

As he was concluding the final chapter of *An tOileánach*, a chapter An Seabhac persuaded him to add, Tomás eloquently expressed his profound respect for the people of the island and the lives they lived:

> I have written minutely of much that we did, for it was my wish that somewhere there should be a memorial of it all, and I have done my best to set down the character of the people about me so that some record of us might live after us, for the like of us will never be again.[53]

These sombre closing words have been quoted thousands of times over the years. They have become an epitaph for the island itself. They express not only Tomás' intent in writing *An tOileánach*, but also his conviction that Blasket life was on the wane and would never be replicated. These were prophetic words indeed.

An Seabhac was successful in bringing Tomás' works to market, securing a publisher for both *Allagar na hInise* and *An tOileánach*. They were released in 1928 and 1929 respectively (see Chapter 11). Yet all the attention that ensued couldn't reverse the trend towards the extinction of the Blasket community.

As for An Seabhac, he had played an indispensable role in Tomás' long literary journey. As Seán Ó Coileáin wrote, he was a 'go-between' connecting two worlds, that of the Great Blasket and Ireland's literary realm.[54] After a long and brilliant career as an educator, writer, editor, businessman and public official, An Seabhac died in Dublin on 19 November 1964.

11. A Literary Outpouring

Once Tomás started writing in earnest, he achieved a remarkable level of output over about twenty years. He published three books under his own name (*Allagar na hInise*, *An tOileánach* and *Dinnseanchas na mBlascaodaí*); a collection of diary entries not included in *Allagar na hInise* was later published as *Allagar II*. In addition, four anthologies of Tomás' prose and verse have been published (*Seanchas ón Oileán Tiar*, *Bloghanna ón mBlascaod*, *Scéilíní ón mBlascaod* and *Cleití Gé ón mBlascaod Mór*). Three stories told by Tomás and others were published in *Béaloideas*, the Journal of the Folklore of Ireland Society.[1] Over 200 of his short pieces are included in these various publications. Tomás' output was wide-ranging, including autobiography, diary, folktales, short stories, poetry, songs and place-name lore.

Tomás was about sixty-one when his first published story appeared in *An Claidheamh Soluis* in 1916. He was seventy-three when *Allagar na hInise* was published in 1928 and seventy-four when *An tOileánach* was published in 1929. He continued writing and publishing until he was in his early eighties, about 1934, when he was physically unable to continue (see Chapter 12).

Tomás was not immune from the emotional turmoil and self-doubt typical of a writer. He wrote of his feelings of insecurity: 'Yes my friend [Ó Ceallaigh], I am able to write again. I stopped for a week as I had written papers of not very

Tomás' first published poem, '*Don Lóchrann*', from the January 1917 issue of *An Lóchrann*.

Do'n Lóċrann.

Fonn: "Alliliú mo ṁáilín."

I.

An teaċt tar n-ais do'n Lóċrann,
   Is cóir dúinn a ṁaiṫ a ṁaoiḋeaṁ,
Mar ní raiḃ ar tír 'á iúngnaiṁ,
   Aċ glórṫa gan mórán críċ'.
Glónan rud an bóṫar,
   Do'n veurṫa 's do'n otairveaḋlaige,
Tá raḋarc na súl do'n óige ann,
   Is tógan le mire a gcroiḋe.

II.

Aoinne a léiġean an Lóċrann,
   Ba cóir do rud maċtnaṁ cruinn,
Go ḃfuil gaċ Gaeḋluinn fúġanta ann,
   Ó gaċ úġdar dá ḃfuil ar tír.
Léiġin-se féin go dlúṫ é,
   Is é rsgrúdaḋ le bárr an pinn,
'S níl ó'n a ceiṫre cúinne,
   Aon rcriúd ann ná fuil go fíor.

III.

An t-óig-fear niġte, gleóiḋte,
   Atá a feolaḋ, is dá cur cuin cinn,
Árd-céimeaċ, léiġeanta, mórḋa,
   Gur bród dúinn, é ḃeiṫ 'nár dtír.
Dá mbeinn-se féin am' ġéirreaċ,
   Agus léar agam le mórán maoin',
Dob feárr liom é 'na léine,
   Ná Éire, le fear gan críc.

IV.

'S níl aon ainnir Gaeḋlaċ,
   Ó Véarra go Cairleán Nua,
Ná go reolfainn féin ar réirre,
   Go dtí an té úd 'á ḃreacaḋ rúd,
Do ḃeirim féin an craoḃ do,
   Sa Ġaeḋluinn dár carad liúm,
Buaḋ is beannaċt Dé aige,
   A n-agaiḋ 'n lae leir a guiḋim do rúd.

Tomás Ua Criomṫain,
An Blascaḋ Mór.

good quality. I was thinking that I had lost direction. Sometimes I feel that what I had written is inferior.'[2] On the other hand, he sometimes expressed enormous confidence: 'Ireland would be in a sickly condition the day that a book by Tomás Dhónaill Mhic Criomhthain [using his father's traditional surname] would be in the shops without being sold.'[3]

When Tomás was writing, Ireland was in the midst of the great political and military turmoil of the early twentieth century. Other ominous forces were also lurking. The first fifteen years of the twentieth century were relatively prosperous on the island but by the time Tomás' two classic books were published in the late 1920s, the island's population had fallen by 20 per cent from its 1916 peak. It would drop another 70 per cent over the next twenty years.[4] Thus, within roughly a generation bracketing the publication of *Allagar na hInise* and *An tOileánach*, the island went from fairly stable to unsustainable.

Tomás' first published literary composition was '*Fiach Fada Mhuintir Oileáin*', based on a story told by his neighbour Thomas 'Maol'. It appeared in the 2 December 1916 issue of *An Claidheamh Soluis*. He quickly followed with a poem, '*Don Lóchrann*', which appeared in the January 1917 issue of *An Lóchrann*, a bilingual monthly edited by An Seabhac. Two months later, his essay '*Ag Díol Éisc*' appeared in the March 1917 issue of the same periodical.

One of Tomás' short works is a description of the incredibly beautiful world of the Blaskets, '*Gort na Trá Báine*'. Piaras Béaslaí, the editor of *An Claidheamh Soluis,* called the piece a 'real jewel' and said that it 'proved that a feeling for nature, akin to that of Wordsworth, existed amongst the Gaelic-speaking people.'[5] This was high praise indeed.

Tomás continued writing for periodicals after the publication of *Allagar na hInise* and *An tOileánach*. He

TAOBH THUAIDH DE'N m-BLASCAOD

"AN LEACA DHUBHACH"

Tá lúb fairrge ar an dtaobh tuaidh de'n mBlascaod. Mór go bhfuil "An Leaca Dhubhach" mar ainm uirti: agus is le linn mo Shean-atar do bheith suas do ghlac an lúb so an ainm-seo. Dob'í "An Leaca Séar" an ainm ársa do bí uirti. Fáth na h-ainme sin: mar níl aon rud do tuitfeadh as láimh duine ná go ragadh amach ar an bhfairrge.

Fáth na h-ainme eile: ba lúb é seo gur draiteadh seilg mhór le fagháil innti ins an am go raibhtas ag cur chun mairceáchtaint do bhaint as. 'Sé cuma gur draiteadh an áit seo ar dtúis, líonta sgadán ag báid-mhóra béal-osgailte ó Daingean Uí Chúisc, ó Chuan Dreag-leatan Fionn-Trágha, agus ó Dreac áiteanna eile.

Ar fagháil na sgadán dóibh do shroiceadar ceanrais eile. 'Sé fearras é sin ná doruigtá, agus do bíodh na báid-mhóra so lán go béal gach maidin, de sgadáin agus d'iasg mhór-ghard, agus ana-ghlaodác aca ar an bhórt so, ins an am-so ó lucht trádá.

Excerpt of Tomás' version of the folktale 'The Sorrowful Cliff' from the *Irish Independent*, 15 June 1926.

regularly corresponded with Fionán Mac Coluim and Cormac Ó Cadhlaigh, sending them stories, poems and proverbs for Irish-language publications. Many went unpublished and are now missing. In addition, his writing was appearing regularly in the *Irish Independent* (see below).

Pádraig Ua Maoileoin wrote that his grandfather was at his best when writing essays where he had fewer practical constraints. Over two-thirds of Tomás' periodical pieces were published before his first book was released. He also had the capacity to write simultaneously on parallel tracts. He published approximately thirty-five stories and poems while he was writing *Allagar na hInise* and another forty or so while he was writing *An tOileánach* and collaborating on the editing of both books.

Interestingly, Tomás doesn't mention his early writing for these Irish-language periodicals in *Allagar na hInise* or *An tOileánach*, despite the autobiographical nature of these works. He might have been expected to brag a bit about his impressive array of published writing.

Tomás' first published book was *Allagar na hInise*. The title refers to the everyday banter or 'cross-talk' between islanders. The book is essentially a selection of entries in a contemporaneous journal of fairly commonplace events that Tomás personally observed over a period of more than four years from 5 December 1918 to New Year's Day 1923. It has significant cultural value because it documents the ordinary lives of the islanders at a time when the island was tipping into decline.

Tomás' diary entries are brief and pithy. Few are longer than a page in length. The subject matter is wide-ranging and includes topics such as the call of the cuckoo, shearing sheep, the price of fish, Irish Home Rule, Shrovetide gossip, the King's speech, Good Friday food, bad news from the mainland, eating lobsters, Tadhg's new donkey, a herb for every disease, springtime toil, expectations dashed and New Year's Day. These topics reflect the flow of daily events. This journal describes island life as it was actually lived.

Allagar na hInise, 1928 edition.

The entries are also quite numerous. The original 1928 Irish version included about one-third of Tomás' total of 552 entries. The 1977 Irish edition includes over 380. The popular 1986 English version, *Island Cross-Talk*, includes 165. *Allagar II* (see below) contains another 168 entries not previously published.

Breandán Ó Conaire wrote that *Allagar na hInise* 'contains outstanding examples of lively dialogue between islanders and of individual characters within the island community, and vivid descriptions of the powers of nature, against which the islanders had little protection.' Leslie Matson's view is that 'Almost every page in *Allagar na hInise* is instinct with the liveliness of the characters being depicted therein. Discussion, argument, sarcastic retorts and witty sallies abound, no doubt heightened by exaggeration and the natural creativity of the writer.'[6]

Allagar na hInise has been published in three versions:

- **1928**: the original Irish-language version of *Allagar na hInise* was published by C.S. Ó Fallamhain in co-operation with the government's Stationery Office. It was finally released about ten years after Tomás started working on it. The book was edited and much abridged by An Seabhac. Pseudonyms were used for many of the characters. The book included a preface by Brian Ó Ceallaigh, dated 'March 1928, Killarney'. Ó Ceallaigh was living on the Continent by that time. It is unclear whether he left this piece with An Seabhac when he departed or sent it to him from Europe; or perhaps it was written on his behalf by An Seabhac.

- **1977**: a more complete Irish version was published by An Gúm, also entitled *Allagar na hInise*. This edition was based on Tomás' original manuscript as edited by his grandson, Pádraig Ua Maoileoin. It includes many of the journal entries omitted by An Seabhac as well as the correct names for the characters.

- **1986**: an English-language version entitled *Island Cross-Talk: Pages from a Diary* was published by the Oxford University Press. It was translated and edited by Tim Enright, who reverted to the original pseudonyms used by An Seabhac.

Some commentators feel that *Allagar na hInise* is actually more interesting than the iconic *An tOileánach*. Ua Maoileoin called it the 'great pearl of Tomás' writing' with 'nicely wrought and rounded scenes with a smooth finish.' He wrote: 'it is in the *Allagar* that I feel the Criomhthanach's pulse. It is there, I think, that he is most comfortable and best able to work. The quilt he is working on, it's a patchwork quilt and it is on the patch that the Criomhthanach is best.'[7]

Allagar na hInise is certainly an impressive work, especially as the author's first book. It provides a penetrating insight into life on the Great Blasket. And, it was a fitting warm-up to what most regard as Tomás' crowning achievement, *An tOileánach*.

An tOileánach, 1967 edition.

Following quickly on the heels of *Allagar na hInise, An tOileánach* was published in 1929. This is generally regarded as the most important book in the Blasket library. An autobiography, it covers a span of seventy years from Tomás' birth in the mid-1850s to the mid-1920s. It is written in typical Tomás style – straightforward prose recounting the author's extraordinary recollections of a life full of community, adventure, hardship and heartache.

An tOileánach is also a kind of social history of the island. It has some anthropological interest and was described by Tim Enright as a 'collective biography'.[8] Similarly, Seán Ó Tuama wrote that it is a biography of the island community.[9] Tomás takes the reader on an intriguing tour through various rites of passage in his own life: birth, childhood, schooling, marriage, children, work, family crises, wakes and old age. He focuses on the progression of events on the island and how they impacted on him.

One minor problem arose before the book was published. The publisher proposed that it should be printed in *cló romhánach* (Roman script). Tomás was not pleased and insisted on its being published in *cló gaelach* (Gaelic script). Nora O'Shea (Nóra Ní Shéaghdha), a former island teacher, wrote in her book *Thar Bealach Isteach* that she was forever arguing with Tomás over the matter. Ultimately, Tomás prevailed.

Ua Maoileoin was actually on the Great Blasket the day the first printed copies of *An tOileánach* arrived in the post. Of his grandfather's reaction, he wrote: 'I remember well the joyousness and pride in his eyes when he opened the first one of them.'[10]

When it came to publishing an English translation of *An tOileánach*, Robin Flower was the obvious person to undertake the task. He had a long history with both Tomás and the island. Unfortunately, the process of translation dragged on much longer than anyone expected. Flower was a busy man and became seriously ill after a fall from a horse in 1933. The intended publisher, Jonathan Cape of London, was unhappy with the delay and dropped the book. Tomás himself was impatient waiting for Flower to finish the job.

Ultimately, Flower's translation, *The Islandman*, was a great success. Nevertheless, Tomás' son Seán wrote to George Chambers that the publication delay 'was a great Loss for us for [Muiris] O'Sullivan's book *Twenty Years A-Growing* [the English language version of *Fiche Bliain ag Fás*] ... took the market from us and that is the Reason Cape gave it up. Flower should have [had] the translation done within nine months but he was sick and could not Have the work done in time. So it can't Be Helped and We do no Blame any Body.'[11]

It is apparent that Tomás was pleased with the results of his collaboration with An Seabhac and Ó Ceallaigh. On 28 May 1928, before either book was published, he wrote a letter to Fionán Mc Coluim enclosing a long song of appreciation to An Seabhac and Ó Ceallaigh for their help in his writing and bringing his books to publication. On 23 May 1929 he wrote to An Seabhac expressing his appreciation to him and Ó Ceallaigh. Finally, on 16 October 1929, he again wrote to An Seabhac: 'My thanks to you ... it was a great thing I had a good backup card [An Seabhac] who could smarten it up.'[12]

An tOileánach has been published in five versions:[13]

- **1929**: the original Irish version edited by An Seabhac was published by C.S. Ó Fallamhain in co-operation with the government's Stationery Office under the title *An tOileánach: Scéal a Bheathadh Féin do Scríobh Tomás Ó Criomhthain*. Further editions were released in 1935, 1967 and 1969.
- **1934**: Flower's English translation of *An tOileánach, The Islandman*, was published by the Talbot Press and Chatto & Windus. It was reprinted in 1937 and 1943. In 1951, it was released again as part of the 'Oxford World Classics' series. It was reissued in 2000.
- **1973**: an Irish edition entitled *An tOileánach*, as edited by Ua Maoileoin, was published by Cló Talbóid. This edition restored some of the controversial material that had been edited out, but eliminated other sections for 'literary reasons'. It was released again in 1980.
- **2002**: a more complete Irish edition of *An tOileánach*, edited by Seán Ó Coileáin, was released by Cló Talbóid. In his introduction, Ó Coileáin expresses his high regard for the earlier editing by An Seabhac.
- **2012**: an English edition, *The Islander, Complete and Unabridged*, translated by Gary Bannister and David Sowby, was published by Gill & Macmillan. It was based on Ó Coileáin's 2002 Irish version.

In addition, *An tOileánach* has been published in German, French, Danish, Italian and Swedish. *The Islandman* has been published in Braille in three large volumes weighing a total of

151 lb. It is indeed a work of international significance. By far, the most widely read version is *The Islandman*.

Breandán Ó Conaire wrote that 'The publication of *An tOileánach*, in particular, had a significant and lasting effect on writing in Irish. Other islanders issued their own autobiographical works, notably Muiris Ó Súilleabháin in 1933 and Peig Sayers in 1936, and this genre became one of the successes of modern Irish language literature.'[14]

An tOileánach was one of a series of Irish language books that were written in the early twentieth century as part of the effort to preserve the Irish language. Tomás mentions his dedication to the advancement of Irish, and he may have had a broad educational purpose in mind. *An tOileánach* was published by an education-oriented government-affiliated publisher and was mandatory reading in selected schools in Ireland for a number of years.

At the end of June 1932, the winners of the literary prizes at the Aonach Tailteann, a national cultural competition, were announced. Tomás was awarded first prize for imaginative prose for *An tOileánach*. He received a statue of the mythical Queen Tailte and a gilded silver medal. The judges said:

> This autobiography is the only great work in Gaelic produced in this · generation. It is unique in Irish literature, and indeed it would be hard to find its like in the literature of the modern world.[15]

The quality and value of the results of Tomás' massive effort over the years had been recognised. Tomás himself said: 'I thought that my work was all useless until I'd see the Queen of Tailteann, and her gold, in front of me on the table here.'[16]

Tomás was initially paid the sum of £58 for the manuscript of *An tOileánach*, a paltry sum of money given the invaluable long-term contribution that this book made to Irish culture.

Reverse of the first prize medal presented to Tomás at the Aonach Tailteann competition in 1932.

After due consideration, he was paid an additional amount, bringing his compensation to £98 exclusive of the English translation rights.

Tomás was a no-nonsense businessman, demanding an accounting of sales and expenses in connection with *An tOileánach*. Similarly, with An Seabhac representing him, he drove a hard bargain for the royalties in connection with *The Islandman*. He once wrote to An Seabhac, 'I'd prefer a pound today while I'm alive instead of 20 and me dead.'[17]

Tomás' next book was *Dinnseanchas na mBlascaodaí*, published in 1935, the year after *The Islandman* was released. This book lists the names, with short descriptions, of almost 400 physical features. For example, Tomás lists over twenty springs and

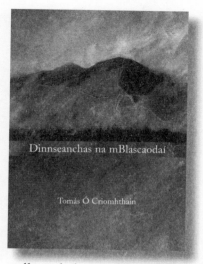

Dinnseanchas na mBlascaodaí, 1999 edition.

wells and the names of twenty cultivated fields in the pre-1907 layout. Essentially, the book comprises place-name lore. Tomás' descriptions reflect his depth of knowledge of the flora and fauna of the islands. In his introduction, Tomás wrote that the book includes the basis for every place that was ever named and its history. The content built on Tomás' research in developing lists of natural features about twenty-five years earlier for Carl Marstrander.

Dinnseanchas na mBlascaodaí has been published by Cois Life in two editions, both in Irish. The original 1935 edition was edited by An Seabhac. In the introduction, Tomás concluded: 'With that I hope the nobles of the Irish language will not be ungrateful to me, as long as I have done as much as I can for the language of my country and my ancestors.'[18] A second edition, published in 1999, was edited by Caoilfhionn Nic Pháidín, who wrote in her Editor's Notes, 'This work is of clear ethnographic origin. The Criomhthanach creates a universe through his accounts of the names of the Blaskets. He breathes life into the people and the animals through the natural features of the land and sea ... It is a spiritual geography.' As Tomás wrote himself: 'Every one of us [the islanders] thought this rock was Paradise, or close to it, and that they would be there as long as the sun shone.'[19]

Seanchas ón Oileán Tiar (*Lore of the Western Island*) is a selection of fifty-two traditional folklore stories and poems that Robin Flower collected from Tomás between 1912 and 1925. Some of these stories were appended to letters from Tomás to Flower over the years. Many were dictated by Tomás from memory while Flower transcribed them in Irish. Without this laborious process, these stories would have been lost.

Flower explained the background of the book in a 1925 letter to Irish scholar R.I Best:

> Tomás and I have been working on the book of stories and it is getting into reasonably good order. I hope to start printing soon after I get back. It is a fascinating collection with the whole life of the Island in the past generation in it, and talking over the tales again and again with Tomás. I have reached a fair understanding of that life which might too stand me in good stead in editing the collection.[20]

Flower published some of what he had transcribed in various periodicals at the time, but most were unpublished when he died in 1946. These stories, poems, prayers and proverbs were edited by Séamus Ó Duilearga and published in 1956, almost twenty years after Tomás' death, by the Education Company of Ireland with the Folklore of Ireland Society. Many of the stories were collected from Tomás as much as sixteen years before his first book was published in 1928.

After Flower's passing in January 1946, his family sent a vast collection of his papers to Ó Duilearga, among them the

Seanchas ón Oileán Tiar,
published in 1956.

SEANCHAS ÓN
OILEÁN TIAR

TOMÁS Ó CRÍOMHTHAIN
agus
ROBIN FLOWER
Séamus Ó Duilearga do chuir i n-eagar.

uncorrected proofs of this book. At their request, Ó Duilearga
edited the work for publication. He also added sixteen other
folktales that Flower had collected from Tomás.

Seanchas consists largely of traditional lore, accounts
of people and adventures on land and sea that Tomás had
learned from various sources. It includes a selection of poems
by Seán Ó Duinnshléibhe as well as verse by other local poets.
There are stories about boats, animals and various adventures;
legends about the local hero Piaras Feiritéar; a selection of
prayers; and a tale about St Gobnait of Dunquin.

In reviewing *Seanchas*, Máire MacNeill wrote: 'The para-
mount interest in the book ... is as a vital document of social
history.'[21] This book has not yet been translated into English.

Bloghanna ón mBlascaod,
published in 1997.

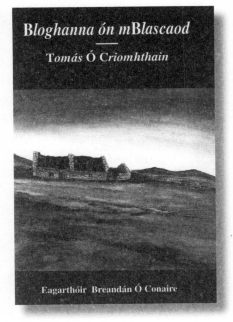

Tomás' first published writings were articles and poems that appeared in Irish-language periodicals and journals such as *Fáinne an Lae*, *An Lóchrann* and *An Claidheamh Soluis*. He published at least 132 such pieces in the eighteen years between December 1916 and December 1934. Tomás' pieces were primarily narrative descriptions of island life, with poetry comprising twenty-three of the total. They were typically short; only ten were over two pages in length.

Breandán Ó Conaire has compiled an anthology of these articles titled *Bloghanna ón mBlascaod*. It was published by Coiscéim in 1997. In his introduction to the book, Ó Conaire wrote:

> It is a diverse collection – essays, interviews, verse, proverbs, letters, diary accounts, folklore and stories

or events, reports and opinions – material that shows the personal traits as well as the literary talents and storytelling skills of the author from the western Island, 'the most western man of all'. We see his independent mind, his worldly religion, his confidence in the value of his own life, his close friendships with his co-islanders, his sharp understanding on the customs and the reactions of his mind, the joy he gets from humour and from the witty words of others even in sharp words, the worthwhile actions of a good person, male or female, his natural mastery of the words, the language and the rhythm of the Irish language.[22]

The periodicals in which they appeared, together with the number of Tomás' contributions to each, are as follows: *Fáinne an Lae* (46), *An Lóchrann* (38), *An Claidheamh Soluis* (22), *Misneach* (16), *An Phoblacht* (4), *Timthire an Chroidhe Naomhtha* (2), *Irish Independent* (2), *An Camán* (1) and *An Scuab* (1).

In 1999, Coiscéim published a collection of 168 diary entries written by Tomás that had not been incorporated in earlier versions of *Allagar na hInise*. This anthology was edited by Pádraig Ua Maoileoin, Tomás' grandson. The dates of the entries range from 11 February 1921 to 1 March 1923.

In his introduction, Ua Maoileoin wrote that he did not know why these particular entries were not previously published, and that they are consistent in subject matter and quality with the entries in the original book. Perhaps An Seabhac, operating under instructions from the original publisher, was simply trying to keep the work to a particular length.

Ua Maoileoin wrote that *Allagar II* finally brings to closure the publication of all the writings of Tomás 'nicely and respectfully'.[23] Actually, there were two more books to come.

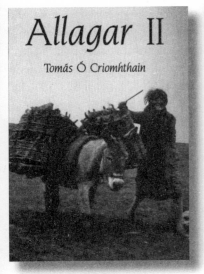

Allagar II, published in 1999.

Cleití Gé ón mBlascaod Mór, published in 1997.

Cleití Gé ón mBlascaod Mór (*Goose Quills from the Great Blasket*) is a collection of twelve stories, all written before 1936. One was written by Tomás and eleven by his son Seán. The book was published by An Sagart in 1997 and edited by Monsignor Pádraig Ó Fiannachta, who obtained the stories from Fr Parthalán Ó Troithe (Bartholomew Troy). Ó Troithe came into the possession of the collection from a friend of Fr Pádraig de Barra (Patrick Barry), a beloved visitor to the island and later to the former islanders living in the Dunquin area. De Barra intended to publish the stories, but he died in 1974 before the arrangements could be made. They were eventually published twenty-three years later.

The first story in the book, written by Tomás, was entitled 'Ón mBlascaod'. The editor renamed it '*An Mórdhach*', the name of the main character in the story, a man named Moore. It includes a reference to Tomás' father Domhnall marrying into the island. Seán's stories include a variety of folklore and contemporary stories. The book has a distinctive format in that the left-hand page carries a photocopy of the handwritten pages of the manuscript. The facing page is the typeset version.[24]

In 2004, Nollaig Mac Congáil assembled an anthology of Tomás' contributions to the *Irish Independent* between 1925 and 1932 entitled *Scéilíní ón mBlascaod [Anecdotes from the Blasket] augus Blúirín as 'Cín Lae Eibhlín Ní Shúilleabháin'*. It was published by Coiscéim. This collection includes twenty-three stories, two of which appear in *Bloghanna ón mBlascaod* and one in *Seanchas ón Oileán Tiar*. The book also includes twenty-one diary entries by Eibhlín Ní Shúilleabháin, the sister of island author Muiris Ó Súilleabháin. This diary was another product of Brian Ó Ceallaigh's encouragement.

Mac Congáil points out that the publication of Tomás' material in the *Irish Independent* during this period suggests that Tomás and other islanders were able to access this

newspaper, perhaps fairly regularly.[25] The *Independent* should be credited with providing a platform for publishing jewels of Irish writing during these years.

Scéilíní ón mBlascaod, published in 2004.

12. The Passing of the Islandman

About four years before Tomás' death, his son Seán, who was still living at home, married islander Eibhlís Ní Shúilleabháin (see Chapter 13). The new couple took up residence with Tomás in the house he had built with his own hands. Tomás was delighted to once again have a '*bean a' tí*', a woman of the house. The dedicated Eibhlís lovingly cared for her father-in-law until his final days. Tomás wrote that he relied a great deal on Seán too: 'he has to stay around the house, for there is little good in me except my tongue.'

Tomás was realistic about his advancing years:

> I am old now. Many a thing has happened to me in the running of my days until now. People have come into the world around me and have gone again. There are only five older than me alive in the Island. They have the pension [having reached the age of seventy]. I have only two months to go till that date – a date I have no fancy for. In my eyes it is a warning that death is coming.[1]

Interestingly, Tomás may have inadvertently forfeited about two years of pension income because of his incorrect understanding of his date of birth (see Chapter 3). He apparently qualified for a pension two years earlier than he began receiving this benefit. One can be sure that this mistake would have made him extremely unhappy.

Tomás in front of his house in about 1933, four years before his death.

As he aged, Tomás became reflective. George Thomson wrote that Tomás 'saw that the world was changing and not, in his opinion, for the better.'[2] Tomás also understood the downside of old age, quoting his friend, the by then long deceased island poet Seán Ó Duinnshléibhe:

> Of all miseries told 'tis the worst to grow old,
> With no man to heed or respect you.[3]

Tomás had learned the lesson that the wise poet Ó Duinnshléibhe had taught him during his salad days. He had, as no islander had before him, preserved his life story and that of the island community for all time.

Tomás maintained his sense of humour as he aged. His old friend the King apparently put on quite a bit of weight as he grew old, and writing to Robin Flower's wife, Ida, Tomás took the opportunity to chide his lifelong friend about his expanding waistline:

> This was a laugh for a lot of them, especially his old partner [Tomás], 'The canoe couldn't carry the King now he is so fat. I told him the other day as he had the name of a King, that he ought to be out helping King George, if he has the name it-self he is short in the drop I suppose he is slow for going out anyway.' But there was no danger that he would take the teasing too far, as the King was married to his own sister, and it was he who sent Flower in Tomás' direction, as he had done with Marstrander before him. He wished him life and health, 'The King, and his family is well. All the Blaskets.' That gave them all a laugh.[4]

Mike Carney remembered visiting Tomás' house in his youth on St Stephen's Day, known as 'Wren Boys' Day', looking for the traditional handout of a treat. Tomás gave him a pinch of sugar. In *An tOileán a Bhí*, islander Máire Ní Ghaoithín wrote: 'Tomás was always very nice to us [children], he was nice to everybody ... he was a kindly, quiet, deep, sensible man.'[5]

The King, who was about two years younger than Tomás, died on 11 June 1929 at the age of seventy-three. His passing must have been a stark reminder to Tomás of his own mortality. Tomás was to live on for another eight years without his dear friend.

George Chambers, the Englishman who visited the island in 1931, became a close friend of Eibhlís (see Chapters 9 and 13). They would later exchange letters for about thirty years. In these letters, Eibhlís provided an intimate picture of Tomás' last years.[6]

In November 1931, Tomás wrote to his son Thomas in America about a visit from An Seabhac. The man who had played such a pivotal role in publishing Tomás' classic works brought him great news. Tomás bragged: '*An tOileánach* is noted all over the world, it is a book that couldnent be found written in any language. 3,000 of them is sold now.' An Seabhac also brought him a supply of tobacco and a bottle of whiskey. Tomás was so excited that he repeated the news about *An tOileánach* in another letter to Thomas in January 1932.[7]

Seán Ó Criomhthain said that his father wasn't sick a day in his life until his last four years.[8] His illness began in the winter of 1933. Eibhlís wrote that his health was ruined by his incessant pipe-smoking. By January 1934, he was bedridden. About that time, Tomás sent a note to Chambers, making a special effort to communicate in English:

> George Chambers, London:
> I want to let you know that I Like you very much. I think it is the only way for doing so is to drop you a few lines But to tell the truth It comes very Difficult on me to write in English for to tell the truth as you know what I am writing I hardly understand it. But if you know Irish Language I tell you That you would get it.

I hope you are enjoying life the same as you want to do so that's what some people would say. But that is not the way may be But I hope not …

The young lads here have an English phrase since you left, you used to say 'Fine morning' and They have the same since.

Good Bye now and Happy Long Life.

T. Crohan[9]

On 5 March and 4 June 1934, Tomás was well enough to write letters to the Department of Education protesting at the elimination of one of the two teaching positions at the island's national school because of declining enrolment. He argued that the junior teacher, Cáit Ní Mhainnín, should be retained because of her twenty-six years of dedicated service, her fluency in Irish and the importance of nurturing the Irish language on the island. Unfortunately, his pleas fell on deaf ears.[10]

At the end of October 1934, six copies of *The Islandman*, the English translation of *An tOileánach*, arrived from the publishers, Chatto & Windus. Tomás was thrilled. In November 1934, he signed a copy of the book for his daughter-in-law Eibhlís.

It appears that Tomás suffered a stroke in mid-1935. Seán Ó Criomhthain said that his father 'got a kind of stroke – his right side failed him'.[11] Seán said Tomás continued writing until his right hand, his writing hand, became paralysed. At one point, he was forced to sign a document with his left hand. Eventually, he couldn't raise his hand over his head.

In a letter to An Seabhac on 4 July 1935, Tomás wrote:

It is to a relative [his son Seán] I am dictating this as I am not well at the moment. The hand which wrote The Islandman cannot put food in my mouth or even close my buttons. I am now a cripple and in all likelihood will be one for the rest of my life. I haven't been well for over a month now ... I feel I will never take the pen in hand again, but perhaps it is not right to complain after all that writing has done for me.[12]

At the end of 1935, Tomás was occasionally able to get up and about. In January 1936, however, he had a setback. Shortly thereafter, he had considerable pain in his legs, and he received the Last Rites of the Catholic Church. In the middle of 1936, he had less pain, but he was still crippled. Chambers sent a parcel the following Christmas. Tomás clung to the contents like a little child for fear of the items being taken away from him. By this time, his memory had nearly failed completely. Nora O'Shea wrote of Tomás' deteriorating condition:

> Until quite recently – it might have been a matter of two years – Tomás could be seen in and out of his little cabin – a solemn look on his face, a faraway lonely look, as though he was forever pondering on the troubles and cares of this harassed world, of his island home and the great world beyond the encircling seas.[13]

Reminiscing about Tomás' last years, O'Shea wrote: 'the first question that a stranger always asked was "Where is the house of the Criomhthain?"' He had become a tourist attraction; everybody wanted a photo of him. 'Even when his health began to fail him, he would often be led like a child to his seat in the yard, just to please the visitor who was anxiously waiting to secure a photo of "the islandman".'

One day Nora herself asked Tomás for a photo. He was reluctant. She said to him 'But, Tomás, you must remember that men like you will not inhabit the island anymore.' Tomás immediately recognised her reference to the famous words

Inside cover of a copy of *The Islandman* inscribed by Tomás for his daughter-in-law Eibhlís in November 1934.

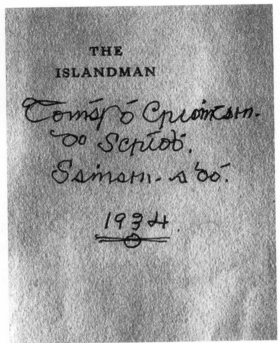

from *An tOileánach* and 'His countenance changed, his face brightened, a smile came on his lips, and he said you may have me.' And thus Nora got her photo of the great man.[14]

Tomás wrote his last letter to An Seabhac on New Year's Day 1937. He must have known that the end was near and he was profuse in his thanks. He wrote 'I wish you every success in your life and everyone belonging to you and God's guidance upon you during your life.'[15]

In early 1937, Eibhlís was well into her first pregnancy. She temporarily relocated to the mainland so as to be close to the doctor, as a precaution. She deeply regretted leaving Tomás, as she had been caring for him throughout his illness. But she felt that she had no choice because of her overriding responsibility to her unborn child.

After his long decline, Tomás died peacefully in his home at seven o'clock on Sunday morning, 7 March 1937. He was eighty-two. It snowed heavily on the day he died, a rarity on the Great Blasket. It was as if God himself was signalling the significance of his passing. Seán Ó Criomhthain said, 'When you would look onto Dunquin, I couldn't see anything but white alps';[16] there was snow on the mountains at the western end of the Dingle Peninsula.

Tomás' official death certificate was registered on 30 May 1997, some sixty years after his passing. It was based on information provided by his granddaughter Niamh. His cause of death is indicated as 'stroke, apparently'.[17]

Seán and Eibhlís' brother Peaidí Mhicil Ó Súilleabháin visited Eibhlís in Dingle and gave her the news that Tomás was dead. She was heartbroken, later writing that Tomás was so helpless at the end that she and Seán were glad that God had taken him.

Seán travelled to the mainland to buy a coffin. He tied it securely on the roof of a friend's car for the trip from Dingle to Dunquin. Back on the island, they laid Tomás' body in the coffin, 'the narrow little bed'. Seán said he was only skin and bones.[18]

A traditional wake was held all day Sunday and all that night in his own house, complete with the traditional keening of women, the drinking of porter and the smoking of clay pipes. Mike Carney attended Tomás' wake before he relocated to the mainland later that year. He recalled that it was a sombre affair, befitting the passing of an island giant.

Tomás departed the Great Blasket for the last time on Monday 8 March at 10 a.m. His coffin travelled to the island slipway along *Bóithrín na Marbh*, the Road of the Dead. It was placed in the stern of a *naomhóg* rowed by three oarsman. His remains were escorted across Blasket Sound by a fleet of *naomhóga*. Prayers were said along the way. Tomás was then laid to rest in the old cemetery adjacent to St Gobnet's church at Baile an Teampaill. Nora O'Shea wrote that 'When the last shovelful of clay had been laid upon the grave the men (among them his son Seán) knelt to say the last prayer over the body of their dead hero.'[19]

Tomás' grave is located in a plot that was generously provided by his former son-in-law, Tomás Ó Maoileoin, his deceased daughter Cáit's husband, who had remarried by this time. Also buried here are Cáit, who died in 1922, and her two young children who died shortly thereafter (see Chapter 13). Tomás' old friend, the last Blasket King, lies nearby. Directly to the west, there is a magnificent view across Blasket Sound to the Great Blasket.

With the Great Blasket nearing the apex of its fame throughout Ireland, Tomás, the person responsible for generating much of that fame, had gone to his heavenly reward.

On 10 March, the *Irish Times* reported on Tomás' passing:

> The death has taken place at his home on the Blasket islands of Mr. Thomas Crogan at an advanced age ... He was extremely popular not only on the islands, but among a very large number of people on the mainland, who had known and appreciated his kindly Gaelic character.[20]

On 11 March, the *Irish Press* reported on Tomás' funeral:

> Tomás Ó Criomhthain, of Blasket Mór, off the Kerry Coast, was borne in a 'naomhóg' across the Blasket Sound to Dunquin, the family burial-ground.
>
> The island fleet of canoes followed in procession.
>
> On the mainland were drawn up a great line of horse-cars, but as he says of his mother's burying, 'it was on the shoulders of men' he was brought to the grave.[21]

A painting of Tomás' grave at Baile an Teampaill with the Great Blasket in the background (Hugh Collins Walsh).

An Seabhac was quoted in the same article as saying that *An tOileánach* was 'the finest book that has ever come out of the Gaeltacht.'

On 12 March, the *Irish Independent* reported on Tomás' death. The story credited three men, Brian Ó Ceallaigh, An Seabhac and Robin Flower, for their respective roles in bringing Tomás' writing to publication.[22]

Shortly after his father's death, Seán Ó Criomhthain, probably still in a state of mourning, gave a decidedly negative interview to *The Kerryman*. In a front page article in its 20 March 1937 edition, Seán's sentiments about the island were summarised as follows:

> [T]he present-day islanders cannot endure the hardship of their predecessors ... The fishing industry, their only means of livelihood, has been a rank failure. In his [Seán's] opinion, from five to seven houses in the Great

In front of Tomás' house shortly after his death in 1937: (l–r) Sheáisí and Seán Ó Ceárna, Eibhlís (Ní Shúilleabháin) Uí Chriomhthain and Tomás' son Seán Ó Criomhthain.

Blasket will be deserted before next Winter. He would leave the island in the morning if he got something to do. Only for the dole, there would be starvation in the island last Winter. The school is being closed owing to a fall in the attendance. There were no marriages for the last four years.

The tourist industry is of no great value. Tourists came to the island for a month or two in the Summer, if weather conditions were favourable. The Blasket Islanders want more than sympathy, or telling them that they are a fine stock and used to hardship.[23]

Looking back on the long span of his experiences on the Great Blasket, Robin Flower was wistful as he penned the Preface to his book *The Western Island* on 15 October 1944:

Excerpt of Tomás' last will and testament bequeathing his worldly assets to his son Seán. The document is signed by Tomás and witnessed by Seán Ó Ceárna and Mícheál Ó Guithín.

The King is dead and Tomás and the greater part of that lamenting company, and all this that follows is the song we made together of the vanished snows of yesteryear.[24]

Flower was again borrowing from the old French proverb that he remembered from an island conversation with the King, Tomás and the island elders that had taken place many years earlier.

Speaking in 1997 at the Blasket Centre (see Chapter 15), Tomás' granddaughter, Niamh (Ní Chriomhthain) Uí Laoithe, recalled the words of her father, Seán Ó Criomhthain:

> Yes I was with Tomás in his good times and bad times. We both saw bad days, as well as a fine day and we shared them both. When worry came to us, then his strengths could be seen – a strength that couldn't be described – but he put his will with the will of God, a strength that grows from spirituality.[25]

Niamh concluded her remarks by reciting a poem composed by islander Mícheál Ó Guithín:

M'Anam Beidh I Leabhar	*My Spirit Shall Live On In a Book*
Labharfad le cách is mé fé cheilt,	I will speak to all while I am unseen
Mar bheadh duine don dtreibh shíoraí	As one from the eternal tribe
Cloisfear mo ghlór ar bheol chách,	My voice will be heard on everyone's lips
Is trí bheol chách a bhead ag tíocht,	And through everyone's lips I will come
Ní bhfaighidh mé choíche bás,	I will never die
Cé go gcuirfear mé fé bhrat sa chill,	Even though I will be buried under a blanket in the graveyard
Ní cuirfear ann ach mo chorpán,	Only my body will be there
Beidh mo ghuth fé bhláth ó aois go haois.	My voice will flourish from age to age.[26]

Tim Enright wrote in his Introduction to the English translation of *Island Cross-Talk*:

> He was aware by then [the time of his death] of his stature as a Gaelic writer, and one of his books has been

translated [*An tOileánach*] ... he had placed his small island, three miles by one, on the literary map of the world ...

Tomás O'Crohan composed his own epitaph, and that of his community, when in *The Islandman* he wrote: 'the like of us will never be again.'[27]

The Great Blasket was evacuated by the Irish government in November 1953. And thus, Tomás' prophetic words of a quarter of a century earlier were duly fulfilled.

13. The Islandman's Descendants

The deaths of so many of Tomás' children at an early age effectively limited the number of his descendants (see Chapter 6). Of his twelve children, only three lived to age thirty-four, and only two lived relatively full lives. He had thirteen grandchildren, two by his son Tomás, eight by his daughter Cáit and three by his son Seán. Six of his grandchildren had no children themselves. His two adult children who lived in West Kerry, Cáit and Seán, both died tragic deaths, from tuberculosis and a car accident respectively. Only one child, Tomás (Thomas), passed away 'normally', at the age of sixty-nine in America. The life stories of these three of Tomás' children help to illustrate the broader story of the Blasket diaspora to the Irish mainland and to America.

Tomás Ó Criomhthain (Thomas T. Crohan)

Tomás' namesake son, Tomás Thomáis Ó Criomhthain, was born on 6 December 1885, the fourth of his twelve children. He was baptised on 20 December 1885. Tomás was enrolled in the National School on 2 February 1895 and completed his studies on 31 July 1900. His attendance at school dropped off considerably in 1898, about the same time that his siblings Máire I and Micheál I came down with measles and ultimately died.

Tomás emigrated to America at the age of twenty-three, sailing from Queenstown to Boston on the SS *Cymric* on 18 April 1909. He was accompanied by two other islanders, Mícheál Ó Conchubhair (Michael Connor) and Mícheál Ó Guithín (Michael Guiheen), his first cousin. All were about the same age and registered on the ship using their anglicised names, Tomás as Thomas Crohan.

Their destination was no surprise: Springfield, Massachusetts. On their arrival, Thomas lived temporarily with his cousin Patrick O'Crohan, his Uncle Pádraig's son, and his family at 37 Essex Street.

Eight years later, Thomas married Cáit Ní Mhainnín, who was born in Cill Úra, Ventry. She had also emigrated to Boston on the SS *Cymric*, arriving on 5 May 1911 and registered under the name of Catherine Manning. They were probably at least acquainted before emigrating. Their wedding was held at Sacred Heart Church on 23 May 1917 and they soon took up residence at 167 Cass Street.

The couple had two children: a son, Thomas J. Crohan, born on 17 March 1918; and a daughter, Catherine, born on 25 April 1920. Thomas became an American citizen on 18 February 1918, and he held a United States passport. Catherine became an American citizen in 1915.

Thomas worked at the Springfield Armory during the First World War as a 'polisher', probably finishing the metal components of various firearms. This government-owned factory was established in 1777 by General George Washington during the American Revolution. Thomas later worked in a similar job at Moore Drop Forging Company. He apparently returned to work at the Armory during the Second World War when his skills would have again been in demand. Catherine worked as a cook for Springfield Public Schools when her child-rearing days were behind her.

Cousins and Blasket islanders Michael Guiheen (left) and
Thomas T. Crohan in Springfield in the 1930s.

After the First World War, the entire family visited the Great
Blasket, staying for eight and a half months. They sailed from
New York to Queenstown on 31 July 1920 aboard the RMS
Baltic. The children were just two years old and three months
old. Tomás wrote: 'One of my sons had been in America for
twelve years. He came home about this time, himself and his
wife and two children.'[1]

In an interesting intersection with Irish history, one of their fellow passengers on the *Baltic* was Archbishop David Mannix of Melbourne, Australia, who was on a trip to Rome via the United States and Ireland. On the night before their departure from New York, Mannix had shared the stage at New York's Madison Square Garden, a huge indoor arena, with Irish President Éamon de Valera rallying support for Ireland's independence. Subsequently, British Prime Minister Lloyd George became concerned that Mannix might stir up trouble in Ireland. Agents of Scotland Yard boarded the *Baltic* and arrested Mannix in Cork harbour before he could disembark. He was transferred to a British destroyer and put ashore on the Cornish coast. He then travelled to London, where he was under virtual house arrest for more than a year.[2]

Tomás wrote of his son's visit to the Great Blasket:

> He only stayed with me half a year when he started across the water again and left me. There was no fishing or anything when they came, but they spent the pound or two that they had brought with them, and what he said was that, if things went on as they were going much longer, he'd have spent every penny he brought with him, or that might be coming to him, and that he'd have nothing left at home or abroad. And I think he was right![3]

The Crohan family returned to Springfield on the SS *Celtic*, sailing from Queenstown to New York on 17 April 1921. There has been some speculation that Thomas may have originally planned a permanent move back to the island with his family. But there is no documentation that the trip was anything more than an extended visit. Tomás does not indicate that he had any expectation that his son was relocating back to the island. Thomas wrote on his US passport application that the purpose of his trip was 'to visit my father'.[4]

Thomas T. Crohan's wife, Catherine Manning (left) with her friend
Máire de Mórdha in Springfield.

When the Crohan family returned to Springfield, they still lived on Cass Street. By 1925, they had moved to 24 Mystic Street near Our Lady of Hope church in the Hungry Hill neighbourhood, a magnet for emigrating Blasket islanders. Their next-door neighbour was Thomas' cousin Michael Guiheen, his travelling companion on his emigration voyage in 1909, and his wife, Mary. Their wives, Catherine and Mary, were sisters.

On miblsscsoo

November. 15.

My Dear Thomas,

I guess it is ti
for me to answer your letter an
heare from ye what way the State
are getting on, or is it improoving su
way better, sre you getting half
time yet or any day more?

Now how is Katherine getting
on, snyway better, or worse, The
youngsters I litte the picliurs ver
much, They are vary nice God
bless them,

Msnny the strangers that cam
heare this Sammer Visiting the Isla
All of them took my picture, I hea
to write my name on the book fo
the whole of them, Professors,
priests, Monks, Brothers, Sisters,
every sort off people,

The "Seabiac" Came in at
last to meet me, and two of his
Brother's the Man at home, an
the other a Professor. The
brought me a bottle of Whiskey
and half a pound of Tobbaco,

The is a fine large Tall man
An "Toilessac" is noted all over the
World, it is a book that couldent
be found Written in any leanguig

Excerpt of a letter in English from Tomás to his son in Springfield dated
15 November 1931.

Tomás and his son maintained a quite frequent correspondence over the years. On 15 November 1931, Tomás wrote to Thomas in Springfield in his halting English:

> Manny the strangers that came heare this summer visiting the Island. All of them took my picture, I had to write my name on the book for the whole of them, professor's, priests, Monks, Brothers, Sisters, every sort of people.[5]

In a letter dated 3 January 1932, after Tomás had achieved a degree of fame as an author, he mentioned to his son the appetite in Ireland for money sent back home from America:

> [B]ut people in this country want's all the dollars in the State's themselves whatever way ye are getting on there. If you would see all the green ribbons that left the post bag lately, you couldent say there is a famine in Springfield or in Hardford [Hartford] either.[6]

After completing his education, Thomas' son, Thomas J., worked at the *Springfield Daily News* as a linotype operator and later served in the United States Army during the Second World War. He met a girl named Mary MacGlasson one night at a dance hall in a suburb of Springfield and inadvertently wound up with her apron in his coat pocket at the end of the event. Mary came to retrieve it the next day, and a romance was on. After the Second World War, the two married and lived in Levittown, a popular post-war master-planned community on Long Island, just outside New York City. Thomas J. worked as a linotype operator for the *Garden City Newsday*. They had no children.

Thomas' daughter, Catherine M., never married and continued to live at the family home on Mystic Street. She worked

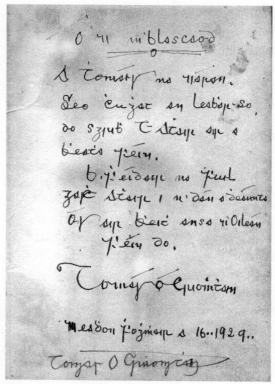

An inscription by Tomás in a copy of *An tOileánach* to his son Thomas T. in Springfield on 16 September 1929. The book is signed by both; Thomas signed in Irish at the bottom.[7]

for forty-one years as a telephone operator at the New England Telephone Company, retiring in 1983. She was a member of the John Boyle O'Reilly Club Ladies' Auxiliary.

During his retirement years in Springfield, Thomas T. sold tickets at the Liberty Theater, a movie house in Hungry Hill. According to Blasket descendant Barbara Carney Ashe, he made a big impression on the next generation of Irish children from the neighbourhood by letting them into the movies for free.

Thomas T. died on 4 July 1954 at the age of sixty-nine. His wife died a year and a half later on 8 January 1956 at the age of sixty-one. Thomas' son Thomas J. died suddenly in 1966 at the relatively young age of forty-eight. His daughter Catherine passed away on 2 September 1999 at the age of eighty.

Cáit (Ní Chríomhthain) Uí Mhaoileoin

Tomás' daughter Cáit Ní Chríomhthain was the fifth of his twelve children, born on 2 November 1887. Cáit enrolled in the national school on 5 June 1893 and completed her schooling on 31 July 1900, although her attendance in her last two years was intermittent.

In 1904, when Cáit was about seventeen, her mother passed away. Thereafter, Cáit played a major role in caring for the family's four younger children. Cáit was the only female in a household comprising five males who ranged in age from eleven to about sixty-five. At first, Tomás was sceptical about Cáit's capability to help out around the house, probably due to her age. Tomás wrote: 'she left two little girls to help me, but there is no great use in the like of them.'[8] Cáit was severely challenged right at the outset. Her sister Máire was sick and died about a year after her mother, on 13 April 1905. The dedicated Cáit continued to play the role of surrogate mother for the next five years, clearly exceeding her father's expectations.

In 1909, Cáit very nearly lost her life in the infamous double drowning of her older brother Domhnall and Eibhlín Nic Niocaill. Cáit's grandson, Pádraig Breathnach, aptly referred to Cáit as 'the girl who *didn't* drown'. It was some consolation to Tomás that Cáit was miraculously resuscitated.

Two years after her near-drowning, Cáit 'married out' of the island. Tomás wrote that a match was made for her by a relative living in Dún Mór, near Dunquin. Her husband was Tomás Ó Maoileoin, her second cousin, who worked on a farm

Cáit (Ní Criomhthain) Uí Mhaoileoin and her family in about 1915. (L–r): Cáit's son Pádraig, her husband Tomás, her daughter Máire and Cáit herself.

in Dún Mór, near Coumeenole. The couple were married on 18 February 1911. Cáit's new home was one of the nearest on the mainland to the Great Blasket. She reputedly enjoyed walking up to the top of the Dún to gaze across Blasket Sound and wave to her family on the island.

Cáit's household included her husband's widowed father, Seán, and his sister Eibhlín. Her family grew rapidly, with the couple having eight children over eleven years. The firstborn, Eibhlín (1912), was moderately mentally impaired. She was followed by Pádraig (1913), Máire (1914), Cáit (1915), Seán (1917), Bríd (1919) Mícheál (1920) and Tomás (1921). When

Cáit (Ní Chriomhthain) Uí Mhaoileoin's eldest son, Pádraig Ua Maoileoin.

Cáit became pregnant for the eighth time, she was already in poor health, suffering from tuberculosis.

On 22 January 1922, at the age of thirty-four and less than two months after the birth of her youngest child, Cáit died from tuberculosis. She left behind her husband, eight children under ten years of age and her father-in-law, Seán. She was buried at Baile an Teampaill in Dunquin. But the family's agony was just beginning. On 28 May her infant son Tomás died, followed by her father-in-law on 1 June. The youngest and oldest of the household were buried in the same week. Three weeks later, on 20 June, her son Mícheál, not yet two years old, died. Within a span of six months, four members of the household had been laid to rest. Tomás and Mícheál were buried with their mother.

When Cáit died, her father Tomás still had fifteen years to live. He described his feelings on Cáit's death in *An tOileánach*:

'Whatever sorrow else befell me, that sorrow of the grave was the crown of them all.'[9] On 8 May 1922, Tomás wrote to his mentor Brian Ó Ceallaigh to sympathise with him on the death of his mother. He told Ó Ceallaigh of Cáit's death, about the four boys and two girls she left behind, and mentioned the nice home she had in Dún Mór.

Cáit passed on her father Tomás' literary talent to her eldest son Pádraig Ua Maoileoin, born on 28 January 1913. Pádraig was educated at the national school in Dunquin, the Christian Brothers School in Dingle, St Brendan's College in Killarney and University College Cork. He joined the Garda Síochána in 1935, working primarily as a translator for thirty years. He later became a very successful broadcaster, author and lexicographer, with five novels, a memoir and many essays to his credit. He won the Oireachtas prize in 1982 for his satirical novel about the exploitation of Blasket culture entitled *Ó Thuaidh!* He also edited and published versions of his grandfather's *Allagar na hInise* and *An tOileánach*.

Cáit (Ní Chriomhthain) Uí Mhaoileoin endured far more than her share of misfortune in her thirty-four years of life. Yet she left an impressive legacy in her children and their many accomplishments.

Seán Ó Criomhthain (Sean O'Crohan)

Tomás' son Seán Ó Criomhthain was the tenth of his twelve children, born on 10 June, 1898. Oddly, Seán once said that he never saw his mother.[10] Since she didn't pass away until he was about six, he probably meant that he did not remember her well. Seán and his father Tomás were extremely close, presumably because of his mother's passing. He was Tomás' second son named Seán, the first having died in a fall off a cliff.

At the time of the 1901 Census of Ireland, the new Ó Criomhthain house was occupied by nine family members. In addition to Tomás, Máire and Seán there were six other siblings living at home. Another daughter was born soon thereafter. By the time of the 1911 Census, their home was a very different place, with only five people occupying the house: Tomás, his brother Pádraig, who had returned from America, and his three sons, Pádraig, Muiris and Seán. Tomás' son Tomás (Thomas) had emigrated to America in 1909 and his daughter Cáit was living on the mainland.

Seán attended the national school on the island between 1902 and 1912. He reported that his first teacher, William Prenderville, was interested in two things: English and drink. Seán developed a great love of reading, a passion that would continue throughout his life. He had access to a wide selection of books in his father's home library. In spite of his great love of the Irish language, Tomás wanted his son to have English as well. Seán said that Tomás considered the ability to speak and write in English 'a valuable jewel'.[11]

Seán had a typical island childhood. He loved to play with his toy *naomhóg*; and after school, he and his friends would play football on the White Strand using a ball made out of a stuffed stocking. During the summer, Seán enjoyed an occasional frolic on the White Strand where he and his friends would take a dip, 'naked as streakers', as he later admitted.[12]

Seán received the sacrament of Confirmation in Ballyferriter when he was a few years older than the normal age. While most of the newly confirmed enjoyed a celebration with bread and tea at Willie Long's shop, Seán and his friends slipped off to Dónal Kane's pub for a sip of something stronger.

Seán appreciated the power and beauty of nature. His extensive knowledge of native fish and birds is evident in his writing. Like many Blasket people, he maintained a sceptical

Seán Ó Criomhthain as a young man in 1924.

attitude about life, and he was very superstitious. He had considerable musical talents; he was a singer with a large repertoire of songs, and he played the fiddle and the melodeon. He was also a talented stepdancer, a skill he learned from his father.

Over the years, Tomás taught Seán the skills of the fisherman and soon after he completed his schooling, he began fishing with his father. This partnership continued for many years, reflecting their close relationship.

In the summer of 1931, a 58-year-old married London businessman, George Chambers, visited the Great Blasket. While touring around the island, he met twenty-year-old Eibhlís' 'Lis' Ní Shúilleabháin and her sister Máire. Eibhlís (born 6 May 1911) was a second cousin of island author Muiris Ó Súilleabháin. For a time, she worked as a domestic at Coláiste Íde, near Dingle, then a teachers' preparatory college. Eibhlís was bright and curious and occasionally read the *Irish Press* and *The Kerryman*. For years, encouraged by Brian Ó Ceallaigh, she kept a still-unpublished diary.

Chambers was deeply affected by Eibhlís, and the two developed a great affection for each other. It is not clear, however, that their relationship ever blossomed into romance. Eibhlís and Chambers maintained an extensive correspondence which continued for about thirty years from 1931 to 1960. Her letters were dated, providing dates for key island events as well as invaluable insights into island life during this period.

In late 1931, Eibhlís wrote to Chambers that she was friendly with a boy on the island. This is her first reference to her developing relationship with Seán. Chambers later asked Eibhlís if she was getting engaged. She explained that on the island, a sweetheart is different from a friend and that engagements were unknown. But she hated the idea of emigrating to America, and she saw marriage to an islander as a way of avoiding it. Chambers was worried that, if Eibhlís

Seán Ó Criomhthain and his wife Eibhlís (Ní Shúilleabháin) Uí Chriomhthain in 1938.

married, her husband would not let her continue writing to him.

On 6 May 1933, aged nearly thirty-five, Seán married Eibhlís in Ballyferriter. It was the day after her twenty-second birthday. The wedding was a major event since no island couple had been married in the previous twelve years. Eibhlís' new father-in-law, Tomás, was also her grand-uncle.

Eibhlís wrote to Chambers of her new life: 'I love my husband and my home, all the world has changed to me, everything for the better.'[13] She wrote that some islanders thought she was foolish to settle down on the island. She also wrote that her new husband appreciated that she was facing much hardship for his sake. After the wedding, Eibhlís moved into the house that Tomás had built for his long-deceased wife, Máire.

The new couple had considerable financial difficulty. The days when one could make a decent living from fishing were over. It was becoming harder to find able-bodied islanders to make up a crew for a *naomhóg*. In this respect the family was fortunate; Eibhlís' three brothers were still living on the island and Seán could collaborate with them in fishing.

Eibhlís soon assumed the role of Tomás' primary caregiver. He was bedridden for several years and very much dependent on her. In early February 1937, the pregnant Eibhlís moved temporarily to Dingle to prepare for the birth of their first child. She stayed with Tomás and Bríd Malone in Burnham on the outskirts of Dingle for five weeks. It was here that Seán brought her the news that Tomás had died. Eibhlís was distraught.

Just about a month later, on 4 April 1937, Eibhlís gave birth to their daughter Niamh. At the beginning of May, Seán brought his family home to the Great Blasket. Eibhlís said of her husband: 'He is a very proud Daddy mind you.'[14] A baby in a cradle was now a rare sight on the island.

Chambers was very generous to the family, frequently sending gifts. There may have been some small improvement in the family's financial position after Tomás' death since Seán became the beneficiary of whatever modest royalties may have been accruing from his father's books. In addition, the Second World War soon caused a rise in the price of fish with a corresponding improvement in their income.

Chambers visited the Great Blasket again in 1938 after Seán and Eibhlís had been married for about five years. It was a happy reunion. Although their correspondence and the flow of Chambers' presents continued for many years, they would never see each other again.

In late 1938, Seán addressed the old controversy involving John Millington Synge's characterisation of the Great Blasket.

Eibhlís (Ní Shúilleabháin) Uí Chriomhthain with her daughter Niamh in the late 1930s.

Seán was only a child when Synge visited in 1905. Seán wrote to Chambers that Synge spoke only the truth. 'All the Blasket people anyhow thought Synge wrote awkwardly about this place and now they do not think so ... I should say ... that he was a clean and decent writer.'[15]

In late 1940, it was decided to open a post office on the Great Blasket. Seán applied for the job of postman, but another islander, Seán Ó Ceárna, was selected. Eibhlís was incensed because her husband was the only married islander who had applied for the job. The new post office and wireless telegraph commenced operation by May 1941.

In January 1941, the national school closed because of declining enrolment. Only five children were attending the school at the time. Since Niamh was nearing school age, this created a major issue for the family. In addition, the family had a scare when Niamh fell ill and medical help could not be brought to the island because of bad weather. And there was another medical scare involving Eibhlís. Yet Seán was procrastinating about moving to the mainland.

Life on the island was not immediately affected by the outbreak of the Second World War, but by Christmas 1941 wartime shortages of basic commodities became an issue. Eibhlís then presented Seán with an ultimatum. Despite Seán's reluctance, Eibhlís was insistent, and Seán had no choice but to give in. He affectionately referred to his bride as the 'Queen'. He said that when your wife is Elizabeth, a 'queen', you have to do what you're told. Accordingly, he began to make preparations to move his family off the island.

One Sunday in the spring of 1942, Seán set off for the mainland to find a new place for his family to live. He wrote: 'Eibhlís warned me not to come back home without finding some site for a house up there, or it would be the worse for me.'[16] Seán visited his aunt and uncle in Muiríoch, near Smerwick Harbour. He soon decided to buy a nearby plot of land that was close to the beach and next door to the family of Muiris Ó Catháin, who had also relocated from the Great Blasket. A man named Jamesy Fitzgerald built the walls of their new house. Seán and a couple of friends then dismantled a house he had purchased on the island and brought its roof across Blasket Sound balanced on two *naomhóga* packed to the gunwale. They transported the load from Dunquin to Muiríoch by lorry and installed the island roof on his new mainland house.

The family finally relocated from the Great Blasket on 14 July 1942. They were the last of the Ó Criomhthains to live on the island. Their move to Muiríoch involved a distance of only about ten miles, but the two places were worlds apart.

Seán and Eibhlís' affection for the island still burned bright, and they experienced some homesickness. They visited the

An older Seán Ó Criomhthain at his mainland home in Muiríoch.

island regularly, staying two or three nights at a time. These visits ended when Eibhlís' parents and brothers moved off the island in 1954, the year after the evacuation. In a letter to Chambers, Eibhlís described their last visit to her family on the island. They could only stay an hour. They laughed and they cried before bidding her family goodbye.

Seán wrote a lament that revealed his deep feelings about the island: 'I saw with my own eyes on the Western Island [the Great Blasket] the finest life I would ever see.'[17] Seán and Eibhlís frequently told their children stories of island life.

Although Seán had long been reluctant to leave his beloved island, he quickly adapted to his new life in Muiríoch. He continued to earn his living primarily by fishing, and later took on physically demanding road repair jobs as well.

When the day's work was done, there were a number of local pubs where Seán could relax over a few pints. Seán wrote that Eibhlís complained that the people he associated with were a bit too rowdy for her taste. There were also several other former Blasket people in Muiríoch to keep him company. He maintained that the islanders sought out their own because they were as different from a mainlander as a lobster from a crab.

Seán was widely recognised as an important source of information on the Great Blasket. Because of his father's renown, many later cultural visitors, looking to connect with a genuine Ó Criomhthain, approached Seán at home or in a pub. This included groups of nuns, brothers and priests. As time wore on, he tired of these demands on his time, writing that he found them irritating. He was sometimes intentionally rude to them to discourage their advances.

In the autumn of 1945, a second daughter named Cáit was born. She was named after Seán's sister, the double drowning survivor, who had died in 1922. Eibhlís reported to George Chambers that she had medical problems after the birth. In early 1948, she delivered a third daughter, named Máire Bríd, but the baby lived just three days. Eibhlís' child-bearing days were over.

In 1952, in an effort to increase the family's income, Seán ventured to Birmingham, England, where he worked as a porter at New Street Station, a railroad hub. Island visitor

George Thomson was then Professor of Greek at the University of Birmingham, and he welcomed his old friend Seán into his home. Thomson's wife recalled Seán expressing amazement at the crowds pouring into the station, reminding him of the seagulls flocking to the island. Seán was uncomfortable in his new environment, however, and he returned home to Muiríoch after a seven-week stint.

Seán had a great penchant for adventure. In 1959, at the age of sixty, he and other West Kerry fishermen attempted to cross the Irish Sea from Rosslare to Wales in a specially built *naomhóg*. This experiment, sponsored by the BBC, was an attempt to determine how Ireland was first populated and how communications were maintained in days of yore. The men wore clothing made of animal skins and ate food thought to be typical of the times. After rowing non-stop for over thirty hours, they were within sight of the Welsh coast when contrary winds and currents forced them to give up.[18] Nevertheless, they had proved a point.

When Niamh reached adulthood, she lived in London for a time, working at St Ann's Hospital, and later emigrated to Hartford, Connecticut, where she worked at Travelers Insurance Company. She returned to West Kerry six years later and became engaged to Tomás Ó Laoithe from Baile an Lochaig, just a few miles from Muiríoch. She returned to Hartford for two more years and then relocated to West Kerry, marrying Tomás on 24 October 1964. The couple raised five children.

Over the years, Niamh remained committed to the preservation of the Great Blasket and was involved with *Fundúireacht an Bhlascaoid* from its formation in 1985. She often voiced her concern about deteriorating conditions on the abandoned island. She was quoted several times in *The Kerryman*, urging the Irish government to conclude negotiations for the acquisition of the island properties. At one point, when the sensitive talks were near collapse, Niamh attended a meeting with government officials to personally express the views of former islanders. She was delighted when the purchase was finalised in 2005.

Seán's younger daughter, Cáit, spent seven years in Dublin, where she was educated at Scoil Chaitriona and St Catherine's College. She then returned to Dingle, where she taught in the local technical school. She married Micheál Ó Conaill from Portmagee on 7 April 1969 and thereafter lived in Killorglin. They have three children.

Seán and Eibhlís were both published writers. Surprisingly, Seán achieved publication before his father. *An Lóchrann*, the monthly Irish-language periodical of the Tralee branch of the Gaelic League, awarded prizes for the best stories submitted by schoolchildren. Stories from five Blasket students were published, including one written by Seán, who won several prizes. It was not until February 1916 that Tomás' first published writing appeared in this same publication. Eibhlís also had an article published in *An Lóchrann* in 1931.

After contributing to various periodicals over the next twenty-five years, Seán wrote a best-selling memoir entitled *Lá Dár Saol,* published in 1969. The book won a prize at the Oireachtas festival. This was forty years after *An tOileánach* was first published. Seán's memoir was later translated by Tim Enright and published in 1992 as *A Day in Our Life*. The book chronicles Seán's early life on the island as it was sliding into decline, the relocation of his family to the mainland and his adventures with his colourful fishermen friends in and around Muiríoch. Its great importance is in documenting the transition of a native island family from the Great Blasket to the mainland.

Niamh (Ní Chriomhthain) Uí Laoithe, Tomás' granddaughter, on her
eightieth birthday, 4 April 2017.

Seán was recognised as a valuable resource on the West Kerry
dialect of the Irish language. He was also a knowledgeable
resource on Blasket life for RTÉ and Raidió na Gaeltachta
(RNG), the Irish-language radio station of which he was an
avid listener. He assisted Muiris Mac Conghail when he was
researching his book *The Blaskets – People and Literature*.

Seán was active in local politics and was a supporter of Fianna Fáil. He hosted a live variety show, *Oíche Sheanchais*, which ran for a week in 1957 at Damer Hall in Dublin and which was a typical evening of island entertainment with song, dance and storytelling. In the early 1970s, he was the captain of a West Kerry team that competed against other fishing communities on a quiz show broadcast on RNG called *Fios Farraige* (*Seafaring Knowledge*).

In September 1971, at the age of sixty, Seán's beloved 'Queen' passed away after battling cancer. He was lost without her. Four years later, he was knocked to the ground by a truck in a hit-and-run accident. He had just begun a walk from his house in Muiríoch to nearby Ballydavid in the early evening of 8 December 1975, the feast of the Immaculate Conception. He was seventy-seven years old. He had survived over sixty years fishing on treacherous seas only to be killed in a random traffic accident on a country road. Seán and his Queen are both buried in the cemetery at Kilmalkedar. Tomás' beloved son and his later-life caregiver were gone.

Many tributes were paid to Seán upon his passing. The poet Seán Ó Ríordáin wrote in the *Irish Times*:

> A strong man in his character, a tough, virile man. He had a thorough understanding of the obligations between men, a man fashioned in a patriarchal mould – a man's man ... I think he had more the aptitude of a scholar than of an author, although his writing was powerful as befits a scholar.[19]

In 1982, seven years after Seán's death, Pádraig Tyers compiled a book called *Leoithne Aniar* (*Westerly Breeze*), based on an eighty-page manuscript about the Great Blasket written by Seán, plus transcripts of interviews with Seán and three other knowledgeable Blasket islanders. This work was translated into English and published in 1998 as *Blasket Memories, The Life of an Island Community*.

A selection of 116 excerpts of the letters to George Chambers from Eibhlís and occasionally Seán written between 8 September 1931 and 30 December 1951 was published in 1978. This book, *Letters from the Great Blasket*, was edited by Seán Ó Coileáin. There were a total of 335 such letters in the book, which contained letters up to 29 June 1960. These letters describe Eibhlís' life as well as many facets of the deterioration of the island community and her father-in-law Tomás' decline in health. It was published in French as *Lettres de la Grande Blasket* in 2011. Niamh told *The Kerryman* that the translation of the book into French would have been beyond her mother's dreams.[20]

While Tomás was a man with both feet firmly planted on the island, his son Seán was a man with one foot planted on the island and the other foot on the mainland. His great significance is that he was a key transitional character in the story of the Great Blasket.

14. Literary Fame and Criticism

Tomás' writing brought a level of fame both to him personally and to the Great Blasket. The Irish literary critic and satirist Brian O'Nolan, also known as Flann O'Brien and Myles na Gopaleen, wrote in his column in the *Irish Times* that *An tOileánach* was 'the superbest book of all the books I have ever read ... its impact was explosive'[1]. *The Kerryman* said 'This is perhaps the most remarkable book published in Ireland for many years.'[2]

Tomás took great satisfaction in his writing. In a copy of *An tOileánach* that he sent to his son Thomas in Springfield on 16 September 1929 (see page 266), Tomás expressed his pride in his inscription, written in Irish: 'Here is this book to you which your father wrote about his own life. Maybe not every father is capable of its writing because of his being here on the island.'[3] Seán Ó Criomhthain said that his father 'never praised his own work,' but that he 'liked the praise as much as anyone else.'[4]

Regrettably, Tomás' experience of celebrity was not without its downside. Some islanders took exception to parts of his narrative and the increasing number of visitors to the now-famous island became somewhat of a nuisance.

And, of course, there was also the scrutiny of scholars and literary critics. Over the nine decades since Tomás' classic books were published, his writing has been extensively dissected, analysed and interpreted. The high level of attention that his works have received is attributable primarily to his prominence as one of the first and most important Irish-language authors. His writing provided a rare and valuable first-person insight into authentic Irish folk culture.

The publication of Tomás' classic books in 1928 and 1929 created quite a stir on the Great Blasket, and the reaction was mixed. The publication of books about the island that were written by one of the island's own was a source of pride, but this sentiment was not unanimous, and there was an undercurrent of controversy.

Some islanders accused Tomás of exaggerating his skills and capabilities, specifically as a fisherman. Others felt that he overstated his father's capabilities and the help he provided to other islanders. Some were critical of certain factual omissions or how particular islanders were portrayed. There was certainly some jealousy at work here.

Tomás' grandson, Pádraig Ua Maoileoin, who stayed in his grandfather's island home numerous times during the post-publication period, observed this reaction at first hand. He pointed out that this kind of criticism was not limited to Tomás' books. Books written by other Blasket authors had also had mixed responses, and the criticism was not unlike the islanders' reaction to John Millington Synge's record of his 1905 visit. Clearly, there was a pattern of the islanders becoming perturbed as they compared the published word with their own personal perception of life on the island. Ua Maoileoin wrote:

> The Blasket books generated controversy and debate on the island. Writers were accused of misrepresentation – 'that is not how it happened'; 'all lies and invention,' Much of this criticism was inspired by envy.[5]

Tomás holding a book. Photograph by Thomas H. Mason.

Tomás wrote in the last chapter of *An tOileánach* about his intent in describing the island and its people:

> I have set down nothing but the truth; I had no need of invention, for I had plenty of time, and have still a good deal in my head ...
>
> I have brought other people besides myself into my story, for, if I hadn't, it would have been neither interesting nor complete. I never disliked any of them, and I've spent my life in their company till to-day without any trouble between us.[6]

Yet there may have been a basis for at least some of this criticism. Mícheál de Mórdha wrote that Tomás 'was never shy in coming forward about the worth of his deeds, but he may have exaggerated his prowess'.[7] Tomás may have either consciously or unconsciously shaded the narrative. It would have been natural for him, for example, to have held a high opinion of the skills and contributions of his parents. Perhaps, in Tomás' view of his job as a storyteller, embellishment was not a violation of the truth, merely a tweaking or slanting of the details.

In other instances, Tomás omitted facts that would have told a more complete story. At least two controversies, for example, stemmed from his account of the double drowning of his son Domhnall and Eibhlín Nic Niocaill. Tomás wrote: 'Another man brought in [rescued] the sister [his daughter Cáit], who was at her last breath.'[8] While this straightforward statement was accurate, it failed to identify islander Peats Tom Ó Ceárna as Cáit's rescuer. Ó Ceárna was later recognised by the government for his heroic efforts. A second controversy arose when Nic Niocaill's mother took exception to Tomás' assertion that his son Domhnall drowned in an attempt to save her daughter while failing to mention that her daughter Eibhlín drowned in an effort to save his daughter Cáit.[9] These inexplicable omissions generated a measure of resentment.

Another controversy involved Seán Eoghain Ó Duinnshléibhe, Tomás' long-time friend and neighbour. Seán Eoghain was upset with Tomás after discovering that the hapless character 'Tadhg' in *Allagar na hInise* was based on him. According to Muiris Ó Ciobháin (Maurice 'Kruger' Kavanagh), the infamous Dunquin publican, an offended Seán Eoghain once told him in his usual brusque style, 'I'd prefer to be chewing dung in my mouth than listening to the red lies told by that little scrap of a man!' According to Leslie Matson, Kruger too believed that the book was 'full of lies'. Kruger said, contradicting a story in *An tOileánach*, that Tomás never went seal-fishing because he was incapable of it.[10] At this point, the truth of the matter is impossible to determine.

All this debate may have created considerable discomfort for Tomás during the final years of his life. He certainly didn't want to quarrel with his neighbours about his writing. One wonders if the unfortunate effect of this situation was to alienate Tomás from the community to some extent. He may have already have withdrawn from full participation in the social life of the community while he focused primarily on his writing.

Beyond debates about Tomás' writing, the island's growing fame and the corresponding increase in visitors to the island was becoming a problem. The growth in tourism had begun before the publication of Tomás' books, as a consequence of the Celtic Revival. In *Allagar na hInise*, an annoyed Tomás wrote of the crowds of visitors to the island:

> It's a Holiday. There's nothing to be seen but naomhógs making for the island from every direction. They move like sea monsters, each of them carrying six or eight people. They don't leave either without their dinner. Someone said that you'd think that the islanders were paid by the Government to prepare tea for them every Sunday and Holiday.[11]

Seán Ó Criomhthain echoed these sentiments, showing little patience with the visitors:

> Visitors galore were calling to the house now, waving *An tOileánach* and *Allagar na hInise* in their fists. They put us off our day's work as they roamed in and out wanting to see the house where the hero [Tomás] was born. That was the way of it year after year.[12]

Máirín Nic Eoin wrote of the stress on the island and its people from the influx of visitors:

> [T]he island's resources are being depleted by these visitors. What is presented as the islanders' natural hospitality and friendliness towards strangers is now being questioned and put to the test by the scale of the intrusion.[13]

Nic Eoin observed the irony in this situation: tourism was contributing to the erosion of the native lifestyle that had made the island popular in the first place.

Despite the controversy on the island, Tomás deserved all the accolades he received. Much of the debate on Tomás' writing relates to nuance and does not undermine the fundamental value and integrity of his works as a whole. As for the irritation related to excessive tourism, this proved to be short-lived as, regrettably, the island continued its downward spiral despite its brief experience of the limelight.

Much of the literary value ascribed to Tomás' writing is attributable to its reputation for authenticity. Tomás' voice is that of a man totally immersed in the traditional Irish culture of the Great Blasket with minimal external distortion. He was the first to describe this unique island community from within, complete with interesting details about its simple lifestyle, rich culture and enormous challenges.

Two of those closest to Tomás' writing have attested to the authenticity of his work. In the foreword to his English translation of *An tOileánach*, Robin Flower wrote that Tomás 'tells his tale with perfect frankness, serving no theory and aiming at no literary effect, but solely concerned to preserve some image of the world he has known'.[14] An Seabhac, in his introduction to *Allagar na hInise,* wrote 'This book is a voice from the Gaeltacht itself ... Tomás is of the Gaeltacht ... He understands the Gaeltacht, what is deep in its heart and the heart of its people.'[15]

Seán Ó Coileáin said: 'there's an authenticity in the book that I don't find anywhere else in modern Irish', describing it as 'the real thing, the bare rock, the foundation'.[16] According to Irene Lucchitti, the significance of Tomás' writing is, in large measure, its 'authenticity'.[17]

Those who embrace the authenticity of Tomás' writing would probably concede that three factors eroded the pure authenticity of Tomás' original manuscripts, at least to some extent. First, Brian Ó Ceallaigh gave Tomás some direction in framing his writing, thereby influencing his output in advance. Second, An Seabhac was a leader in the Celtic Revival. Some of his editing of the manuscripts was inevitably influenced by his political outlook and his sense of propriety. And finally, Tomás' authenticity was compromised to a degree in the translation of the original manuscript from Irish to English by Robin Flower (see below). Nevertheless, on the whole, the body of Tomás' writing remains an authentic insider's voice on a unique Blasket community that has long since vanished.

Tomás wrote in the oral tradition of the storytellers of the island. He was a storyteller, not a historian. In the genre of folktales, pure accuracy in the details was sometimes sacrificed for the sake of a fundamental truth or underlying message. Furthermore, he sometimes provided slightly different versions of the same event, occasionally exercising a degree of literary licence in his writing. Some involved a storyteller refining his story over time, and some may reflect modifications to suit different audiences.

For example, he gives two slightly different versions of the story of the woman threatening to throw her child off a cliff

A justifiably proud Tomás holding one of his books in the mid-1930s, a few years before his death.

at a bailiff, one in *An tOileánach* and the other in *Seanchas an Oileáin Tiar*. In both cases, no rent is collected, but Tomás changed some of the details for the sake of more emphatically portraying the anger and bravery of the island women in *An tOileánach*. And, of course, there is some possibility that Tomás didn't sing the controversial '*Caisleán Uí Néill*' at his wedding; he could have added this vignette when he was writing *An tOileánach* over forty years later.

This phenomenon is not unusual in folklore. Críostóir Mac Cárthaigh, for example, wrote that he is aware of twelve separate versions of the folktale of the 'Sorrowful Cliff' ('*An Leaca Dhubhach*'), two provided by Tomás himself (see an Irish-language excerpt from one such version on page 229).[18]

As indicated throughout this work, Tomás was certainly less than precise on dates, for example incorrectly stating the date of his birth. Such errors likely resulted, in part, from the lack of access to any documentation of the facts.

All of this raises the issue of whether authenticity requires historical 'truth' and accuracy. Cathal Ó Háinle takes the view that there is 'quite exquisite literary truth rather than historical truth' in some elements of Tomás' writing; Tomás 'does not destroy historical truth ... [he] deforms it in the interest of imaginative truth.'[19]

Tomás wrote in a very simple and direct style. He characterised himself in heroic fashion, as he describes overcoming various challenges. His prose is concise and unadorned, perhaps borrowing from his letter-writing habit where getting to the point was important. He simply reported his version of events without much emotion and moved on to the next episode in his saga. His minimalist style is focused on the current episode rather than on the broad sweep of his story. He had a well-developed sense of humour, and comical anecdotes are woven into the narrative. For the most part, he avoided extensive elaboration and focused on relaying what he perceived to be the underlying message. Seán Ó Coileáin observed that he matured as a writer over time.[20] This is evident in *An tOileánach* – its later sections are more polished. Tomás' writing sometimes had a poetic flavour, perhaps due to the influence of his mentor Seán Ó Duinnshléibhe.

Tomás' classic books have fundamental differences. *Allagar na hInise* is a diary written contemporaneously with the events described. *An tOileánach* is an autobiography relying on his memory of events that occurred as much as half a century earlier. After finishing *Allagar* and moving on to *An tOileánach,* Tomás was forced to adjust his writing style. His diary entries as well as his many short submissions to periodicals involve stand-alone vignettes. In his autobiography, Tomás was required to sustain a consistent narrative describing the span of his life. Despite having made this adjustment, *An tOileánach* retains a staccato flavour, with Tomás constantly moving from episode to episode with minimal segues in between.

In comparing these books, Muiris Mac Conghail wrote:

> The *Allagar* text is an expansive narrative with a considerable amount of dialogue, crafted to provide further information and perhaps a 'colouring' on somebody's character. Ó Criomhthain was able to draw on his powers of recall when writing dialogue. *An tOileánach*, on the other hand, is a somewhat stern book ... Tomás describes his fellow islanders in a fairly detached way, noting many of their foibles, their drinking habits when in Dingle, and their physical courage when in danger.[21]

Pádraig Ua Maoileoin goes one step further. He suggests that Tomás' four major books (*Allagar na hInise, An tOileánach,*

Dinnseanchas na Blascaodaí and Seanchas on Oileán Tiar) are written in four different styles, depending on the nature and subject matter of the book.[22]

Beyond that, four unique aspects of Tomás' writing style are notable:

- Tomás was seldom forthcoming about his feelings on personal matters such as his marriage and the deaths of family members. He often reported all too briefly and dispassionately on the facts of a difficult personal situation. To some extent, this may be a reflection of his stoicism. But beyond that, it may have been that he was unsure of precisely how to express his feelings. He was more comfortable relying primarily on his version of the facts.

- Tomás often conveys an ironic attitude toward women, perhaps reflecting the paternalistic attitude of the time. He occasionally portrays them as hectoring and wrote that they talk too much and are unintelligible. Sometimes he criticises and then backs off. He praises his mother, although we rarely hear her voice. We never hear his wife's voice. Tomás doesn't explain this attitude – perhaps it is unconscious. The reader gets the impression that he may have been influenced by a marriage match that went against his true feelings. On the other hand, his grandson, Pádraig Ua Maoileoin, praised Tomás for 'fine descriptions of people, particularly women'. He once said, 'Tomás was a woman's man.'[23]

- In both *Allagar na hInise* and *An tOileánach*, Tomás makes almost no effort to describe the Great Blasket itself. He simply drops the reader into this unique island setting with little context. This is particularly odd because the harsh environment of the island is a major factor in so much of the story. He probably assumed, erroneously, that his readers would be familiar with the island, reflecting his narrow understanding of the world beyond the island.

- Tomás frequently used proverbs and wise sayings in everyday conversation, considered a sign of eloquence in his day. One of his favourites was that 'expectations are often disappointed', which he used in various forms. Another is 'the dead don't feed the living.'[24] He once emphasised the importance of proverbs when he interrupted and ended an argument by insisting, 'You can't better the proverb.'[25]

Robin Flower was perhaps in the best position to observe Tomás' literary style as it evolved:

> He has told me that, in writing this book, he aimed at a simple style, intelligible to every reader of Irish, using nothing of the 'cruadh-Ghaoluinn,' the 'cramp-Irish' of the pure literary tradition. This aim he has achieved. For the narrative runs easily in the ordinary language of the island, with only an occasional literary allusion of a straightforward kind.[26]

Providing more context, Flower wrote that:

> [Tomás] was peculiarly adapted by the whole bent of his mind to act as an observer as well as a vigorous participant in all the events of his isolated world ...
>
> The great value of this book is that it is a description of this vanishing mode of life by one who has known no other ...
>
> [F]rom his earliest days, he was keenly observant, watching and judging the people about him, eagerly alive to their tricks of character, and appreciating to the full the humours and tragedies of their life ...

This critical alertness is very noticeable in his use of his native language. Those who, like myself, have had the privilege of his friendship and instruction have often wondered at the neatness and precision of his explanations of the meaning of words and phrases, his ready production of synonyms and parallels out of a vast vocabulary, the finish and certainty of his phrasing in ordinary conversation.[27]

The erudite George Thomson, who was also in a position to assess Tomás' style in the context of his personality, wrote:

Tomás was reticent by nature. His narrative style was incisive and unemotional. In his books he seems to be feeling his way, uncertain how much of himself to reveal. His marriage was arranged for him ... His family life was clouded by adversity but, apart from [Domhnall's drowning] ... he passes over it in a couple of paragraphs ...

Tomás looks back at the past with a certain aloofness ...

Tomás' outlook ... was medieval ... He considered that the old men he remembered from his youth were better men than those now growing up ...

Tomás records the events of his life just as they occurred without conscious selection and without embellishment. This does not mean that his account of the facts is purely objective ... it bears the stamp of a strong personality.[28]

Many other prominent scholars have commented on Tomás' writing style:

- **Thomas Barrington (1937):** 'The style is spare but enhanced by a kindly irony. The story is told with austerity. Sentimentalism is shunned like a plague. It has tremendous power because of this simplicity. It strives to create no literary effect.'[29]

- **J.A. Brooks (1956):** 'He is quite unconscious of literary artifice, and makes no attempt to beguile us. His style is spare, precise and touched with irony; and I have read no other modern Irish author whose prose matches his.'[30]

- **Declan Kiberd (2003)**, in an interview with RTÉ: 'This is an autobiography by a person who is reticent to talk about his own thoughts. Tomás presents himself as a typical islander; not special. He is like Hemingway. He exhibits grace under pressure – e.g. very brief description of the death of his children. He curbed his self-indulgence. He didn't want to disclose the content of his own mind. His writing was the antithesis of focus on personality and individualism.'[31]

- **Pádraig Ua Maoileoin (2003):** 'As I said somewhere "as well worked and polished as stones on the shore." That was the way he placed the words. He was a stone mason, you understand, and a wordsmith, if you like. He had a great respect for words. Not unnatural or ungainly words that people would find too difficult. Tomás didn't use strange words but the ordinary words of his speech, the ones he liked and savoured most. He knew other people would have a taste for them as well. He understood words, that is to say, how to fit them together in a suitable way as he would fit stones into a wall or in the building of a house.'[32]

- **Thomas Shea (2010):** 'Tomás O'Crohan is best appreciated as a self-conscious performer who underplays, rather than flaunts, his potent literary artistry.' Shea said he demonstrates literary creativity by utilising bawdy humor and the third person, by elaborate evocative metaphors, as well as by his overall shaping of the narrative.[33]

- **Máirín Nic Eoin and Fintan O'Toole (2015):** 'His [Tomás'] story is certainly what it purports to be ... He provides a unique insider's account of the personal, social and economic life of a tightly knit coastal community, one subsisting on the periphery of national life and preserving a deep oral culture ... His story, indeed, is much more communal than personal: the values that underpin it are always collective ones ... His sparse style is a conscious aesthetic effect.'[34]

- **Breandán Ó Conaire (2015):** 'His mastery of the written language and of the resources of the language itself, and his skills in the oral traditions of scéalaíocht and seanchas, bring an additional poetic and literary quality to the sociological importance of Ó Criomhthain's accounts.'[35]

The *Sunday Independent* urged its audience to read *The Islandman*, and offered its impressions of the narrative:

> Tomás O'Crohan emerges from this book as a very lovable and a very gentle and noble character. He has lived his years imprisoned by the sea. These years have been one unending struggle to wring from his rocky patch of land and from the ocean the barest existence for himself and those depending on him ...
>
> It should not be supposed, however, that the life of Tomás O'Crohan and his neighbours was nothing but a round of grinding toil and uninterrupted misery. Far from it. There is, indeed, a good deal more laughter than tears in the story as a whole.[36]

Interestingly, the whole tone of *An tOileánach* changes after Tomás' marriage. The narrative shifts from the relatively carefree days of his youth and his flirting behaviour to the more serious duties of family. He also begins to experience tragedies, and his outlook is more subdued and wistful. The tone changes again in the last chapter, added at the request of An Seabhac. It has the feel of a eulogy for the island with Tomás becoming reflective about his life and legacy.

In summarising the various published reviews of *An tOileánach* with respect to Tomás' writing style, Breandán Ó Conaire wrote:

> Not only was the importance of the subject matter of the book highlighted in the reviews, but also the quality of the storytelling and the narrating, on the thorough mastery of the vocabulary and expressions of the Irish language throughout. The lively telling was praised as full of life and spirited energy, but all reined in by the complete craftsman, the carved descriptions, clipped, strong, astute, real natural language, the clever, witty conversation, the understanding of drama in the narrating of the story and the functional, active phrase, without an idle word or a syllable out of place, as well as the hardness, substance, bare tension in the language, language that is a mirror to the life and the personality of the author.[37]

By way of comparing Tomás' literary style with island writers Peig Sayers and Muiris Ó Súilleabháin, Alan Titley said that while these three authors and their classic books focus on the same small island, they are very different in outlook, imagination, treatment, acceptance and philosophy.[38] All three were excellent storytellers long before they were authors. But each was quite distinctive in their writing style, perhaps reflecting the generation gaps between them.

An tOileánach is a literary classic of world-class stature. Most literary criticism of Tomás' writing focuses on *An tOileánach* and most of the reviews were very positive. *Allagar na hInise* is generally regarded as less important, but several critics rank it as superior to *An tOileánach*. The following is a summary:

- *The Irish Times* (**1930**): 'Not since the days of Defoe has an island been brought so vividly before us as Tomás Ó Criomhthain has brought An Blascaod Mór ... *An tOileánach* is a wonderful book and a testimony to the vitality of the Gaelic language.'[39]

- *Irish Independent* (**1934**): 'The book gives us a vivid picture of that way of living, and every turn of its phrase is a revelation of Tomás; he does not sweep up the shavings of another man's workshop; again and again we get the sparks as they are hammered out on the anvil of his own experience.'[40]

- *The Irish Press* (**1934**): 'Thomas O'Crohan has written one of the few immortal books of the age.'[41]

- **Daniel Binchy** (**1934**): 'On the whole ... Mr. Sugrue [An Seabhac] had done his work [editing Tomás' manuscripts] with considerable skill, and all those who take any interest in Irish literature are deeply in his debt.'[42]

- **Tomás Barrington** (**1937**): 'This is a wonderful book, without doubt the greatest that has come out of Ireland in many a year.'[43]

- **Seán Ó Ciarghusa** (**1937**): '*The Islandman* was the best book that had come out of the Gaeltacht. I would say that it is the best book that has come out of Ireland in our time.'[44]

- **Marie Cruise O'Brien** (**1977**): 'In *An tOileánach*, the writing has a flavour, a quality of goodness you can almost taste.'[45]

Tomás' writing has been the subject of several sceptical reviews as well:

- **Ernest Blyth (1933)**: 'It [*An tOileánach*] is the best An Gúm has done and I don't think there are more than a couple of books in modern literature in Irish better than it. Nevertheless, it is not a masterpiece.'[46]
- **Seán Ua Ceallaigh (1934)**: '[*An tOileánach* is] perhaps the most over-rated book, despite its somewhat unique nature, ever issued by the Irish press.'[47]
- **Mark Quigley (2003)**: Tomás's output were political documents. He was influenced and perhaps manipulated by multiple parties with a nationalist political agenda.[48]

Tomás and his island colleagues were not immune from satire. In June 1933, *Dublin Opinion*, a satirical magazine, lampooned the Great Blasket with a cover illustration of an island with cartoon characters at typewriters and pen and ink, along with a publisher rowing a boat crammed full of manuscripts to the mainland. The caption at the bottom reads: 'Literary Wave Hits the Islands.' This caricature mocks the Great Blasket for its proliferation of native writers, all following in the footsteps of Tomás.

In 1941, Brian O'Nolan, writing under the pseudonym Myles na Gopaleen, published a full-blown parody of *An tOileánach* entitled *An Béal Bocht*. It was translated into English and published in 1973 as *The Poor Mouth: A Bad Story about the Hard Life*. The main character, Bonaparte O'Coonassa, is an amalgam of island writers, including Tomás and Muiris Ó Súilleabháin. While na Gopaleen referred to his book as a 'prolonged sneer', he said it was his abiding respect for *An tOileánach* that motivated him to write the book.[49]

Front cover of the June 1936 issue of *Dublin Opinion* lampooning the literary productivity of the Great Blasket. The mock sign on the island reads: 'Short courses in novel writing.'

The Islandman, Robin Flower's English translation of *An tOileánach*, is by far the most widely read edition of Tomás' classic. Flower had a series of advantages as a translator. He had a close personal relationship with Tomás that developed over more than twenty years. He had taken dictation from Tomás for hours on end while collecting folklore, and he was intimately familiar with his speech and writing patterns. Flower's command of Irish had by then improved to the point where he could communicate clearly and precisely with Tomás.

Daniel Binchy wrote that Flower was the ideal interpreter:

> [A]s all who are even vaguely familiar with Irish studies know, it would have been impossible to find anyone with better qualifications ... And he has risen nobly to the occasion, producing a masterly translation in which the sensitiveness of the poet and the accuracy of the scholar are blended in perfect harmony.[50]

Flower himself described his approach to the translation of *An Oileánach* when a literal translation would have been impossible because of the unique Irish dialect and idiom:

> It seemed best therefore to adopt a plain, straightforward style, aiming at the language of ordinary men who narrate the common experiences of their life frankly and without any cultivated mannerism.[51]

Flower's last visit to the Great Blasket was not until 1939, two years after Tomás' death, and they had corresponded for many years before the translation began. Thus, Tomás was available to Flower for consultation, if needed, during the translation process. Further, Flower wrote in his Foreword to *The Islandman* that An Seabhac had reviewed the translation,

Tomás seated outside his home in the mid-1930s.

and presumably any comments he had were reflected in the final manuscript. Flower clearly understood the shortcomings of a translation as against the original: 'rouge is no substitute for a natural complexion.'[52]

The *Sunday Independent* wrote: 'Dr. Robin Flower ... has given a first-rate rendering of this great book into English, especially in the way he has succeeded in preserving so much of the rich idiom and colloquial charm of the original.'[53] The *Irish Press* called it an 'exquisite'[54] translation and Declan Kiberd 'an excellent translation.'[55] John McGahern wrote:

> I was always puzzled by the difference between the original and Robin Flower's translation. I was inclined to blame this on the literalness of the translation; and it was only when I tried to translate parts of it myself that I came to realize how good a translation Flower's actually is.[56]

The Kerryman credited Flower for his knowledge of the Great Blasket and of Tomás which they said served him well:

> The fine translation now being published is the work of Dr Robin Flower, who is himself a stylist and writer, and who has furthermore lived for long periods on the island. He is intimately acquainted with the author and with all the circumstances of life on the Blaskets.[57]

Flower's translation is not without its critics. Despite his praise for the book (see above,) J.A. Brooks, writing in the *Irish Times* in 1956, said:

> The English translation gives no idea of the greatness of the book. The translator was the late Dr. Robin Flower, who was an excellent Irish scholar, and a stylish writer of English, and yet his translation was a failure ... he tried to retain the Irish idiom and construction; but what was plain and direct in Irish was quaint in English. I believe that 'The Islandman' is one of those untranslatable books which must be read in the original.[58]

In his usual blunt style, Brian O'Nolan wrote in the *Irish Times*: 'A greater parcel of bosh and bunk than Flower's "Islandman" has rarely been imposed on the unsuspecting public. The English translation gives no sense of the full flavour of the story.'[59] Seán Ó Coileáin said that 'translating is problematic; particularly this type of writing. Life and language are *ONE*.'[60] Ciaran Ross wrote: 'one cannot overemphasize the irony of reading Blasket writing in English, because it is the language that comprehensively supplanted the original language [Irish] and its lived world which the Blasket story-teller seeks to evoke and relive.'[61]

Less attention has been paid to Tim Enright's translation of *Allagar na hInise* as *Island Cross-Talk*. The *Irish Examiner* said that Enright 'successfully captured the poignancy of a traditional way of life now beginning to erode drastically.'[62]

Many scholars have identified overtones of Greek literature in the storytelling and writing of the Great Blasket. They have suggested that several broad themes and stylistic features of Homer's *Iliad* and *Odyssey* have found their way into Tomás' writing as well as that of Peig Sayers and Muiris Ó Súilleabháin.

Blasket visitor and Greek scholar George Thomson saw direct parallels between the two cultures, separated by centuries: 'The island of Ithaca had little to offer besides mountain pasture – "It is a rough place," says Odysseus, "but a fine nurse of men." One might say the same of the Blasket Island.' He quotes Nestor, the oldest of the chiefs who fought at Troy, as saying 'There is no man living today who would be a match for them.'[63] He points out that these are the exact words of Tomás in describing the men of the Great Blasket:

The conversation of those ragged peasants [on the Great Blasket], as I learned to follow it, astonished me.

It was as though Homer had come alive. Its vitality was inexhaustible, yet it was rhythmical, alliterative, formal, artificial ...[64]

Thomson may have been the first to identify the parallels between the Great Blasket and ancient Greece, but he was not the last:

- J.V. Luce (1969) wrote extensively on the subject, delineating the similarities, for example: 'Homer would not, I think, have found anything strange in O'Crohan's characterization of the King of the Blasket.'[65]
- Tim Enright (1993), in his introduction to Seán Ó Criomhthain's *A Day in Our Life*, wrote: 'The ancient Greeks taught us to look at the world without illusion for self-pity; in Homer man rises without despairing to meet the challenges and suffering which are his lot. That is the very spirit of Tomás.' In his introduction to *Island Cross-Talk* (1986), Enright pointed to the words of Homer's *Iliad*, 'The day will come when sacred Troy shall perish,' and Virgil's *Aeneid*, 'We Trojans are no more', which eerily resemble Tomás' famous words at the end of *An tOileánach*, 'the like of us will never be again.'[66]
- Declan Kiberd (2001) explained: 'Most of the tales that were learned by Tomás Ó Criomhthain had been given oral narration for centuries before they were written down: to that extent they were like those of Homer, not least in that terse understated and concrete idiom which seemed always to tremble on the brink of poetry.'[67]

Obviously, Tomás and the other island authors had only minimal knowledge of the writings of ancient Greece. There was certainly no attempt on their part to impart a style other

Tomás in 1924, photographed by Carl Wilhelm von Sydow.

than their own. They were simply describing a community which happened to exhibit many of the same cultural features as the Greek classics, particularly in the heroic nature of their folktales.

There has been a vigorous ongoing debate among critics and scholars as to whether Tomás writing constitutes 'literature' or some other type of narrative, perhaps of a cultural or anthropological nature.

Literature is generally defined as written works of high quality with long-term significance. By this definition, both *Allagar na hInise* and *An tOileánach* clearly qualify as literature. Brian Ó Ceallaigh was perhaps the first to comment on the matter. In his description of how Tomás came to be an author, he wrote:

> He [Tomás] reveals the life around him simply and as it really is. The panorama of daily happenings passes before Tomás as before a sociologist and a thinker ... A whole state and kind of existence, unknown to the modern world, is represented in his work. And it is represented by a mind whose sky has always been the sky of the Blaskets, and never any other.
>
> This picture of life is true. Therefore, it is literature.[68]

And even more emphatically:

> Tomás is a writer, a fisherman, a farmer with one cow, and a stonemason too. He handles words as he handles stones: he makes pictures with them. This book is a picture of the Western Island [the Great Blasket] and a true picture. Therefore it is literature.[69]

Scholar Daniel Binchy visited Tomás on the island after *Allagar na hInise* was published and while he was finalising *An tOileánach*. Binchy wrote:

> Personally I have always been profoundly sceptical of the value of modern Irish as a literary medium: this book [*An tOileánach*] has at least convinced me that it can be both a sensitive and a powerful medium in the hands of a writer like Tomás ...

As an autobiography, as the record of a singularly attractive personality, and as a literary achievement of rare beauty and strength, his book deserves to live.[70]

Brian O'Nolan, writing in the *Irish Times,* described the original Irish edition of *An tOileánach* as 'majestic'. He also said that the book was 'an extremely noble salute from them about to go away'; 'The Irish is perfectly free, lucid, unaffected, not at all trying to be quaint or funny'; and 'every page is a lesson how to write, it is all moving and magnificent.'[71]

Also in the *Irish Times*, Catherine Foley wrote: 'The book is regarded as a classic and a cornerstone in the canon of Irish literature.'[72] Irene Lucchitti wrote that Tomás the author was 'a skilled, deliberate, knowledgeable craftsman of literature' and that his published writing 'demands an unequivocal recognition ... as works of literature'.[73] In their book *The Irish Novel in Our Time*, Patrick Rafroidi and Maurice Harmon wrote: 'his book is reckoned – and rightly so – to be the masterpiece of Gaeltacht literature.'[74]

Much of this discussion seems to turn on the standard being applied. A direct comparison of Tomás' writing with the writing of acknowledged Irish literary masters who wrote in English, such as James Joyce, Oscar Wilde, William Butler Yeats, George Bernard Shaw, would most likely result in his work coming up short. While his metaphors are vivid, his narrative tends to be choppy and sometimes repetitive. Perhaps he takes his terse approach to an extreme. But for an author with his modest background describing in his native Irish a fading community from within, the result is brilliant.

Almost eighty years after his death, Tomás' writing stands as eloquent testimony to the memory of the long-gone Blasket community. In 2015, the *Irish Times* and the Royal Irish Academy collaborated in a series called 'Modern Ireland in 100

Artworks', with one work representing each year, beginning in 1916. Not surprisingly, *An tOileánach* was the selection for 1929, the year it was published. The subtitle of the article seems to settle the debate: 'The fisherman's account of life on Great Blasket is a milestone in Irish-language literature.'[75]

15. The Legacy of the Blasket Islandman

Tomás was an extraordinary man by almost any measure. And, of course, he was an Irish writer of enormous significance. His primary legacy is his extensive portfolio of powerful writing, which will live for ever as testimony to a bygone way of life. In his books, stories and poems, he bequeathed a captivating saga that beautifully illustrates authentic Irish folk culture. The value of his writing in documenting the life of the Great Blasket community is unsurpassed.

Robin Flower wrote of the significance of Tomás' classic autobiography, *An tOileánach*:

> It was the first attempt by a peasant of the old school, practically uneducated in the modern sense, though highly trained in the tradition of an ancient folk culture, to set out the way of his life upon his remote island from childhood to old age.[1]

In Flower's *The Western Island,* he introduced Tomás with a poem that provides a personal insight into his close friend's character. He wrote of the symbiosis of Tomás and the island, his precise craftsmanship, his command of words, as well as his loneliness:

Tomás

I loitered there, and he
Built up the turf-rick with how careful hands;
Hands that had built a thousand ricks and now
Worked delicately with a deft unconsciousness.
Below us the Great Island
Fell with white-shining grasses to the cliffs,
And there plunged suddenly
Down sheer rock-gullies to the muttering waves.
Far out in the bay the gannets
Stopped and turned over and shot arrowy down,
And, beyond island, bay, and gannets falling,
Ireland, a naked rock-wave, rose and fell.
He had lived on the Island sixty years
And those years and the Island lived in him,
Graved on his flesh, in his eye dwelling,
And moulding all his speech,
That speech witty and beautiful
And charged with the memory of so many dead.
Lighting his pipe he turned,
Looked at the bay and bent to me and said:
'If you went all the coasts of Ireland round,
It would go hard to you to find
Anything else so beautiful anywhere;
And often I am lonely,
Looking at the Island and the gannets falling
And to hear the sea-tide lonely in the caves.
But sure 'tis an odd heart that is never lonely.'[2]

Tomás was a pivotal figure in the emergence of Irish as a modern, literary language. Seán Ó Criomhthain once said of his father's contribution to the Celtic Revival: 'I imagine that if Tomás were alive today there would be no man in Ireland as

Statue of Tomás outside the Blasket Centre in Dunquin.

pleased as himself because of the success of the [Irish] language movement as well as other things ... I'd say that he'd feel like the King of Ireland.'[3]

Writing in *The Star* in 1929, Eoin Mac Neill, co-founder of the Gaelic League, political leader and Irish language scholar wrote:

> Here is one of the clearest signs that Ireland has begun to live again – thainig anan I n-Eirinn. This book [*An tOileánach*] is a vital thing, an act of national life, a healthy national growth of the national organism. It is something more than life, it is a victory of life in the struggle for life. It has in it the germ cells of more life, better life, fuller life, stronger and more lasting life.
>
> It is Irish from cover to cover, not Irish merely in language, but Irish also in its tradition, in its outlook, in its subject, which is the daily normal life of a community as Irish as it has been left possible to be ...
>
> I pity the Irishman to whom this book is foreign.[4]

Tomás was a complicated, multidimensional human being. He was intelligent, perceptive, persistent, self-aware and self-confident, stoic and resilient, articulate, broadly skilled and visionary. He was imbued with Irish folk culture and he had a gift for words. He had an ironic sense of humour. He was a hard man, rigid and boastful. He was blunt, but he could also be quite engaging. He realised his own significance and he was sometimes dismissive of others.

Seán Ó Tuama wrote: 'he is an island Renaissance man of Crusoe-like versatility – fine dancer, hunter, fisherman, singer, house-builder, poet, turf cutter, storyteller ... There is a circumspection, a sternness in him, a moralistic detachment.'[5] George Thomson described Tomás as behaving with 'a certain detachment, sympathetic, but gently ironical'.[6] He exuded a somewhat cool, aloof and observant manner that might be typical of a scholar.

As he aged, Tomás may have been socially isolated to at least some degree. He described two situations where he was apparently excluded from what would normally have been collaborative community efforts: the construction of his new house, which he undertook without help; and the salvage of the wreck of the *Quebra*, when he was not invited to join a work crew.

On St Patrick's Day 1943, in a speech marking the fiftieth anniversary of the founding of the Gaelic League, Taoiseach Éamon de Valera articulated his vision of an ideal Ireland based on what he called 'frugal comfort'.[7] In many respects, Tomás was the embodiment of de Valera's concept of a simple and rugged but culturally fulfilling life in a mostly rural Ireland.

Seán Ó Coileáin said Tomás was as hard as a rock and as old as the mist. Of his classic works, he said *An tOileánach* is on an epic scale and that *Allagar na hInise* is unrelenting and uncompromising.[8]

The unveiling of Tomás' memorial headstone at Baile an Teampaill. An Seabhac is on the left.

Over the years, Tomás captured the social, cultural and political implications of the Celtic Revival and the birth of an independent Ireland. And he took these momentous events to heart. In the 1901 Census, he signed his name as 'Thomas Crohan'; in the 1911 Census, however, he signed his name as 'Tomás Ó Criomhthain', an apparent affirmation of his own personal cultural and political evolution. He was the only islander to sign his name in Irish.[9]

On 3 November 1957, An Seabhac unveiled a granite memorial to Tomás at his grave in the old Dunquin cemetery at Baile an Teampaill. Funding for the headstone was raised by a committee chaired by An Seabhac. The solicitation was signed by the president of the Gaelic League, religious leaders, university professors, a judge of the High Court of Ireland and distinguished artists and writers.

Tomás's grave at Baile an Teampaill with the inscription 'the like of us will never be again' in Irish. Note the error in the year of his birth – 1856 rather than 1854.

The headstone was designed and hand-carved by craftsman Séamus Murphy of Cork. Its shape is reminiscent of the ancient beehive huts of West Kerry and the Great Blasket. On the face is an image of fish, a symbol of Christianity and the trade Tomás practised. On the reverse is a *naomhóg*.

At the ceremony, Tomás Ó Muircheartaigh, the president of the Gaelic League, spoke of the role of the Gaeltacht in keeping the Irish language alive, and Seán Ó Criomhthain thanked all those responsible for creating the memorial. The *Irish Press* published a fitting tribute:

> That old man, remembering the days of his youth, the simple, dignified life of the islanders, wrote a book that is of immense value in any study of our history.
>
> His people were poor people, living frugally by hazardous currach-fishing on wild seas, by farming meagre patches of land islanded between rocks.
>
> Their chief contact with the cities of the world would have been not with Dublin or London but with Chicago,

New York, Boston – places that in their folklore acquired almost a mythological significance.

But their lives followed a pattern that had been drawn in the early ages of our civilisation, and the quietude of their days was enlivened by song and poetry and ancient story, by simple and earnest faith. All of this Tomás Ó Criomhthain preserved in the pages of his autobiography.

The Blaskets are silent now and the hearths are cold around which Ó Criomhthain's people sat on wild winter nights and told stories as old and as noble as Homer. But this book and his memorial in Dunquin remind us, even in the age of science and man-made satellites, that man's true happiness is in order and faith and in the ancient simplicities of the land and the sea and the changing seasons.

For his own lonely storm-swept home and for the whole island of Ireland this was Ó Criomhthain's contribution to civilisation.[10]

On 21 March 1997, sixty years after his death, another celebration of Tomás' life and work was held at the recently opened Blasket Centre. They keynote speaker was Mary Robinson, the President of Ireland. A full-length play, *The Islandman*, based on Tomás' life, was presented.

Tomás' significance in Ireland is evident in two very public tributes to him: two commemorative postal stamps bore his image, and a commemorative £20 banknote bore his words.

Tomás will live on forever as one of the giants of Irish-language literature of the early twentieth century. Among his peers are Máirtín Ó Cadhain of Connemara, Fr Peadar Ua Laoghaire of Cork, brothers Séamus Ó Grianna and Seosamh Mac Grianna of Donegal, Pádraic Ó Conaire of Galway, and Muiris Ó Súilleabháin and Peig Sayers of the Great Blasket Island.

Descendants of Seán Ó Criomhthain with President Mary Robinson on 21 March 1997. Cáit (Ní Chriomhthain) Uí Chonaill, Mary Robinson and Niamh (Ní Chriomhthain) Uí Laoithe (l–r) are at the centre.

Tomás' legacy includes six major achievements:

- **Gave a voice to the common man.** Tomás wrote an account of life on the Great Blasket from the inside at the dawn of the twentieth century. He was a simple fisherman and farmer who wrote brilliantly in his native tongue. Despite being essentially self-taught, he had a large vocabulary and used it to create vivid imagery. His writing was grounded in the reality of the community. Tomás lives on as the personification of the island.

- **Furthered Ireland's transition from oral to written storytelling.** Tomás was one of the very first practitioners of Irish folk storytelling to transition to a written format. He understood that the traditional role of the poet and

One of two postage stamps issued on 1 July 1957 marking the centenary of Tomás' birth. He was the first writer in Irish so honoured.

Rough facsimile of an Irish £20 banknote with a faint excerpt from *An tOileánach* in the background behind the map of the Blaskets, issued on 4 February 1980. On the face was a portrait of William Butler Yeats.

storyteller had its inherent limitations. Too often, as the tellers of these stories passed away, their folktales disappeared with them. He saw that the written medium had the important advantage of permanency.

- **Chronicled the life of the Blasket community.** Tomás perceived that life on the Great Blasket was fading away. He described the story of the island community so that there would be a record of this one-of-a-kind enclave. His works facilitated the spread of the story of the Great Blasket worldwide. He helped record the dynamics of the island community for posterity.

- **Documented island folklore.** Tomás transcribed many traditional folktales that would have been lost without his personal intervention. These tales include selected works of Blasket poet Seán Ó Duinnshléibhe and Tomás 'Maol' Ó Ceárna as well as tales he learned from other islanders. These folktales are important reminders of an authentic Irish folk culture that was on the wane.

- **Advanced the cause of Irish language and culture.** Tomás was convinced of the intrinsic value of the Irish language as a manifestation of the distinctive culture and history of the Irish people. His writing helped to illustrate that the Irish language could be the vehicle for great literature. He advanced the noble cause of the Celtic Revival. And he provided the people of the Irish Free State, then in its infancy, with a heroic image of what it means to be Irish.

- **Inspired other Blasket authors.** Tomás was the first of the Blasket writers. His example led to at least eleven other native islanders publishing books in Irish – a rare feat indeed for such a small and isolated community.

Regrettably, Tomás' writing and the fame that came with it was insufficient to save the Blasket community itself. The economic forces that were at work, as well as the intractable problems of poor transportation and communication, were simply too powerful to overcome. By the time of Tomás' passing in 1937, the island was well on its path of decline. Tomás himself anticipated the inevitable result of this process in his immortal words: *'mar ná beidh ár leithéidí arís ann'* ('for the like of us will never be again').[11]

Interestingly, Seán Ó Criomhthain said that his father never thought that there wouldn't be any people living on the island

The ruins of Tomás' home in 2015.

Tomás' home as restored in 2017.

– that it would be abandoned. His famous words were actually intended to convey his conviction that his island successors wouldn't be like him. Tomás thought they would be smarter, more clever and they wouldn't need to work as hard. It was his personal 'like' that he envisioned dying out – not that the island would be deserted.

By devoting himself to his writing, Tomás provided us with a lovely portrayal of a vanishing community, so that he and his community could live on after they had passed away. Tomás himself accomplished his objective of a form of immortality: to be remembered after his death. Tomás clearly saw his writing in the context of posterity. As he wrote in the closing paragraphs of *An tOileánach:*

> One day there will be none left in the Blasket of all I have mentioned in this book – and none to remember them. I am thankful to God, who has given me the chance to preserve from forgetfulness those days that I have seen with my own eyes and have borne their burden, and that when I am gone men will know what life was like in my time and the neighbours that lived with me.[12]

Clearly, all who love Ireland are beneficiaries of Tomás' precious legacy.

Tomás, with Robin Flower, gesturing skyward.

A Comparative Timetable

European History						1914 First World

Irish History		1845–47 Great Famine	1879 Year of the Yellow Meal	1879–90 Land League	1891–1922 Celtic Revival		1916 Easter Rising

Great Blasket Population	1841 153	1851 97	1871 130	1881 136	1891 132	1911 160	1

Tomás Ó Criomhthain Milestones	1854 Tomás Born	1878 Tomás Marries	1904 Wife Dies	1907 Marstrander Visits	1910 Flower Visits	1916 First Published Article	19 Ó Cea Vis

Tomás' Age		23	50	52	55	61	6

326

| | | 1939 | 1945 | | |
| | | Second World War | | | |

19–21	1922	1922–23	1937	1949	1953
War of	Irish Free State	Irish	Constitution	Republic	Great Balsket
pendence	Established	Civil War	Adopted	Declared	Evacuated

| | | 1926 | 1936 | 1946 | | 1953 | 1954 |
| | | 143 | 110 | 45 | | 22 | 0 |

18	1928	1929	1934	1935	1937	1986
ng	*Allagar na hInise*	*An tOileánah*	*The Islandman*	*Dinnseanchas*	Tomás	*Island*
cripts	Published	Published	Published	*na mBlascaodaí*	Dies	Cross-Talk
ins				Published		Published

| 3 | 74 | 75 | 79 | 80 | 82 | |

Endnotes

Abbreviations

Blasket Island Reflections (Póirtéir)	*Reflections*
The Blasket Islands – Next Parish America (Stagles & Stagles)	*Next Parish*
Blasket Lives (Matson)	*Lives*
Blasket Memories (Tyers)	*Memories*
The Blaskets – People and Literature (Mac Conghail)	*People*
Dáithí de Mórdha, the Blasket Centre (interview)	Dáithí de Mórdha
A Dark Day on the Blaskets (Ó Dubhshláine)	*Dark Day*
A Day in Our Life (O'Crohan)	*Day*
The Hidden Life of Tomás Ó Crohan (Lucchitti)	*Hidden*
Irish Tourism – Image, Culture, Identity (Cronin and O'Connor)	*Tourism*
An Island Community (de Mórdha)	*Community*
Island Cross-Talk (O'Crohan)	*Cross-Talk*
Island Home (Thomson)	*Home*
The Islander (O'Crohan)	*Islander*
The Islandman (O'Crohan)	*Islandman*
Letters from the Great Blasket (Ní Shúilleabháin)	*Letters*
National Library of Ireland	NLI
Nua Aois, 1970, 'Agallamh le Seán Ó Criomhthain'	*Agallamh*
An tOileánach Léannta (Nic Craith)	*Léannta*
On an Irish Island (Kanigel)	*Irish Island*
Primary Education on the Great Blasket (Nic Craith)	*Primary Education*
Seanchas ón Oileán Tiar (Ó Criomhthain and Flower)	*Seanchas*
The Western Island (Flower)	*Western*

Dedication

1   Kurtzman, *Left to Die.*

Endnotes

Chapter 1. Tomás Ó Criomhthain: The Blasket Islandman

1   *Western*, p. 12.
2   *Islandman*, p. ix.
3   Binchy, 'Two Blasket Autobiographies', p. 547.
4   *Memories*, p. 111.
5   *Community*, p. 34.
6   *Islandman*, p. ix.
7   *Western*, p. 15.
8   *Islandman*, pp. 244–5.

Chapter 2. A Blasket Homeland

1   *National Geographic Traveller*, Summer 1986, p. 61.
2   Smith, *The Ancient and Present State of the County of Kerry*, p. 183.
3   *Memories*, pp. 7–8.
4   *Islandman*, p. viii.
5   *Ibid.*, pp. 242–3.
6   *Ibid.*, p. 26.
7   Marstrander, *Impressions from Ireland*, p. 21.
8   Michael Carney, Springfield, Massachusetts, interview.
9   *Islandman*, p. vii.
10 *Day*, p. 2.
11 *Islandman*, pp. 242–3.
12 *People*, p. 11.
13 Foster, 'Waking the Dead: The Islandman and the Irish Revival', p. 58.
14 Londe & Fox, *The Cracked Lookingglass*, Shea, 'The Blasket Writers', p. 80.
15 Other native Blasket authors include: Tomás' son, Seán Ó Criomhthain; Tomás' daughter-in-law Eibhlís (Ní Shúilleabháin) Uí Chriomhthain; Mícheál 'An File' Ó Guithín; Máire Ní Ghuithín; Muiris Ó Catháin; Seán Sheáin Í Chearnaigh; Seán Pheats Tom Ó Ceárnaigh; Seán Ó Catháin; Eibhlín Ní Shúilleabháin; Michael Carney; and Gearoid Ó Catháin.
16 *Memories*, p. 174.
17 Carney & Hayes, *From the Great Blasket to America*, p. 17.
18 Dáithí de Mórdha.
19 Blasket Centre, Dunquin.
20 *Irish Press*, 23 April 1947, p. 1.
21 *The Kerryman*, 19 July 1947, p. 1.
22 *Irish Independent*, 17 September 1952, p. 7.
23 Mícheál Ó Cinnéide, Wexford, interview.

Chapter 3. The Ó Criomhthain Family

1   *Islandman*, pp. 1, 3.
2   Ó Conaire, *Tomás an Bhlascaoid*, Ó Conaire, 'Nótaí Cúlra', pp. 16–18.
3   Two women named Cáit Ní Shé from the Great Blasket were baptised in 1811; it is unclear which was Tomás' mother.
4   *Islandman*, pp. 2–3.
5   *Ibid.*, p. 1.
6   *Ibid.*, p. 168. Tomás wrote that his father died at the age of seventy, but he was probably eighty.
7   *Ibid.*, pp. 169–70. Tomás wrote that his mother died at the age of eighty-two, but she was probably seventy-eight.
8   *Ibid.*, pp. 2, 33.
9   *Next Parish*, p. 67.
10 *Islandman*, pp. 2, 26–9, 188, 195.
11 *Ibid.*, pp. 3–4.
12 *Ibid.*, p. 65.
13 *Ibid.*, p. 68. Tomás wrote that six of his siblings were living in 1880: three on the Great Blasket (Tomás, Cáit and Máire) and three in America (Pádraig, Eibhlín and Nóra). Seán and Eibhlís were deceased by this time.
14 *Ibid.*, pp. 13–15, 20.
15 *Ibid.*, pp. 20–1.
16 *Ibid.*, pp. 20–1, 64–5. An extensive search yielded no official record of Máire's return voyage.
17 *Ibid.*, p. 65
18 Ó Guiheen, Mícheál, *Diary*.
19 *Islandman*, pp. 19, 41, 68.
20 *Ibid.*, pp. 64–5.
21 *Ibid.*, p. 65.
22 *Ibid.*, pp. 67–8.
23 *Ibid.*
24 *The Islander* indicates that Pádraig stayed in America for seven years, not ten (p. 207). An extensive search yielded no official record of ship's passage for Pádraig on his two round trips to America or the one-way trips of his sons Pádraig and Seán.
25 *Islandman*, pp. 171–3.
26 *Ibid.*, p. 172.
27 *Ibid.*, p. 240.
28 *Ibid.*, p. 14.
29 *Ibid.*, pp. 64, 68–71, 119–128.
30 *Ibid.*, p. 1.
31 *Ibid.*, pp. 23–4.

Endnotes

32   *Ibid.*, pp. 6, 11, 23.
33   *Ibid.*, p. 216.
34   *Ibid.*, pp. 2, 33–34.
35   *Ibid.*, pp. 34, 81.
36   *Ibid.*, pp. 33–4, 89–91, 114.
37   *Cross-Talk*, pp. 26, 27, 106, 153.

Chapter 4. Coming of Age on the Great Blasket

1   *Islandman*, p. 23.
2   *Ibid.*, p. 2.
3   *Ibid.*, p. 6.
4   *Ibid.*, pp. 6, 11–12.
5   *Ibid.*, pp. 7–9.
6   *Ibid.*, pp. 36–7, 41.
7   *Ibid.*, pp. 41–5.
8   *Ibid.*, pp. 75–9.
9   *Ibid.*, p. 100.
10   *Ibid.*, pp. 237–8.
11   *Ibid.*, p. 13.
12   *Primary Education*, pp. 83–84.
13   *Ibid.*, p. 95.
14   *Islandman*, p. 18.
15   *Ibid.*, pp. 15–16.
16   *Ibid.*, pp. 21, 35.
17   *Ibid.*
18   *Ibid.*, pp. 38–9.
19   *Ibid.*, p. 18.
20   *Ibid.*, pp. 21, 47.
21   *Ibid.*, pp. 59–60.
22   *Ibid.*, pp. 60–2.
23   *Ibid.*, pp. 39–40.
24   This estimate of the duration of Tomás' schooling is based on *Islandman*, pp. 59–62 and 146, adjusted for a corrected birth date of 21 December 1854.
25   *Islandman*, p. 245.
26   *Ibid.*, pp. 47–9.
27   *Ibid.*, pp. 62–3.
28   *Ibid.*, pp. 94–7.

Chapter 5. Marriage and Family

1   *A Pity Youth Does Not Last*, p. 31.
2   *Reflections:* Booklet, pp. 36–7; *Islander*, pp. 42–3.
3   *Islandman*, pp. 92–3.
4   *Ibid.*, p. 93.
5   *Ibid.*, pp. 80, 65, 178.
6   *Allagar II*, p. 60.
7   *Islandman*, pp. 34, 37–8.
8   *Ibid.*, p. 80.
9   *Ibid.*, pp. 80–2.
10 *Ibid.*, pp. 102–3; *Islander*, pp. 116–17.
11 *Islandman*, p. 113; *Islander*, p. 162.
12 *Islandman*, pp. 103–10.
13 *Islander*, p. 162.
14 *Islandman*, pp. 129–30.
15 *Ibid.*, pp. 144–5.
16 *Ibid.*, p. 113.
17 *Ibid.*, pp. 187–8.
18 *Ibid.*, pp. 144–5.
19 *Community*, p. 49.
20 *Islander*, p. 172.
21 Shea, 'The Islander: A More Provocative Tomás O'Crohan', p. 100.
22 *Islandman*, p. 145.
23 *Islander*, pp. 178–9.
24 Songs in Irish: http://songsinirish.com/p/caislean-ui-neill-lyrics.html.
25 Seán Ó Coileáin, Cork, interview; *Lives:* Tomás Ó Criomhthain.
26 Noonan, *Biography and Autobiography: Essays on Irish and Canadian History and Literature*, Ó Háinle, 'Deformation of History in Blasket Autobiographies', pp. 139–41; *Irisleabhar Mhá Nuad*, 1985, pp. 184–109.
27 *Islandman*, p. 146.
28 *Ibid.*, p. 147.
29 *Ibid.*, pp. 147, 218.
30 *Ibid.*, pp. 156–8.
31 Ó Conaire, *Tomás an Bhlascaoid*, An Seabhac, 'Tomás Ó Criomhthain, Iascaire agus Údar'. p. 203.
32 *Islandman*, p. 147.
33 *Ibid.*, pp. 29, 189.
34 *Ibid.*, p. 195.
35 Measurements per drawings prepared for Office of Public Works by Paul Arnold, Architects, Dublin, 2015.
36 *Islandman*, pp. 31–2, 101, 187.

Endnotes

37 Ó Conaire, *Tomás an Bhlascaoid*, Ó Conaire, *Tomás an Bhlascaoid*.
38 *Sunday Independent*, 14 March 1937, p. 12.
39 *Islandman*, pp. 86, 92–3, 148–63, 166.
40 *Ibid.*, pp. 146–7, 167–9.
41 *Ibid.*, pp. 228, 234–5.

Chapter 6. Tragedy Stalks the Ó Criomhthain Family

1   *Sunday Independent,* 14 March 1937, p. 12.
2   *Islandman*, pp. 91, 186, 218.
3   *Dark Day,* p. 144 (collected from Méiní (Ní Shé) Uí Dhuinnshléibhe by Mícheál Ó Guithín).
4   *Islandman*; *People*, pp. 131–2; *Lives*: Tomás Ó Criomhthain, Máire (Ní Chatháin) Uí Chriomhthain, Cáit (Ní Chriomhthain) Ua Mhaoileoin and Domhnall Ó Criomhthain. Death certificates courtesy of Pádraig Breathnach, Carrickmacross.
5   *Islandman*, p. 186. Seán I fell off the cliff in 1887, not 'about 1890'.
6   *Ibid.*, pp. 147, 186.
7   *Ibid.*, pp. 196–7.
8   *Ibid.*, p. 147.
9   *Ibid.*, p. 197.
10 *Ibid.*, p. 218.
11 *Ibid.*
12 *Dark Day*, pp. 97–8.
13 *Ibid.*, p. 110.
14 *Islandman*, p. 198.
15 *Ibid.*
16 Ó Conaire, *Tomás an Bhlascaoid*, Ó Criomhthain, Seán, 'Tomás Ó Criomhthain,' p. 146.
17 *Islandman*, p. 197.
18 *Dark Day*, pp. 154–5.
19 *An Claidheamh Soluis*, 30 July 1910.
20 Death Certificate courtesy of Pádraig Breathnach, Carrickmacross.
21 *Islandman*, pp. 238–9.
22 *Irish Island*, 'Another Island' (RTÉ), p. 52.

Chapter 7. A Blasket Life

1   *Seanchas*, pp. 10–12.
2   *Islandman*, pp. 88–9.
3   *Ibid.*, pp. 97–101, 147.

4   *Ibid.*, pp. 152–3.
5   *Seanchas*, pp. 11–12.
6   *Islandman*, pp. 153–5.
7   *Ibid.*, pp. 167, 176.
8   *Ibid.*, pp. 228–30.
9   *Ibid.*, pp. 165–6.
10 *Ibid.*, pp. 102, 187.
11 *Community*, pp. 280–9.
12 *Islandman*, p. 220.
13 *Ibid.*, p. 155.
14 *Seanchas*, p. xi; *Islandman*, pp. 225–6.
15 *Cross-Talk*, pp. 1, 148.
16 *Ibid.*, pp. 32, 54, 99, 116, 133, 148.
17 *Ibid.*, p. 204.
18 *Islandman*, p. 243.
19 *Western*, p. 23.
20 *Community*, pp. 261–71; Irish Wrecks Online: County Kerry.
21 *Islandman*, p. 6.
22 *Ibid.*, pp. 4–5.
23 *Ibid.*, pp. 9–10.
24 *Ibid.*, pp. 5, 190–4.
25 *Ibid.*, pp. 71–3.
26 *Ibid.*, p. 239.
27 *Ibid.*, p. 5.
28 Ó Muircheartaigh, *Oidhreacht an Bhlascaoid*, Ó Dubháin, 'Báillí agus Callshaoth', pp. 19–20.
29 *Islandman*, pp. 201–7.
30 *Ibid.*, pp. 214–15.
31 *Seanchas*, p. 49.
32 *Islandman*, pp. 215–16.
33 *Ibid.*, pp. 52–4.
34 *Ibid.*, pp. 54–5.
35 *Ibid.*, pp. 166–7.
36 *Ibid.*, pp. 55–7.
37 *Ibid.*, p. 233.
38 *A Galician in Ireland*, p. 35.
39 *Islandman*, pp. 233–5.
40 *Memories*, p. 78.
41 *Cross-Talk*, p. 199.
42 *Islandman*, pp. 235–6.
43 *Bloghanna ón mBlascaod*, p. 26.
44 *Islandman*, p. 141.

Endnotes

45 *Seanchas*, pp. 55–8, Ó Scannláin; *Poets and Poetry of the Great Blasket*, pp. 84–7.
46 Jordan, *The Pleasures of Gaelic Literature*, pp. 25–38.
47 *Islandman*, pp. 82–3; *Islander*, p. 92
48 Ó Guithín, Mícheál, *Diary.*
49 Ryan, *Irish Rosary*, p. 73.
50 *Memories*, p. 42.
51 *Islandman*, p. 237.
52 *Cross-Talk*, p. 110.
53 *Ibid.*, p. 122.
54 *Ibid.*, p. 109.
55 *Allagar na hInise* (1977), p. 72.
56 *Islandman*, pp. 100, 147, 198, 244.
57 *Cross-Talk*, p. 208.
58 *Irish Folktales*, p. 121; *Cross-Talk*, p. 155.
59 Ó Guithín, Mícheál, *Diary.*
60 *Islandman*, pp. 51, 237, 242.
61 *Ibid.*, pp. 68–71, 106–13, 115–28, 133, 243.
62 *Ibid.*, pp. 173–5.
63 *Ibid.*, pp. 133–9, 208–14.
64 *Ibid.*, p. 243.
65 *Ibid.*, p. 27.
66 *Ibid.*, pp. 34–5.
67 *Ibid.*, pp. 133–6.
68 *Ibid.*, pp. 55–6; *Islander*, pp. 51–2.
69 *Islandman*, pp. 156–63; *Islander*, pp. 186–99.
70 *Landed Estates Database, Cable & Undersea Communications*; Shea, 'A More Provocative Tomás O'Crohan,' pp. 104–105.
71 *Islandman*, p. 30.
72 Ó Muircheartaigh, *Oidhreacht an Bhlascaoid*, Ua Maoileoin, 'Allagar an Chriomhthanaigh', pp. 213–14.
73 *An Caomhnóir, Rí an Oileáin*, 1990, pp. 13–14.
74 *Islandman*, p. 17.
75 *Allagar na hInise* (1977), pp. 40–41.
76 *Cross-Talk*, p. 12.
77 *An Caomhnóir*, 'Rí an Oileáin', 1990, pp. 13–14.
78 *Lives:* Pádraig Peats Mhicí Ó Catháin.
79 Ó Muircheartaigh, *Oidhreacht an Bhlascaoid*, Ua Maoileoin, 'Allagar an Chriomhthanaigh', p. 212.
80 *Cross-Talk*, pp. 32, 51, 134, 136, 157, 168–73, 188, 208.

Chapter 8 Inspiration, Irish Literacy and Early Writing

1   *Islandman*, p. ix.
2   *Cross-Talk*, p. 191.
3   *Islandman*, pp. 55–6.
4   *Ibid.*, pp. 49–51. Maurice Brick of Gorta Dubha, West Kerry and New Rochelle, New York remembers a slightly different version of this event. His recollection is that the Dunquin men had already taken what booty they could. The Gorta Dubha men were looting the remainder of the ship's cargo when their own boat accidently overturned. They were forced to seek refuge on the ship, which eventually sank. The Dunquin men refused to help them, resulting in the loss of the twenty-one lives.
5   *Islandman*, pp. 66–7.
6   *Lives:* Tomás 'Maol' Ó Ceárna.
7   *Western*, p. 70; *Home*, pp. 32–3.
8   *Islandman*, pp. 86–7.
9   *Ibid.*, p. 140.
10   *Ibid.*, p. 152.
11   *Ibid.*, p. ix; *An tOileánach* (2002), p. xxx.
12   *Western*, p. 100.
13   *People*, pp. 141–2.
14   *Islandman*, pp. 215–16; *An tOileánach* (2002), p. xxx.
15   *Day*, p. 3; *Home*, pp. 29–30.
16   *Inventing Ireland: The Literature of the Modern Nation*, p. 153; *Irish Island*, p. 13.
17   *Anáil an Bhéil Bheo,* p. 241.
18   *Islandman*, p. 240.
19   *Ibid.*, p. 223.
20   *Ibid.*, p. 241.
21   *Ibid.*, p. 224.
22   *Ibid.*, p. 225.
23   *Ibid.*
24   *Lives:* Tomás Ó Criomhthain.
25   *Islandman*, p. 223; *Cross-Talk*, pp. 1–2.
26   *Léannta*, Chapter 3.
27   Ó Conaill, *Library of Tomás Ó Criomhthain; Léannta*, p. 75.
28   *Cross-Talk*, pp. 166, 188.
29   Foster, 'Waking the Dead: The Islandman and the Irish Revival', p. 56.
30   *Memories*, pp. 115–16.
31   *Léannta*, pp. 29–32; NLI: MS G 1224, MS 24,394 (submissions to Mac Coluim), MS G 1228 (submissions to Ó Cadhlaigh), MS 15,785 (letters from Tomás), MS G 1,020–2 (three boxes of Tomás' documents).

Endnotes

32   *Léannta*, pp. 29–32, 54–5, 75.
33   *Memories*, pp. 78, 89.
34   Royal Irish Academy, MS 4 B 40; Ó Conaire, *Tomás an Bhlascaoid*; Ó
     Coileáin, 'Tomás Ó Criomhthain, Brian Ó Ceallaigh agus An Seabhac',
     p. 234.
35   *Islandman*, p. 241; NLI: MS G 1,022; *Agallamh*, pp. 26, 30–1.
36   *Islandman*, pp. 244–5; *Reflections:* CD1.

Chapter 9. Influential Island Visitors

1   *A Brief Account of the Rise and Progress of the Change in Religious
     Opinion Now Taking Place in Dingle and the West of the County of
     Kerry, Ireland*, p. 54.
2   *Home*, p. 31.
3   *Lives:* Tomás Ó Criomhthain.
4   *Léannta*, p. 28.
5   *Allagar na hInise* (1977), pp. 19–20.
6   *Reflections:* CD1.
7   *Irish Island*, p. 8.
8   *Hidden*, p. 115.
9   *Memories*, pp. 90–1.
10   *Islandman*, pp. 223–4.
11   *Irish Island*, p. 39.
12   *Hidden*, p. 49.
13   *People*, p. 136.
14   *Memories*, p. 92.
15   *Irish Island*, p. 48.
16   *Western*, p. 12.
17   *People*, p. 139.
18   *Islandman*, p. 238.
19   *Western*, p. viii.
20   *Seanchas*, p. xi; *Léannta*, p. 43.
21   *People*, p. 40.
22   *Léannta*, p. 44.
23   *Irish Times*, 12 June 1931, p. 6; *Irish Island*, pp. 191–2, 246.
24   *Irish Island*, p. 224.
25   *Irish Press*, 23 January 1946, p. 4.
26   *Irish Island*, p. 48.
27   *People*, p. 139.
28   *Ibid.*
29   *Islandman*, p. 240.
30   *Memories*, p. 93.

31 *Home*, pp. 119–50.
32 NLI: MS G 1,020; *Islander*, p. 292.
33 Binchy, 'Two Blasket Autobiographies', pp. 546–7, 552.
34 *An Irish Talk – Kerry*, p. ix; *Revue Celtique*, Volume 47, pp. 212–14.
35 *A Galician in Ireland*, p. 31.
36 O'Faolain, *An Irish Journey*, pp. 142–3.

Chapter 10. A Published Author in the Making

1   *Islandman*, p. 239; *People*, pp. 140–2.
2   Mac Conghail, 'Brian Ó Ceallaigh, Tomás Ó Criomhthain and Sir Roger Casement', p. 183; Reid, *The Lives of Roger Casement*, p. 291.
3   NLI: MS G 1,022 & MS 15,785; *Léannta*, pp. 48–9 & 59.
4   *Cross-Talk*, p. 4; *Allagar na hInise* (1977), p. 20.
5   *Sunday Independent*, 14 March 1937, p. 12.
6   *Cross-Talk*, p. 4.
7   *Memories*, p. 116.
8   *Allagar na hInise* (1977), p. ix, 6; *Sunday Independent*, 14 March 1937, p. 12.
9   *Léannta*, pp. 107–8.
10 *Cross-Talk*, p. 2.
11 *Memories*, pp. 113–14.
12 *Léannta*, p. 109.
13 NLI: MS G 1,022; *People*, p. 142; Ó Conaire, *Tomás an Bhlascaoid*, Ó Coileáin, 'Tomás Ó Criomhthain, Brian Ó Ceallaigh agus An Seabhac', p. 244.
14 *Islandman*, pp. 239–40.
15 NLI: MS G 1,022; *People*, p. 142; *Léannta*, p. 109.
16 *Léannta*, pp. 111–12.
17 Ó Conaire, *Tomás an Bhlascaoid*, Ó Coileáin, 'Tomás Ó Criomhthain, Brian Ó Ceallaigh agus An Seabhac', p. 237.
18 *Cross-Talk*, p. 4.
19 NLI: MS G 1,022.
20 NLI: MS G 1,022 and 15,785; Ó Conaire, *Tomás an Bhlascaoid*, Ó Coileáin, 'Tomás Ó Criomhthain, Brian Ó Ceallaigh agus An Seabhac', pp. 235, 248–9.
21 *Sunday Independent*, 14 March 1937, p. 12.
22 *Irish Island*, p. 58.
23 *Memories*, pp. 114–15.
24 *Memories*, p. 113; *Agallamh*, pp. 25–31.
25 NLI: MS G 1,020 (b).
26 *Agallamh*, p. 28.

Endnotes

27 Feiritéar, *Deireadh An Áil*; Ó Conaire, *Tomás an Bhlascaoid*; Ó Coileáin, 'Tomás Ó Criomhthain, Brian Ó Ceallaigh agus An Seabhac', p. 241.

28 *Reflections:* Booklet, p. 38.

29 Mac Conghail, 'Brian Ó Ceallaigh, Tomás Ó Criomhthain and Sir Roger Casement', p. 176.

30 NLI: MS G 1022; Ó Conaire, *Tomás an Bhlascaoid,* Ó Coileáin, 'Tomás Ó Criomhthain, Brian Ó Ceallaigh agus An Seabhac', pp. 258–259.

31 NLI: MS G 1022; Ó Conaire, *Tomás an Bhlascaoid,* Ó Coileáin, 'Tomás Ó Criomhthain, Brian Ó Ceallaigh agus An Seabhac', pp. 247–8.

32 *People*, p. 143.

33 Ó Muircheartaigh, *Oidhreacht an Bhlascaoid,* Mac Conghail, 'Páirtí Thomáis Chriomhthain', p. 165.

34 *Irish Independent*, 31 December 1936, p. 14.

35 *Hidden*, p. 184.

36 *Sunday Independent*, 14 March 1937, p. 12.

37 *Memories*, p. 113.

38 Ó Conaire, *Tomás an Bhlascaoid*, Ó Coileáin, 'Tomás Ó Criomhthain, Brian Ó Ceallaigh agus An Seabhac', p. 235.

39 Ó Muircheartaigh, *Oidhreacht an Bhlascaoid*, Mac Conghail, 'Páirtí Thomáis Chriomhthain', pp. 164–5; *Sunday Independent,* 14 March 1937, p. 12.

40 *Ceiliúradh an Bhlascaoid #2*, Ó Coileáin 'An tOileánach – Ón Láimh go dtí an Leabhar', p. 27.

41 *Ibid.*; Ó Conaire, *Tomás an Bhlascaoid,* Ó Coileáin, 'Tomás Ó Criomhthain, Brian Ó Ceallaigh agus An Seabhac', pp. 254–6; *Ceiliúradh an Bhlascaoid #2*, Ó Coileáin 'An tOileánach – Ón Láimh go dtí an Leabhar', pp. 33, 39, 42; University College Cork: MS U 115, Box 18.

42 *Islander*, p. xix.

43 Stewart, '*An tOileánach* – More or Less', pp. 235, 239–40.

44 *Islandman*, pp. 26.

45 *Islander*, p. 299.

46 Ó Conaire, *Tomás an Bhlascaoid, Iascaire agus Údar,* pp. 203–204; Barrington, 'Telescope and Microscope', 1937, p. 29.

47 *Ceiliúradh an Bhlascaoid #2*, Ó Fiannachta, 'An Spreagadh chun Pinn', p. 86.

48 Ó Conaire, *Tomás an Bhlascaoid*, Ó Conaire, 'An tOileánach I gCló,' p. 270.

49 Sjoestedt, 'Review of Tomás Ó Criomhthain's *An tOileánach* and *Allagar na hInise*'.

50 *Irish Island*, pp. 136, 138–9.

51 Ó Conaire, *Tomás an Bhlascaoid,* An Seabhac, 'Tomás Ó Criomhthain, Iascaire agus Údar,' p. 204.

52 *Cross-Talk*, pp. 4–5.

53 *Islandman*, p. 244.

54 Ó Coiléain, 'An Seabhac agus Scríbhneoirí an Bhlascaoid', p. 97.

Chapter 11. A Literary Outpouring

1 *Béaloideas:* 'Tuirse na nGaibhne', edited by An Seabhac, (Volume 1, June 1927, pp. 80–2), 'Sgéalta O'n Mblascaod', edited by Robin Flower, (Volume 2, Number 1, 1929), 'Measgra Ón Oileán Tiar', edited by Flower, Robin, and Séamus Ó Duilearga, (Volume 25, Number 71, 1957, pp. 46–107).

2 Ó Conaire, *Tomás an Bhlascaoid*; Ó Coiléain, 'Tomás Ó Criomhthain, Brian Ó Ceallaigh agus An Seabhac', p. 240.

3 *Ibid.*, p. 243.

4 The Great Blasket Island population in various years: 176 (1916); 143 (1926); 110 (1936); and 45 (1946) as per *People*, pp. 34–5, *Next Parish*, pp. 48–50; *Community*, pp. 353–4.

5 *Sunday Independent*, 14 March 1937, p. 12; *Allagar na hInise* (1977), p. x.

6 *Lives*: Tomás Ó Criomhthain.

7 *Reflections*, Booklet, pp. 38–39.

8 *Day*, p. 4.

9 Foster, 'Waking the Dead: The Islandman and the Irish Revival', p. 50.

10 Ní Shéaghdha, *Thar Bealach Isteach*; *Léannta*, p. 116.

11 *Letters*, pp. 26–7.

12 An Seabhac Archives, Kerry County Library, Tralee; Fionán Mc Coluim Archives, National Folklore Collection, University College Dublin; Ó Conaire, *Tomás an Bhlascaoid*; Ó Coiléain, 'Tomás Ó Criomhthain, Brian Ó Ceallaigh agus An Seabhac', pp. 255–9.

13 Cronin *et al.*, *Anáil an Bhéil Bheo*, pp. 241–54. John Eastlake provides an extensive analysis of the publication history of *An tOileánach* in 'The (Original) Islandman?: Examining the Origin in Blasket Autobiography' in Cronin *et al.*, *Anáil an Bhéil Bheo*.

14 *Irish Times*, 14 February 2015, p. 47 and accompanying online article, Royal Irish Academy, *Dictionary of Irish Biography*.

15 Ó Muircheartaigh, *Oidhreacht an Bhlascaoid*, Ó Conaire, 'Foilsiú An tOileánach', pp. 190.

16 *Ibid.*

17 Ó Conaire, *Tomás an Bhlascaoid*, Ó Conaire, 'An tOileánach I gCló', p. 276.

Endnotes

18 *Dinnseanchas na mBlascaodaí* (1935), Introduction.
19 *Dinnseanchas na mBlascaodaí* (1999), pp. xi–xiii.
20 NLI: MS 11,000; *Léannta*, p. 101.
21 Mac Neil, 'Seanchas ón Oileán Tiar', p. 169.
22 *Bloghanna ón mBlascaod*, p. xi.
23 *Allagar II, Focal Beag ón Eagarthóir.*
24 Background information on *Cleití Gé ón mBlascaod Mór* provided by Tomás' grandson-in-law, Mícheál Ó Conaill, Killorglin.
25 *Scéilíní ón mBlascaod*, p. 13.

Chapter 12. The Passing of the Islandman

1 *Islandman*, pp. 240, 244.
2 *Home*, p. 61.
3 *Islandman*, p. 215.
4 *Léannta*, p. 19.
5 *An tOileán a Bhí*, p. 59.
6 From a collection of 335 typewritten versions of letters from Eibhlís and Seán to George Chambers at 64 Temple Fortune Way, London, courtesy of Tomás' granddaughter Cáit (Ní Chriomhthain) Uí Chonaill, Killorglin.
7 Letters from Tomás to his son Thomas in Springfield, 15 November 1931 and 3 January 1932, Blasket Centre, Dunquin.
8 *Agallamh*, p. 33.
9 *Letters*, p. 28.
10 Letters from Tomás to the Department of Education, 5 March and 4 June 1934; *Primary Education*, 126–9.
11 Feiritéar, *Deireadh An Áil.*
12 An Seabhac Archives, Kerry County Library, Tralee; Ó Conaire, *Tomás an Bhlascaoid*, Ó Coileáin, 'Tomás an Bhlascaoid, Tomás Ó Criomhthain, Brian Ó Ceallaigh agus An Seabhac', pp. 259–60.
13 *An Caomhnóir*, 1977, 'The Passing of the Islandman', p. 7.
14 *Ibid.*
15 An Seabhac Archives, Kerry County Library, Tralee; Ó Conaire, *Tomás an Bhlascaoid*; Ó Coileáin, 'Tomás Ó Criomhthain, Brian Ó Ceallaigh agus An Seabhac', p. 260.
16 Feiritéar, *Deireadh An Áil.*
17 State Records, Dingle Registration Area, Health Service Executive, Death Certificate, 30 May 1997.
18 Feiritéar, *Deireadh An Áil.*
19 *An Caomhnóir*, 1977, O'Shea, 'The Passing of the Islandman', p. 7.
20 *Irish Times*, 10 March 1937, p. 8.

21   *Irish Press*, 11 March 1937, p. 9.
22   *Irish Independent*, 12 March 1937, p. 10.
23   *The Kerryman*, 20 March 1937, p. 1.
24   *Western*, p. viii.
25   *Ceiliúradh an Bhlascaoid #2*, (Ní Chriomhthain) Uí Laoithe, 'Ag Uaigh Thomáis Uí Chriomhthain,' pp. 137–140.
26   *Ibid.*, p. 140.
27   *Cross-Talk*, pp. 8–9.

Chapter 13. The Islandman's Descendants

1   *Islandman*, p. 240.
2   *Irish Times*, 24 September 2015.
3   *Islandman*, p. 240.
4   US Passport Application, Thomas T. Crohan, 8 May 1920.
5   Letter from Tomás to his son Thomas in Springfield, Blasket Centre, Dunquin, 15 November 1931.
6   Letter from Tomás to his son Thomas in Springfield, Blasket Centre, Dunquin, 3 January 1932.
7   This book part of Tomás' granddaughter Catherine Crohan's estate and was donated to the Blasket Centre in 1993.
8   *Islandman*, p. 218.
9   *Ibid.*, pp. 238–9.
10   *Memories*, p. 111; Ó Conaire, *Tomás an Bhlascaoid, Ó Criomhthain*, Seán, 'Tomás Ó Criomhthain,' p. 144.
11   *Agallamh*, p. 33.
12   *Lives:* Seán Ó Criomhthain.
13   *Letters*, p. 20.
14   *Ibid.*, p. 24.
15   *Letters*, pp. 57–8; *Memories*, p. 78.
16   *Day*, p. 28.
17   *Ibid.*, p. 14.
18   *Irish Examiner*, 26 March 1959, p. 6.
19   *Irish Times*, 10 December 1975, p. 14.
20   *The Kerryman*, 3 March 2011, p. 8.

Chapter 14. Literary Fame and Criticism

1   *Irish Times*, 3 January 1957.
2   *The Kerryman*, 13 October 1934, p. 25.
3   Inscription from Tomás to his son Thomas in Springfield, 16 September 1929, the Blasket Centre, Dunquin.

Endnotes

4   *Agallamh*, p. 31.
5   *The Blaskets*, p. 35.
6   *Islandman*, p. 242.
7   *Community*, p. 250.
8   *Islandman*, p. 198.
9   *Dark Day*, p. 163.
10 *Lives:* Tomás Ó Criomhthain and Seán Eoghain Ó Duinnshléibhe.
11 *Allagar na hInise* (1977), p. 91.
12 *Day*, p. 23.
13 *Tourism*, pp. 162–4.
14 *Islandman*, p. vii.
15 *Cross-Talk*, pp. 1–2, 5.
16 *Irish Island*, p. 131 (Ó Coileáin, Cork, interview).
17 *Hidden*, pp. 13, 15–19.
18 Mac Cárthaigh, '"The Road under the Sea"', p. 82; *Irish Independent* 15 June 1926, p. 4.
19 Noonan, *Biography and Autobiography: Essays on Irish and Canadian History and Literature,* Ó Háinle, 'Deformation of History in Blasket Autobiographies,' pp. 139–41.
20 Ó Coileáin, Cork, interview.
21 *People*, p. 146.
22 Ó Conaire, *Tomás an Bhlascaoid*, Ua Maoileoin, 'An Criomhthánach,' p. 156.
23 *Reflections*, Booklet, pp. 38–9; *Islandman Translated*, p. 191.
24 *Islandman*, pp. 68, 91, 186, 217.
25 *Western*, p. viii.
26 *Islandman*, p. ix.
27 *Ibid.*, pp. v–viii.
28 *Home*, pp. 57–58, 61, 65.
29 Barrington, 'Telescope and Microscope', p. 116, O'Leary, *Gaelic Prose in the Irish Free State*, p. 141.
30 *Irish Times*, 19 December 1956, p. 5.
31 *Reflections:* CD1.
32 *Reflections:* Booklet, p. 38, CD1.
33 Shea, 'Literary Craftsmanship in Tomás O'Crohan's *The Islandman*', pp. 1–2.
34 *Irish Times*, 19 December 1956, p. 5.
35 *Irish Times*, 14 February 2015, p. 47 and accompanying online article, Royal Irish Academy, *Dictionary of Irish Biography*.
36 *Sunday Independent,* 14 October 1934, p. 9.
37 *Comhar*, Ómós do Thomás Ó Chriomhthain (2), April 1977, p. 20.
38 *Reflections:* CD1.

39 *Irish Times*, 24 January 1930, p. 3.

40 *Irish Independent*, 7 November 1934, p. 10.

41 *Irish Press*, 9 October 1934, p. 6.

42 Binchy, 'Two Blasket Autobiographies', p. 548.

43 Barrington, 'Telescope and Microscope', p. 116.

44 *The Leader*, 20 March 1937.

45 Jordan, *The Pleasures of Gaelic Literature*, Cruise O'Brien, '*An tOileánach*', p. 26.

46 *Irish Independent*, 4 April 1933.

47 *Catholic Bulletin and Book Review*, January 1934, p. 55

48 Quigley, 'Modernity's Edge', pp. 382–406.

49 *Irish Times*, 3 January 1957, p. 6.

50 Binchy, 'Two Blasket Autobiographies', p. 549.

51 *Islandman*, p. x.

52 *Ibid.*, pp. x–xi.

53 *Sunday Independent*, 14 October 1934, p. 9.

54 *Irish Press*, 9 October 1934, p. 6.

55 Kiberd, *Irish Classics*, p. 529; *Irish Times*, 4 November 2000, p. 11.

56 McGahern, 'An tOileánach/The Islandman', p. 7.

57 *The Kerryman*, 13 October 1934, p. 25.

58 *Irish Times*, 19 December 1956, p. 5.

59 *Ibid.*, 3 January 1957, p. 6.

60 *Reflections:* CD1.

61 Ross, 'Blasket Island Autobiographies', p. 117.

62 *Irish Examiner*, 4 April 1986, p. 12.

63 *Home*, pp. 70–1.

64 Thomson, *Marxism and Poetry*, pp. 38–9.

65 Luce, 'Homeric Qualities in the Life and Literature of the Great Blasket Island', p. 154.

66 *Day*, p. 13; *Cross-Talk*, p. 1; *Iliad*, vi. 448; *Aeneid*, ii. 324–6.

67 Kiberd, *Irish Classics*, p. 522.

68 *Sunday Independent*, 14 March 1937, p. 12.

69 *Cross-Talk*, p. 3; *Allagar na hInise* (1977), p. x.

70 Binchy, 'Two Blasket Autobiographies', pp. 552, 560.

71 *Irish Times*, 3 January 1957, p. 6, 24 January 1951, p. 4, 17 January 1955, p. 6 (all from O'Nolan's occasional column 'Cruiskeen Lawn').

72 *Ibid.*, 4 January 2003, p. 39.

73 *Hidden*, p. 22.

74 Rafoidi and Harmon, *The Irish Novel in Our Time*, p. 38.

75 *Irish Times*, 14 February 2015, p. 47.

Endnotes

Chapter 15. The Legacy of the Blasket Islandman

1 *Islandman*, p. v.
2 *Western*, p. 14.
3 *Memories*, p. 116.
4 *The Star*, 24 August 1929, p. 1.
5 Foster, 'Waking the Dead: The Islandman and the Irish Revival', p. 52.
6 *Home,* p. 56.
7 RTÉ Archives, Address by Éamon de Valera, 17 March 1943.
8 Ó Coileáin, Cork, interview.
9 Census of Ireland, 1901, 1911; *Community*, p. 348.
10 *Irish Press*, 2 November 1957, p. 6.
11 *An tOileánach* (2002), p. 328.
12 *Islandman*, p. 244.

Other Sources and Further Reading

Other Sources:

The following are additional sources of information listed by chapter.

Chapter 1. Tomás Ó Criomhthain: The Blasket Islandman

de Mórdha, Mícheál, *An Island Community – The Ebb and Flow of The Great Blasket Island*, trs. from Irish by Gabriel Fitzmaurice (Liberties Press, Dublin, 2015) (also Chapters 2–4 and 6–9)

Ó Conaire, Breandán (ed.), *Nua Aois,* University College Dublin, 1970 (also Chapters 5, 8 and 11)

Chapter 2. A Blasket Homeland

Biuso, Thomas, *Blascaodaigh i Meiriceá – Blasket Islanders in America*, Fundúireacht an Bhlascaoid, Dingle, 1989

Carney, Michael with Hayes, Gerald, *From the Great Blasket to America – The Last Memoir by an Islander* (The Collins Press, Cork, 2013) (also Chapter 7)

Hayes, Gerald, with Kane, Eliza, *The Last Blasket King, Pádraig Ó Catháin, An Rí* (The Collins Press, Cork, 2015)

Lucchitti, Irene, *The Islandman – The Hidden Life of Tomás O'Crohan* (Peter Lang AG, Bern, Switzerland, 2009) (also Chapters 7–10 and 14)

Mac Cóil, Liam and Ó hUiginn, Ruairí (eds), *Bliainiris* 7 MacConghail, 'Scoil an Mhisiúin san Oileán Tiar' (Carbad, Ráth Chairn, County Meath, 2007)

Mac Conghail, Muiris, *The Blaskets – People and Literature – A Kerry Island Library* (Town House, Dublin, 1998) (also Chapters 3-4 and 8-10)

Ní Shúilleabháin, Eibhlís, *Letters from the Great Blasket* (Mercier Press, Cork, and Irish American Book Company, Boulder, CO, 2008) (also Chapters 11–13)

Other Sources and Further Reading

Nic Craith, Máiréad, 'Primary Education on The Great Blasket Island: 1864–1840', *Journal of the Kerry Archeological and Historical Society*, Volume 28, 1999 (also Chapters 4, 8 and 12–13)

Ó Cochláin, Pádraig and Ó Gallchóir, Andrias, *Report to the Minister for Lands*, 22 December 1948

O'Crohan, Seán trs. Tim Enright, *A Day in Our Life – The Last of the Blasket Islanders* (Oxford University Press, Oxford, 1993) (also Chapters 7 and 13)

O'Crohan, Tomás, trs. Robin Flower, *The Islandman* (Talbot Press, London, and Chatto & Windus, Dublin, 1934; Penguin Books, London, 1943; Oxford University Press, Oxford, 1951) (also Chapters 3, 7 and 9-10)

Ó Maoileoin, Pádraig, *The Blaskets* (Office of Public Works, Stationery Office, Dublin, undated) (also Chapters 7 and 10)

Ó Súilleabháin, Muiris, trs. Moya Llewelyn Davies and George Thomson, *Twenty Years A-Growing* (J.S. Sanders & Co., Nashville, TN, 1998)

Póirtéir, Cathal (producer), *Blasket Island Reflections*, RTÉ Radio Documentary, Compact Disks and Booklet, Dublin, 2003 (also Chapters 5, 8-9, 11 and 14)

Stagles, Ray and Stagles, Joan, *The Blasket Islands – Next Parish America* (O'Brien Press, Dublin, 1998) (also Chapters 3, 5 and 7)

Thomson, George, *Island Home – The Blasket Heritage* (Brandon, Dingle, 1998) (also Chapter 7)

Transcripts of the Proceedings of Dáil Éireann, Houses of the Oireachtas, Volume 104, 25 February 1947 and 12 March 1947, Dublin

Tyers, Pádraig, *Blasket Memories, The Life of an Irish Island Community* (Mercier Press, Cork, 1998) (also Chapters 4–5, 7–10 and 12–13)

'View from the Pier, Ireland Peer to Pier' – Interview with Dáithí de Mórdha, 2013, www.viewfromthepier.com/2013/09/04/daithi-de-mordha_-archivist_great-blasket-centre

Wartime Research Group of Ireland, *Wartime Aircraft Crashes in County Kerry: 1939–1945*, http://homepage.eircom.net/~wrgi/tableker.html

WorldCat, www.worldcat.org/ (also Chapter 11)

Chapter 3. The Ó Criomhthain Family

Ballyferriter Parish Register (also Chapters 5 and 13)

City Directories: Hartford, Connecticut (1914), Holyoke, Massachusetts (1869, 1897), New Britain, Connecticut (1913)

City of Springfield, Massachusetts, Registries of Births and Deaths

de Mórdha, Dáithí, interview (also Chapter 5)

Griffith's Valuation Survey, County Kerry, The Great Blasket Island: 1847–1864, National Archives of Ireland

Matson, Leslie, *Blasket Lives: Biographical Accounts of 125 Blasket People*, Unpublished research, Blasket Centre, Dunquin, 2005: Tomás 'Maol' Ó Ceárna, Eibhlín (Ní Ghuithín) Uí Ceárna, Tomás Ó Criomhthain, Máire (Ní Chatháin) Uí Chriomhthain, Seán Eoghain Ó Duinnshléibhe, Máire (Ní Shé) Uí Duinnshléibhe, Cáit (Ní Chriomhthain) Uí Ghuithín, Máire (Ní Chriomhthain) Uí Shúilleabháin (and various other chapters)

Magee, Betty Shea of Windsor, Connecticut (descendent of Diarmid 'The Rake' Ó Se), interview

Massachusetts State Vital Records Registry (also Chapter 13)

Matson, Leslie, *Méiní, The Blasket Nurse* (Mercier Press, Cork, 1996) (also Chapters 5–8)

Ó Coileáin, Seán, 'An Seabhac agus Scríbhneoirí an Bhlascaoid', *Béaloideas* (the journal of the Folklore of Ireland Society), 2015 (also Chapter 10)

Ó Conaire, Breandán (ed.), *Tomás an Bhlascaoid,* Ó Conaire, 'Nótaí Cúlra', Ó Criomhthain, Seán, 'Tomás Ó Criomhthain', Ua Maoileoin, 'An Criomhthánach' (Clo Iar-Chonnacht, Indreabhán, Conamara, 1992) (also Chapters 5–7 and 11)

Ó Conaire, Breandán, 'Tomás an Bhlascaoid, Nótaí Cúlra' 1 and 2, *Comhar*, August and September, 1977

Ó Crohan, Tomás, trs. Garry Bannister and David Sowby, *The Islander* (Gill & Macmillan, Dublin, 2012) (also Chapters 9–10)

Ó Criomhthain, Tomás and Flower, Robin, ed. Séamus Ó Duilearga, *Seanchas ón Oileán Tiar* (Comhlucht Oideachais na h-Éireann, Baile Átha Cliath, 1956) (also Chapters 7, 9 and 14)

Ó Muircheartaigh, Aogán (ed.), *Oidhreacht an Bhlascaoid,* Ó Coileáin, 'An tOileánach' (Coiscéim, Baile Átha Cliath, 1989)

Register of the Blasket National School, National Archives of Ireland (also Chapters 5-6 and 13)

Ship's Manifests: SS *City of Boston*; SS *England;* SS *Pennsylvania*; SS *Scythia*; SS *Cymric*; SS *Celtic*; HMS *Baltic* (also Chapter 13)

State Records, Dingle, Volume 5

Chapter 4. Coming of Age on the Great Blasket

History of the Roman Catholic Diocese of Kerry, www.dioceseofkerry.ie

Lives: Pádraig Peats Mhicí Ó Catháin

Nic Craith, Máiréad, *An tOileánach Léannta* (An Clóchomhar, Baile Átha Cliath, 1988) (also Chapters 8–11)

Ó Catháin, Gearóid Cheaist with Ahern, Patricia, *The Loneliest Boy in the World – The Last Child of the Great Blasket Island* (The Collins Press, Cork, 2014)

Ó Conaire, Breandán, Dublin, interview

Other Sources and Further Reading

O'Donnell, Kelly Frances, "'The Like of Us Will Never Be Again": A Comparative Analysis of the Contributions of the Blasket Authors: Peig Sayers, Tomás Ó Criomhthain, and Muiris Ó Súilleabháin', University of Connecticut, Honors Scholar Thesis, 2011 (also Chapter 7)

Ó Muircheartaigh, Aogán (ed.), *Oidhreacht an Bhlascaoid*, Ó Mainín, 'Scoileanna an Oileáin'

Chapter 5. Marriage and Family

Birth Registry, District of Ventry (also Chapter 13)

Ní Chéilleachair, Máire (ed.), *Ceiliúradh an Bhlascaoid #2: Tomás Ó Criomhthain – 1855–1937,* Ó Coileáin, 'An tOileánach – Ón Láimh go dtí an Leabhar' (An Sagart, An Daingean, 1998) (also Chapter 10)

Ó Criomhthain, Tomás, ed. Pádraig Ua Maoileoin, *Allagar na hInise* (Oifig an tSolathair, An Gúm, Baile Átha Cliath, 1977)

O'Crohan, Tomás, trs. Tim Enright, *Island Cross-Talk, Pages from a Blasket Island Diary* (Oxford University Press, Oxford, 1986) (also Chapter 15)

Ó Conaire, Breandán (ed.), *Tomás an Bhlascaoid,* An Seabhac, 'Tomás Ó Criomhthain, Iascaire agus Údar', Ó Criomhthain, Seán, 'Tomás Ó Criomhthain' (also Chapter 10)

Ó Dubhshláine, Mícheál, *Inis Mhic Uibhleáin* (Brandon, Dingle, 2009)

Office of Public Works, *Archeological Assessment and Instrument Survey on the Great Blasket Island, Co. Kerry*, Aegis, Dublin, 2010

Chapter 6. Tragedy Stalks the Ó Criomhthain Family

Birth Registry, Dingle Union.

Foster, John Wilson, *Between Shadows: Modern Irish Writing and Culture* (Irish Academic Press, Dublin, 2009)

Irish Independent, 'The Girl Who Was Loved by Pearse', 21 May 1974

Lives: Cáit (Ní Chatháin) Uí Chathasa, Domhnall Ó Criomhthain, Cáit (Ní Chriomhthain) Ua Mhaoileoin

Carney, Michael, Springfield, Massachusetts, interview (also Chapter 12)

Ó Dubhshláine, Mícheál, *A Dark Day on the Blaskets* (Brandon, Dingle, 2003) (also Chapter 7)

Chapter 7. A Blasket Life

Flower, Robin, *The Western Island – The Great Blasket* (Oxford University Press, Oxford, 2000)

Foley, Foley, Patrick, *The Ancient and Present State of the Skelligs, Blasket Islands, Donquin and the West of Dingle* (Cló-Chumann, Dublin, 1903)

Irish Wrecks Online (website): County Kerry, www.irishwrecksonline.et/Lists/KerryListA.htm

Irisleabhar Mhá Nuad, 2001

Keane, Pádraic, Sligo, interview

Ó Criomhthain, Tomás, ed. Breandán Ó Conaire, *Bloghanna ón mBlascaod* (An Chéad Chló, Baile Átha Cliath, 1997) (also Chapter 10)

Ó Criomhthain, Tomás, ed. Caoilfhionn Nic Pháidín, *Dinnseanchas na mBlascaodaí* (Cois Life, Baile Átha Cliath, 1999)

Ó Muircheartaigh, Aogán (ed.), *Oidhreacht an Bhlascaoid*, Ua Maoileoin, 'Allagar an Chriomhthanaigh', Ó Háinle, 'Peig, Aonghus Ó Dálaigh agus Macbeth' (also Chapter 12)

Chapter 8. Inspiration, Irish Literacy and Early Writing

Eastlake, John, 'Orality and Agency: Reading an Irish Autobiography from the Great Blasket Island', *Oral Traditions*, Volume 24, Number 1, 2009 (also Chapters 9 and 14)

Kanigel, Robert, *On an Irish Island* (Alfred A. Knopf, New York, 2012) (also Chapters 9-11 and 14)

Ní Chéilleachair, Máire (ed.), *Ceiliúradh an Bhlascaoid #2; Tomás Ó Criomhthain – 1855–1937,* Ó Conaill, 'Cébh É Tomás Ó Criomhthain?' (An Sagart, An Daingean, 1998) (also Chapter 10)

Ó Conaire, Breandán (ed.), *Tomás an Bhlascaoid*, Ó Coileáin, 'Tomás Ó Criomhthain, Brian Ó Ceallaigh agus An Seabhac' (also Chapters 9–10)

O'Leary, Philip, *Gaelic Prose in the Irish Free State: 1922–1939* (Pennsylvania State University Press, University Park, PA, 2004) (also Chapter 14)

Shea, Thomas F., 'The Islander: A More Provocative Tomás O'Crohan', *New Hibernia Review*, Volume 18, Number 3, 2014

Chapter 9. Influential Island Visitors

Chambers, George, *The Lovely Line and Other Verses* (Oyster Press, Colchester, UK, 1950)

de Mórdha, Mícheál (ed.), *Ceiliúradh an Bhlascaoid #14: John Millington Synge* (Coiscéim, Baile Átha Cliath, 2012)

Flower, Robin, *The Irish Tradition* (Lilliput Press, Dublin, 1994)

Moreton, Cole, *Hungry for Home – Leaving the Blaskets: A Journey from the Edge of Ireland* (Penguin Group, New York, 2000)

Ó Conaill, Mícheál, Killorglin interview

Ó Conaire, Dublin, interview

Ó Lúing, Seán, 'Carl Marstrander (1883–1965)', *Journal of the Cork Historical and Archeological Society*, Volume LXXXIX, Number 248, Cork, January–December 1984

Chapter 10. A Published Author in the Making

Ó Criomhthain, Tomás, ed. Pádraig Ó Siochfhradha, *An tOileánach* (Mhuinntir C.S Ó Fallamhain and Oifig an tSoláthair, Baile Átha Cliath, 1929)

Harrison, Alan, 'Blasket Literature', *Irish University Review*, Volume 31, Number 2, 2001

Mac Conghail, Muiris, 'Brian Ó Ceallaigh, Tomás Ó Criomhthain and Sir Roger Casement', *Journal of the Kerry Archeological and Historical Society*, Volume 23, 1993

Ó Conaire, *Tomás an Bhlascaoid*, Ó Conaire, 'An tOileánach I gCló' (also Chapter 11)

Ó Muircheartaigh, *Oidhreacht an Bhlascaoid*, Mac Conghail, 'Páirtí Thomáis Chriomhthain', Ó Conaire, 'Foilsiú An tOileánach' (also Chapter 11)

Ó Coileáin, Seán, Cork, interview

Reid, B.L., *The Lives of Roger Casement* (Yale University Press, New Haven, CT, 1976)

Robin Flower Papers, National Folklore Collection, University College Dublin.

Ross, Ciaran, 'Blasket Island Autobiographies: The Myth and Mystique of the Untranslated and Untranslatable', *Translation and Literature*, Volume 12, Number 1, Spring 2003

Chapter 11. A Literary Outpouring

Foster, John Wilson, *The Cambridge Companion to the Irish Novel* (Cambridge University Press, Cambridge, 2006)

Chapter 12. The Passing of the Islandman

O'Shea, 'The Passing of the Islandman', *An Caomhnóir*, Fundúireacht an Bhlascaoid, 2012

Ó Conaire, *Tomás an Bhlascaoid*, Feirtéar, 'Sochraid Thomáis Uí Chriomhthain'

Ní Chéilleachair, Máire (ed.), *Ceiliúradh an Bhlascaoid #2; Tomás Ó Criomhthain – 1855–1937*, (Ní Chríomhthain) Uí Laoithe, 'Ag Uaigh Thomáis Uí Chriomhthain' (An Sagart, An Daingean, 1998) (also Chapter 10)

Feiritéar, Breandán, producer, *Deireadh An Áil: The Last of the Brood – The Last of the Blasket Islanders* (RTÉ, 1966) (also Chapter 13 and 15)

Breathnach, Pádraig, Cáit (Ní Chríomhthain) Uí Mhaoileoin's grandson, Carrickmacross, interview

Chapter 13. The Islandman's Descendants

Ashe, Barbara Carney, Longmeadow, Massachusetts, interview

Breathnach, Pádraig, *The Girl who Didn't Drown – A Biographical Profile of Cáit (Ní Criomhthain) Uí Mhaoileoin,* Unpublished, 2015

Cronin, Michael and O'Connor, Barbara (eds), *Irish Tourism – Image, Culture and Identity* (Channel View Publications, Clevedon, UK, 2003) (also Chapter 14)

City Directory: Springfield, Massachusetts, 1940

Foley, Mary, Springfield, Massachusetts, interview

Lives: Seán Ó Criomhthain, Eibhlís' 'Lis' (Ní Shúilleabháin) Uí Chriomhthain

Millman, Lawrence, *Our Like Will Not be There Again: Notes from the West of Ireland* (M. Evans & Co., Lanham, MD, 2015)

Springfield Union, 24 May 1917, 5 July 1954, 10 January 1956, 20 April 1966

Springfield Union-News, 3 September 1999

Uí Chonaill, Cáit (Ní Chriomhthain), Killorglin, interview

Uí Laoithe, Niamh (Ní Chriomhthain), Dingle, interview

US Army Enlistment Records, Thomas T. Crohan, 20 April 1942

Chapter 14. Literary Fame and Criticism

Foster, John Wilson, 'Waking the Dead: The Islandman and the Irish Revival', *Irish Renaissance Annual*, Spring 1982

Ó Conaire, Breandán, *Myles na Gaeilge – Lámhleabhar ar Shaothar Gaeilge Bhrian Ó Nualláin* (An Clóchomhar, Baile Átha Cliath, 1986)

Quigley, Mark, 'Modernity's Edge: Speaking Silence on the Blasket Islands', *Interventions*, Volume 5, Number 3, 2003

Chapter 15. The Legacy of the Blasket Islandman

Department of Posts and Telegraphs, Dublin, 'New Commemorative Issues,' February 1957

Tomás Ó Criomhthain Memorial Solicitation, An Seabhac, Chairman, December 1956

Further Reading

Books

Castro del Rio, Plácido Ramón, *A Galician in Ireland* (Fundación Plácido Castro, Pontevedra, Spain, 2003)

Céitinn, Seosamh, *Tomás Oileánach* (An Clóchomhar, Baile Átha Cliath, 1992)

Other Sources and Further Reading

Coohill, Joseph, *Ireland: A Short History* (3rd edn) (Oneworld Publications, London, 2013)

Cronin, Nessa, Crosson, Seán and Eastlake, John (eds), *Anáil an Bhéil Bheo: Orality and Modern Irish Culture* (Cambridge Scholars Publishing, Cambridge, 2009)

de Mórdha, Dáithí and de Mórdha, Mícheál, with Ciarán Walsh, *The Great Blasket, A Photographic Portrait* (The Collins Press, Cork, 2013)

de Mórdha, Mícheál, *Scéal agus Dán Oileáin* (Coiscéim, Baile Átha Cliath, 2012)

Fennelly, Anita, *Blasket Spirit – Stories from the Islands* (The Collins Press, Cork, 2009)

Glassie, Henry, *Irish Folktales*: Ó Criomhthain, Tomás and Flower, Robin, 'No Man Goes Beyond his Day' (Pantheon Books, New York, 1985)

Gorky, Maxim, trs. Ronald Wilkes, *My Childhood* (Penguin, London, 1913)

Hamsun, Knut, trs. W.W. Worster, *The Growth of the Soil* (Random House, New York, 1917)

Jordan, John (ed.), *The Pleasures of Gaelic Literature* (Mercier Press, Cork, with RTÉ, Dublin, 1977)

Kiberd, Declan, *Inventing Ireland: The Literature of the Modern Nation* (Harvard University Press, Cambridge, MA, 1997)

Kiberd, Declan, *Irish Classics* (Harvard University Press, Cambridge, MA, 2000)

Kiberd, Declan and Matthews, P.J., *Handbook of the Irish Revival – An Anthology of Irish Cultural and Political Writings 1891–1922* (Abbey Theatre Press, Dublin, 2015)

Kurzman, Dan, *Left to Die – The Tragedy of the USS Juneau* (Pocket Books, New York, 1994)

Londe, Greg and Fox, Renee (eds), *The Cracked Lookingglass* (Princeton University Library, Princeton, NJ, 2011)

Loti, Pierre, as translated from French, *An Iceland Fisherman* (CreateSpace Independent Publishing Platform, 2014)

Mac Clúin, Seóirse, *Réilthíní Óir* (Comhlucht Oideachais na h-Éireann, Dublin, 1922)

McCourt, Malachy, *History of Ireland* (Running Press, Philadelphia, 2004)

Mason, Thomas H., *The Islands of Ireland, Their Scenery, People, Life and Antiquities* (Mercier Press, Cork, 1967)

Ní Ghaoithín, Máire, *An tOileán a Bhí* (An Clóchomhar, Baile Átha Cliath, 1978)

Ní Ghuithín, Máire, *Bean an Oileáin* (Coiscéim, Baile Átha Cliath, 1986)

Ní Shéaghdha, Nóra, *Thar Bealach Isteach* (Oifig an tSolathair, Dublin, 1940)

Noonan, James (ed.), *Biography and Autobiography: Essays on Irish and Canadian History and Literature* (Carleton University Press, Ottawa, Canada, 1993)

Ó Cadhain, Máirtín, trs. Liam Mac Con Iomaire and Tim Robinson, *Graveyard Clay – Cré na Cille* (Yale University Press, New Haven, CT, 2016)

Ó Catháin, Muiris, *Ar Muir is ar Tír – On Land and Sea* (An Sagart, An Daingean, 2010)

Ó Ceárna, Seán Pheats Tom, *Fiolar an Eireaball Bháin* (Coiscéim, Baile Átha Cliath, 1992)

Ó Criomhthain, Tomás, *Allagar na hInise*, original manuscript (National Library of Ireland: MS G 1,022, Dublin)

Ó Criomhthain, Tomás, ed. Pádraig Ó Siochfhradha, *Allagar na hInise* (Mhuinntir C.S Ó Fallamhain and Oifig an tSolathair, Baile Átha Cliath, 1928)

Ó Criomhthain, Tomás, ed. Pádraig Ua Maoileoin, *Allagar II* (Coiscéim, Baile Átha Cliath, 1999)

Ó Criomhthain, Tomás, *An tOileánach*, original manuscript (National Library of Ireland: MS G 1,020 (b) – Dublin)

Ó Criomhthain, Tomás, ed. Pádraig Ua Maoileoin, *An tOileánach* (Cló Talbóid, Baile Átha Cliath, 1973)

Ó Criomhthain, Tomás, ed. Seán Ó Coileáin, *An tOileánach* (Cló Talbóid, Baile Átha Cliath, 2002)

Ó Criomhthain, Tomás, ed. Pádraig Ó Siochfhradha, *Dinnseanchas na mBlascaodaí* (Oifig Díolta Foillseacáin Rialtais, Baile Átha Cliath, 1935)

Ó Criomhthain, Tomás and Seán, ed. Pádraig Ó Fiannachta, *Cleití Gé ón mBlascaod Mór* (An Sagart, An Daingean, 1997)

Ó Criomhthain, Tomás, ed. Nollaig Mac Congáil, *Scéilíní ón mBlascaod agus Blúirín as 'Con Lae Eibhlín Ní Shúilleabháin* (Coiscéim, Baile Átha Cliath, 2004)

Ó Cruadhlaoich, Gearóid, *Oileáin agus Oileánaigh, Iris na hOidhreachta 7* (An Sagart, Dingle, 1995)

O'Dowd, Kate Keane, trs. Tadhg Ó Dúshláine, ed. Tracey Ní Mhaonaigh, Tracey, *The Lone Seagull* (Cuallacht Cholm Cille, National University of Ireland, Maynooth, 2011)

O'Faolain, Sean, *An Irish Journey* (Longmans, Green and Co., London, 1940)

Ó Fiannachta, Pádraig, *Oileáin agus Oileánaigh* (An Sagart, An Daingean, 1995)

Ó Giolláin, Diarmuid, *Locating Irish Folklore: Tradition, Modernity, Identity* (Cork University Press, Cork, 2000)

Other Sources and Further Reading

Ó Grianna, Seamus, ed. Nollaig Mac Congáil, *The Sea's Revenge* & Other Stories (Mercier Press, Cork, 2003)

O'Guiheen, Mícheál, trs. Tim Enright, *A Pity Youth Does Not Last: Reminiscences of the Last Blasket Island Poet* (Oxford University Press, Oxford, 1982)

O'Guiheen, Mícheál, *Diary* (Unpublished, National Library of Ireland MS G 1021 (c), Dublin)

Ó Scannláin, Séamas (ed. and trs.), *Poets and Poetry of the Great Blasket* (Mercier Press, Cork, 2003)

Ó Tuama, Seán, *Repossessions: Selected Essays on the Irish Literary Heritage* (Cork University Press, Cork, 1995)

Rafroidi, Patrick and Harmon, Maurice (eds), *The Irish Novel in Our Time* (Publications de l'Université de Lille III, France, 1976)

Sayers, Peig, trs. Séamus Ennis, *An Old Woman's Reflections, The Life of a Blasket Island Storyteller* (Oxford University Press, Oxford, 2000)

Sayers, Peig, trs. Bryan McMahon, *Peig, The Autobiography of Peig Sayers of the Great Blasket Island* (Syracuse University Press, Syracuse, NY, 1974)

Smith, Charles, *The Ancient and Present State of the County of Kerry* (ECCO Print Editions, Hampshire, United Kingdom, Undated, First Published in 1756)

Smith, Sidonie and Watson, Julia, *Reading Autobiography, A Guide for Interpreting Life Narratives,* University of Minnesota Press, 2010

Stagles, Ray and Redican, Sue, *The Blasket Island Guide* (O'Brien Press, Dublin, 2011)

Stewart, James, *Boccaccio in the Blaskets,* Officina Typographica, Galway, 1988

Synge, John Millington, *In Wicklow and West Kerry* (Dodo Press, Gloucestershire, UK, 1912)

Synge, John Millington, *Playboy of the Western World and Riders to the Sea* (Dover Publications, Inc., New York, 1993)

Thompson, Mrs David Peter, *A Brief Account of the Rise and Progress of the Change in Religious Opinion Now Taking Place in Dingle and the West of the County of Kerry, Ireland* (Seeley, Burnside and Seeley, London, 1846)

Thomson, George, *Marxism and Poetry* (International Publishers Co., New York, 1946)

Tyers, Pádraig (ed.), *Leoithne Aniar* (Cló Dhuibhne, Baile an Fheirtéaraigh, 1982)

Tyers, Pádraig, *West Kerry Camera* (The Collins Press, Cork, 2006)

Ua Laoghaire, Peadar, *Niamh* (Muintir na Leabhar Gaedhilge, Baile Átha Cliath, 1907)

Ua Laoghaire, Peadar, *Scéal Séadna* (Muintir na Leabhar Gaedhilge, Baile Átha Cliath, Dublin, 1904)

Walsh, Clarán and de Mórdha, Dáithí, *The Irish Headhunter, The Photograph Albums of Charles R. Browne* (Stationery Office, Dublin, 2012)

Journals, Periodicals, Theses

Barrington, Thomas, 'Telescope and Microscope', *Bonaventura: A Quarterly Review*, Volume 1, Number 1, Summer 1937

Binchy, Daniel A., 'Two Blasket Autobiographies', *Studies: An Irish Quarterly Review*, Volume 23, Number 92, December 1934

Biuso, Tom, 'Looking into Blasket Island Photographs', *Éire-Ireland: A Journal of Irish Studies*, Volume 19, Number 4, 1984

De Rosa, Roisin, 'The Great Blaskets Betrayal', *An Phoblacht*, 23 September 1999

Fennell, Chris, 'Tradition and Modernity on Great Blasket Island', *Ireland*, University of Illinois at Urbana-Champaign, 2014

Flower, Robin (ed.), 'Measgra ón Oileán Tiar', *Béaloideas* (the Journal of the Folklore of Ireland Society). Volume XXV, 1957

Flower, Robin (ed.), 'Sgéalta ón mBlascaod', *Béaloideas* (the Journal of the Folklore of Ireland Society), Volume II, 1930

Harris, John, 'Orality and Literacy in Tomás Ó Criomhthain's Literary Style', *Canadian Journal of Irish Studies*, Volume 19, Number 2, 1993

Hyde, Douglas, 'The Necessity for De-Anglicizing Ireland', *Language, Lore and Lyrics: Essays and Lectures*, Academic Press, Dublin, 1986

Lucchitti, Irene, 'Islandman Translated: Thomas O'Crohan, Autobiography & the Politics of Culture', University of Wollongong, New South Wales, Australia, 2005

Lucchitti, Irene, 'Tomás O'Crohan's Autobiography: A Cultural Analysis of Robin Flower's English Translation', *Brazilian Journal of Irish Studies*, Special Issue Number 5, June 2003

Luce, J.V., 'Homeric Qualities in the Life and Literature of the Great Blasket Island', *Greece and Rome*, Second Series, Volume 16, Number 2, 1969

Lysaght, Patricia, 'Paradise Lost? Leaving the Great Blasket', Béaloideas (the journal of the Folklore of Ireland Society), Volume 74, 2006

Mac Cárthaigh, Críostóir, '"The Road Under the Sea" – Legend Formation and Development', *Béaloideas* (the journal of the Folklore of Ireland Society), Volume 83, 2015

Mac Cárthaigh, Críostóir, 'Supernatural Maritime Narratives in a West Kerry Fishing Community: Problems of Genre Classification, Context and Interpretation', University College Dublin, 2015

Mac Neil, Máire, 'Seanchas ón Oileán Tiar', *Journal of American Folklore*, Volume 71, Number 280, April–June 1958

Other Sources and Further Reading

Mac Neill, Eoin, 'Thainig Anam I n-Eirinn', *The Star*, 24 August 1929

McGahern, John, '*An tOileánach/The Islandman*', *Canadian Journal of Irish Studies*, Volume 13, Number 1, June 1987; and *Irish Review*, Volume 6, Spring, 1989

Marstrander, Carl, *Impressions from Ireland*, trs. K.H. Moe, Norwegian Geographical Society, Raidió Teilifís Éireann, Dublin, undated

National Geographic Traveller, 'Dingle – Ireland, Country Style', National Geographic Society, Summer 1986

O'Cahill, Donal, 'Goodbye to the Blaskets', *American Mercury*, April 1954

Ó Catháin, Pádraic, 'Tír na nÓg – Land of the Young', *An Caomhnóir*, Fundúireacht an Bhlascaoid, 2012

Ó Ciarghusa, Seán, 'Tomás Ó Criomhthain Obituary', *The Leader: A Review of Current Affairs, Politics, Literature, Art and Industry*, 20 March 1937

Ó Ciosáin, Niall, 'The Blasket Island Literature', *Irish Economic and Social History*, Volume XX, 1993

Ó Conaire, Breandán, 'Flann O'Brien, Myles na gCopaleen and the Irish Cultural Debate', *Studia Hibernica*, Number 35, 2008–2009

Ó Conaire, Breandán, 'Ómós do Tomás Ó Criomhthain, An tOileánach agus na Léirmheastóirí', 1, 2, 3, *Comhar, March, April and June*, 1977

Ó Coileáin, Seán, 'Tomás Ó Criomhthain, Brian Ó Ceallaigh agus An Seabhac', *Scríobh*, Volume 4, ed. Seán Ó Mórdha, 1979

Ó Dhálaigh, Nóra, *Aisling, Whiskey on Water, or Taking a Drop, c.* 1975

Ó Dubhda, Seán, *Cogadh na Talún i gCorca Duibhne*, National Library of Ireland, 1944

Ryan, John J.M., *Irish Rosary*, January 1935

Shea, Thomas F., 'Literary Craftsmanship: Tomás O'Crohan's *The Islandman*', *Irish Studies Working Papers*, Volume 10, Number 4, 2010

Shea, Thomas F., 'Review of *The Islandman: The Hidden Life of Tomás O'Crohan*, by Irene Lucchitti', *Irish Studies Review*, Volume 11, Number 9, 2011

Sjoestedt, Marie Louise, *An Irish Talk – Kerry*, School of Advanced Studies, Ministry of Education, Paris, 1938

Sjoestedt, Marie-Louise, 'Review of Tomás Ó Criomhthain's *An tOileánach* and *Allagar na hInise*', *Revue Celtique*, Volume 47, 1930

Stewart, James, '*An tOileánach* – More or Less', *Zeitschrift für Celtische Philologie*, Volume 25, University of Bonn, 1976

Synge, John Millington, 'In West Kerry: The Blasket Islands', *The Shanachie – An Irish Miscellany Illustrated*, Second Number, Volume 2, 1907

Newspapers and Magazines

An Claidheamh Soluis
Evening Echo

Irish Examiner
Irish Independent
Irish Press
Irish Times
The Kerryman
Kerry Reporter
An Phoblacht
Springfield Republican, *Springfield Union* and *Springfield Daily News*
Time
Sunday Independent

Archives, Websites and Other Sources

An Bunachar Náisiúnta Beathaisnéisí Gaeilge, www.ainm.ie

Blasket Centre Archives, Dunquin, County Kerry

Census of the City of Springfield, Massachusetts

Census of Ireland, 1901 and 1911, National Archives of Ireland, www.census.nationalarchives.ie

Cobh Heritage Centre, *Emigration & Famine,* www.cobhheritage.com

History of the Atlantic Cable & Undersea Communications, www.atlantic-cable.com

Landed Estates Database, National University of Ireland Galway. Estate: Fitzgerald (Knight of Kerry), http://landedestates.nuigalway.ie/LandedEstates

Ó Conaill, Mícheál, *Library of Tomás Ó Criomhthain: An Inventory*, Killorglin, 25 January 2017

Ó Conaire, Breandán, *Dictionary of Irish Biography: Tomás Ó Criomhthain,* 14 February 2015, https://www.ria.ie/news/publications-art-and-architecture-ireland-dictionary-irish-biography/modern-ireland-100-5

RTÉ, *Another Island: A Portrait of the Blasket Islands,* Muiris Mac Conghail, interview with Pádraig Ua Maoileoin, video documentary, Dublin, 1984

Songs in Irish (website), 'Caisleán Uí Néill', http://songsinirish.com/p/caislean-ui-neill-lyrics.html

Stewart, Bruce, *Ricorso, A Knowledge of Irish Literature, 1990–2010*, www.ricorso.net/

United States Census, US Department of Commerce, Washington, DC

Acknowledgements

Writing a biography of this nature requires the collaboration of many people, each with their own critically important contribution. I am deeply grateful for the expert assistance and kind support of a very special group of people who share my passion for the Great Blasket Island.

First and foremost, I am indebted to Niamh (Ní Chriomhthain) Uí Laoithe, Tomás' granddaughter, for permission to use copyrighted material in this work. Likewise, I appreciate the considerable help of her sister Cáit (Ní Chriomhthain) Uí Chonaill and Cáit's husband Micheál Ó Conaill. I will never forget the late afternoon when the four of us gathered for conversation about the island and about Tomás himself. Micheál was especially helpful in tracking down family history details over many months and in carefully reviewing the draft manuscript.

I am also thankful to Pádraig Breathnach, the grandson of Tomás' daughter Cáit (Ní Chriomhthain) Uí Maoileoin, for his extensive contributions to this work. Pádraig graciously shared with me his broad knowledge of the genealogy of the Ó Criomhthain family, suggested new sources of background information and made many cogent comments on multiple drafts. Eileen de Lapp, another descendant of Cáit, also furnished information on the Ó Criomhthain family tree.

Dáithí de Mórdha, formerly the director of the Blasket Centre and now with Raidió na Gaeltachta, played a critical role in researching this book. His knowledge of the Blaskets is encyclopaedic. This book would absolutely not have been possible without his help and guidance. His father, Micheál de Mórdha, the retired director of the Blasket Centre, provided a wealth of in-depth insight and wise counsel. The recently appointed director, Doncha Ó Conchúir, has also been extremely helpful.

My great friend Micheál Ó Cinnéide, originally of Moorestown, West Kerry and currently of Wexford, gave continuous help and encouragement in this undertaking. He also painstakingly reviewed several drafts of the manuscript and helped with translation. Micheál's highly constructive suggestions, including the comparative timetable, were invaluable. His enthusiasm for the project provided steady forward momentum, for which I am very grateful. His brother, Lorcán Ó Cinnéide, provided invaluable feedback and his sister Dairena Ní Chinnéide helped with translation.

I am particularly indebted to Leslie Matson of Waterford for his extensive research into the lives of the people who inhabited the Great Blasket: *Blasket Lives: Biographical Accounts of 125 Blasket People*. This unpublished research was vital in getting to know Tomás, his family and his neighbours. I appreciate his permission to quote from his work.

Three wonderful Blasket descendants in the Springfield, Massachusetts area – Mary Foley, Mairéad Shea, the late Maureen Carney Oski and Barbara Carney Ashe – all shared their memories of the island and their forebears. Mary Foley, in particular, was indispensable in tracking Blasket families in the United States. Betty Shea Magee of Windsor, Connecticut, the great-granddaughter of Diarmuid 'The Rake' Ó Sé, was very helpful in providing information about his life and times. Maurice Brick, originally from Gorta Dubh, West Kerry and now of New Rochelle, New York reviewed the folktale told

Acknowledgements

by Tomás involving his native village and contributed an alternative version.

Four distinguished Blasket scholars generously shared their considerable and detailed knowledge of Tomás and his writing: Seán Ó Coileáin, now retired from University College Cork, Breandán Ó Conaire, now retired from Dublin City University, Máiréad Nic Craith of Heriot-Watt University, Edinburgh, Scotland and Thomas Shea of the University of Connecticut. Their insightful contributions based on their many years of in-depth Blasket research are greatly appreciated.

Special thanks to Críostóir Mac Cárthaigh, Director of the National Folklore Collection, University College Dublin and a Blasket scholar in his own right; James Harte of the Manuscripts Department, National Library of Ireland; Mike Lynch, Archivist at the Kerry County Library in Tralee; and Maggie Humberston, Head of Library and Archives at the Lyman & Merrie Wood Museum of Springfield History in Springfield, Massachusetts. These very capable professionals provided informed guidance on a whole range of resources on the Blaskets, its people and their descendants.

I am also grateful to Oxford University Press, Mercier Press, the National Archives of Ireland, the Blasket Centre and Máiréad Nic Craith for permission to incorporate copyrighted material.

Thanks as well to Anna Ní Choirbín from Corr na Móna, County Galway, a Fulbright Language Teaching Assistant at Elms College in Chicopee, Massachusetts, for her expert work in the translation of multiple source documents from Irish to English.

And finally, I extend my gratitude to my spouse, Maureen Carney Hayes, a second-generation Blasket descendant, for her boundless love and support in this endeavour and in our always exciting life in general.

Photo Credits

Photographs and images incorporated herein are presented courtesy of the following:

An Post: pp. 221, 321
The Blasket Centre: pp. xviii, 2, 22, 26, 29, 60, 69, 96, 100, 109, 120, 126, 134, 148, 181, 182, 198, 237, 251, 261, 263, 264, 266, 278, 292, 317, 323 (2), 325
Board of Trinity College Dublin:
- John Millington Synge Collection: p. 56
- Charles R. Browne Collection: pp. 12, 36
Pádraig Breathnach: p. 268
Central Bank of Ireland: p. 321
Coiscéim: pp. 241, 243, 244
Cois Life: p. 238
Comhlucht Oideachais na Éireann, Tta. (Education Company of Ireland): p. 240
Conradh na Gaeilge: p. 104
Dublin Institute for Advanced Studies: p. 194
Ann Flower: p. 183
Gerald Hayes: p. 318
Michael Hayes, pp. 10, 315
The Kerryman, p. 28
Niamh (Ní Chriomhthain) Uí Laoithe: pp. 256, 282, 320
The Mason Family (photos by Thomas Mason): pp. 189, 287
The MacMonagle Archive: p. 246

Photo Credits and Permissions

Maura Llewelyn O'Sullivan Kavanagh: p. 193

National Archives of Ireland: pp. 34, 85, 106

National Folklore Collection, University College Dublin:

- George Chambers: pp. 43, 274, 276
- Tomás Ó Muircheartaigh, p. x
- Carl von Sydow: pp. 86, 164, 272, 309
- Thomas Waddicor: p. xiii
- Other: p. 305

National Library of Ireland:

- Manuscripts Collection: pp. 210, 213
- Photo Archives – Coleman Doyle Collection: pp. 52, 53

National Monuments Service/Department of Arts, Heritage and the Gaeltacht: p. 19

Oxford University Press: p. 87

Plácido Castro Foundation: p. 197

The Ross Family (photo by John Ross): p. 27

RTÉ Archives: p. 269

University of Oslo: p. 177

Hugh Collins Walsh and Doug James: p. 254

Every reasonable effort has been made to secure permission from the copyright holders of all photographs and other material presented in this book. Any omissions are unintentional and regretted. The publisher will be happy to hear from any copyright holders not acknowledged and will rectify any errors or omissions in future editions.

Index

Index

Index